Jackie Perseghetti

David C Cook
transforming lives together

FAITH FACTOR OT
Published by David C. Cook
4050 Lee Vance View
Colorado Springs, CO 80918 U.S.A.

David C. Cook Distribution Canada
55 Woodslee Avenue, Paris, Ontario, Canada N3L 3E5

David C. Cook U.K., Kingsway Communications
Eastbourne, East Sussex BN23 6NT, England

David C. Cook and the graphic circle C logo
are registered trademarks of Cook Communications Ministries.

ISBN 978-0-7814-4458-3

Cover and interior design by BMB Design/Scott Johnson

Printed in USA
First Edition 2007

3 4 5 6 7 8 9 10

063010

For You, Lord

Contents

Acknowledgments

This single page out of the entire book is one I find most difficult to write for it cannot possibly contain the gratitude and thanks I owe to so many. You are all dear to me and deeply appreciated whether your name makes it to the confines of this page or not. You know who you are.

To the editors at Cook Communications Ministries, both past and present, thank you for believing in this project and helping to make it the best it can be. Special thanks to Jeannie Harmon for her wonderful work on the original *Caution: Dangerous Devotions*. Jeannie, who could have imagined that it would one day be translated into Portuguese! Also, special thanks to Mary McNeil whose vision helped make *Faith Factor* a reality. Mary, your passion, patience, hard work, and friendship won't be forgotten. Although every author cringes at editorial "red ink," I'd like to express my appreciation to Jennifer Lonas for her insightful comments and great suggestions. Lastly, a special thank you to Diane Gardner, a very patient supervising editor who worked with me to meet hefty deadlines. Diane, not only are you an awesome editor, but you are gracious as well. Thank you from the bottom of my heart.

To my friends and faithful prayer warriors who stood in the gap: Janis Wright, Marla Hartzell, Jeannie Roddy, Felice Gerwitz, Rebekah Fairchild, Darlene Jones, Cinda Hammond, Pam Bidwell, women in my BSF small group, and our Home Growth group—you will never know how much your prayers and encouragement have meant!

To my dear family, thank you for your encouragement and love:

Doug, not only are you the best husband in the world, but also my dearest friend. Thank you for all those evening walks to clear my head and wonderful foot rubs to revive my weary body! I love you and couldn't have done this without your support.

Ben, your interest and asking how the book was coming along was a source of encouragement to keep me chugging away when my fingers and brain were protesting. Thanks for helping to keep me focused. Of all the sons in the world, if I could choose just one … I'd choose you—all the time.

Bethany, not only were you helpful while home on breaks, but your encouragement continued across the miles. Thank you for all your help, suggestions, enthusiasm, and prayers. More than a daughter, you are a friend.

Dad and Mom, thank you for your faithful support through your many prayers and reminders to "take care of myself."

Finally, no words contrived by man could describe the debt of gratitude and love I owe to the One who has truly made all this possible. It is to Him alone I dedicate this book. I love you, Lord. May this book be used for Your glory and to point many towards You.

Your nearness is my good … (Psalm 73:28)

Introduction

Why Faith Factor?

A popular saying I once heard states, "Faith is walking to the edge of all the light that you have—and taking one more step." And that's exactly what God is calling you and me to do today. But it's not a blind leap of faith. God has given us all the light we need, and that light is found in His Word, the Bible. All we need to do is read, understand, and apply God's Word to our lives. That's the purpose of this book.

Some of you who are familiar with my former titles, *Caution: Dangerous Devotions* and *Caution: More Dangerous Devotions,* may be wondering, *Are* Faith Factor OT *and* Faith Factor NT *different?* To that I would say yes! While maintaining the same quality of retelling the biblical text, these two books have been updated and expanded to include more background information, cultural explanations, more sidebars, and, in the case of this book, the entire Old Testament (rather than just through the book of Psalms). You will also find comparative timeline tidbits that place biblical and secular history side by side, as well as online access to more devotional lessons we simply had no room to squeeze into the books. You can find those lessons online at *www.cookministries.com/FaithFactor* as well as a convenient topical index for both devotionals.

It's my prayer that *Faith Factor OT* and *Faith Factor NT* will ignite your heart and grow your faith—and may all the glory for that go to God alone.

Walk on!

> "The apostles said to the Lord, 'Increase our faith!'
> "He replied, 'If you have faith as small as a mustard seed ...'"
> (Luke 17:5–6)

> "It's impossible to please God apart from faith. And why? Because anyone who wants to approach God must believe both that he exists and that he cares enough to respond to those who seek him" (Heb. 11:6 MSG).

Genesis

Where is the best place to start anything? At the beginning! Appropriately, the word Genesis means "origin" or "beginning." In this book we'll read about the beginning of the world, humans, sin and God's judgment, languages, and nations. Genesis is the very foundation upon which the whole Bible stands. Those who don't want to acknowledge God often attack this book, but don't let their unbelief influence your opinion. As you read through Genesis, keep your eyes on the truth found here.

Genesis was written by Moses, although he wasn't born until about three hundred years *after* the events in this book happened! Is this a problem? No. God may have allowed long life spans for the first man, Adam, and his descendants so that firsthand accounts of historical events could be passed from generation to generation. For instance, Shem (one of Noah's sons who lived through the flood) could have passed along historical records to Abraham. Since both oral and written records existed in Abraham's day, Moses would later have access to accurate information. Regardless of how God revealed His word to Moses, the message of Genesis is one God didn't want us to miss.

As you journey through this first book of the Bible, keep your eyes open. Genesis has lots of twists and turns, ups and downs, and even a few bumps. Some of the terrain may look familiar, while some may seem confusing and a little disorienting. But don't let that discourage you. There are some important roads to explore in this book that will keep you from getting lost later on. So stay the course and keep your eyes and heart open to what God wants to teach you. When you finish your journey through Genesis, you'll be stronger in your faith because of the experience!

Check out a bonus lesson online at www.cookministries.com/FaithFactor: "My Way or the Highway" (taken from Genesis 9-11), which talks about being wise in your own eyes.

TIMELINE TIDBITS: Along the bottom o

Said and Done!
Taken from Genesis 1

Foundation

Just as you need to get yourself ready each morning before starting your day, so you need to prepare your heart before reading God's Word. The best way to do this is to spend a few minutes in prayer. It doesn't need to be a long prayer—a simple sentence expressing your heartfelt desire to God will do. Each time you read God's Word, ask Him to open your eyes and teach you.

Focus

Have you ever wondered where we really came from? Did God really create us, or are we the result of a "big bang" and a long period of evolution?

"In the beginning God ..." Notice that the Bible doesn't begin with "In the beginning ... life." From the very first verse of Genesis, God wants us to know that He is the One who created the heavens and the earth. How we respond to that news is our choice. We can either reject it or accept it as fact. When the world was created, was anyone around besides God to verify what happened? Can science either prove or disprove Genesis 1:1? The answer to both of these questions is no.

In the beginning, God created. Because of His power and creativity, it took only a spoken word on His part to bring everything into existence.

his book are Timeline Tidbits,

This is the God of the universe; this is the message He wants us to know. We aren't a clump of cells that happened to group together and form life on our own. God specifically tells us that He created the heavens and the earth and the life found on the earth. God wants us to know that He is responsible for creation—all of it.

How did God do it? First, Scripture tells us that He created everything in six days and then rested on the seventh. Was He tired? No. God rested because He was finished and wanted to provide an example for us to follow. That's the basis for our week to this day—days of work followed by a time of rest. (It's interesting to note that almost all known cultures throughout history have revolved around a seven-day week!)

On the first day of the week, God created night and day by separating the light from the darkness. On day two, He created our atmosphere with just the right mix of elements to support life. On day three, God gathered the waters to form the seas and created dry land. He also created plants and trees. God looked at what He had made and was pleased. Day four brought the creation of the sun, moon, and stars, which gave light to the earth and marked days, years, and seasons.

Now the stage was set for God's next act of creation. On day five, He brought into existence the birds of the air and the creatures of the sea. He made them complete and perfect, with everything they would need to produce more of their kind. He then created all the animals and insects on day six—but He didn't stop there. On that same day God unveiled His crowning achievement: He created people. Up until now, God had spoken everything into existence. But when it came to man, He did

Adam (pronounced ah-dahm) is the Hebrew word for "human being." It's related to another Hebrew word, Adamah (pronounced uh-dah-muh), which is the word for "ground." Interestingly, all the chemicals in our bodies are the same chemicals found in dirt!

God spoke into existence everything in our universe—except for man. God formed Adam with His own hands and, in a very intimate way, blew the breath of life into him. It was almost like divine CPR!

something very hands-on and personal. He shaped man from the dust of the ground and then breathed life into him (see Gen. 2:7). Then He created Eve from Adam.

Unlike the animals God created, He created humankind with souls. He did this so we could have relationships with Him. God gave us a will so we can choose our emotions—so we can love—and a superior mind so we can communicate with words. This is where human life began. It didn't take millions of years for us to evolve!

So what about evolution? Evolution is a theory that humans evolved (came into being) from lower life forms over a span of millions of years by trial and error. Not surprisingly, the more scientists learn about the complexities of the human body, the more they're abandoning the idea of evolution and investigating the idea of "intelligent design" or some kind of creative act. God has been telling us all along it is He who created everything.

Footwork

Note: Anything worth having usually requires some effort. In this section, you'll need to use a little energy. But don't panic! Your Bible is all you'll need. Just look up the Scripture verses and answer the questions that follow. Doing this will build your spiritual muscles and make you strong in the Lord. Really!

Turn to Genesis 1:1 in your Bible. (Go ahead; look it up and read it!) What does it say? "In the beginning" mentions the creation of something: time! This verse also mentions the creation of space and matter—our universe and all that's in it. (It's interesting to note that most other cultures, histories, religions, and sciences recognize that time, space, and matter already existed before they did, though they don't know how it all happened.) Also, notice what this verse doesn't say. It doesn't try to prove that God exists. That's because it was written in the beginning when no one doubted God.

side-by-side. Due to various cal-

Fruit

Science textbooks contain both facts and theories. Theory is different from fact. Don't be fooled into thinking that evolution is a scientific fact. It's not. All scientists know that a theory must be tested to be considered scientifically accurate. That is, the theory and the conditions it is tested under must be repeatable in a laboratory under exact conditions. The theory of evolution isn't based solely on scientific evidence; rather it's based on a belief system that rules God out. Evolution isn't pure science; it's a form of religion. So whose word would you rather believe? The word of those who weren't around when things began and can't reliably explain how matter came into being, or the word of the Creator Himself, who was there and made everything? Think about it.

Don't Look at *Me!*
Taken from Genesis 2—3

Foundation

Stop and pray before you b~~~~ ~~~~ lesson. Ask God to open
~~~~ ~~~~ ~~~~ t He wants to show you in
~~~~ t loving God.

~~~~ gretted? You're

~~~~ was so perfect just moments ago! What happened? Adam and
~~e both wondered. They suddenly felt ashamed and wanted to hide from
God—the very One who created them. The peace they once enjoyed in
their hearts had vanished. Something was dreadfully wrong.

Adam's mind was racing as he thought about his life up to this point. God
had given him the task of caring for the garden, studying what God had
created, and naming all the animals. While observing the animals, Adam had
noticed that each one had a mate, yet there was no mate suitable for himself.
A smile came to Adam's face as he remembered how God had met that
need. He placed Adam into a deep sleep, took one of his ribs, and fashioned
a companion especially for him. When Adam awoke, there stood Eve! She
was a perfect match for him! But then Adam's smile quickly faded. He knew
that he had been created to walk in the cool of the garden with a loving God,
but now all he wanted to do was hide!

Sin literally means "to miss the mark." It is living independently of God and relying on yourself as your own authority. Sin isn't just breaking God's law; it's betraying God Himself.

Eve was tempted by wanting great pleasure, wanting what she didn't have, and wanting to advance her own cause ("the lust of the flesh, the lust of the eyes, and the pride of life"[1 John 2:16, KJV]). Jesus was tempted in the same ways, but didn't give in (Matt. 4:1–11).

Eve also felt guilty about what she had done. She had never experienced such a horrible feeling before. Why had she listened to that serpent? Why hadn't she obeyed that one simple rule God had given her?

The serpent told her the fruit from the tree of knowledge was really the most desirable thing in the garden. He even promised that it would make her like God! All that power and knowledge seemed irresistible. And the fruit looked so delicious! What harm could it do to take a bite? Perhaps God had been mistaken or hadn't really meant what He said about the consequences of eating the fruit. Besides, the serpent had assured her she wouldn't die if she ate it. So, perhaps God had been mistaken or didn't really mean what He said.

Eve grabbed the fruit and took a bite. Then she turned around and offered some to Adam as well. After eating the fruit, something inside them changed. Instead of wanting to be with God, they were afraid of Him.

"Adam, where are you?" God called out, knowing exactly where he and Eve were and what they had done. He had created them with a free will to choose, and the forbidden tree was a test of their obedience and love for Him. Would they choose God's way or their own way? God knew the answer. They had been tempted and had chosen their own way above His.

"Did you eat from the forbidden tree?" God questioned.

Adam panicked. "Don't look at *me*!" he said, pointing a blaming finger. "Eve gave me the fruit to eat."

Eve quickly added, "Don't look at *me!* The serpent said it would be all right!"

Because of Adam and Eve's disobedience, sin had entered their lives. As a result, they faced separation from God and had to leave the garden forever. Not only that, but the land they worked would now be cursed, and they would experience pain, sorrow, and death. What had promised to be so pleasing brought only regret.

It would be sad if the story ended here, but it doesn't. Even in the midst of Adam and Eve's denial—"Don't look at *me!*"—God stepped in and said, "Yes, I know. Instead, look to *Me.*"

As Adam and Eve left the garden, God didn't abandon them. He provided clothing for them to wear made out of animal skins (the first animal sacrifice), which would serve as a constant reminder that sin comes with a cost.

Footwork

Open your Bible to Genesis 3:14–15. As a result of Adam and Eve's sin, God also cursed the serpent. What does verse 14 say? Now look at verse 15 and read about the threat to Satan and the promise to mankind! The offspring (or seed) of the woman—Jesus, who would be born of a virgin—would crush the serpent's head (completely destroy the work of Satan).

Fruit

Satan twisted God's truth in order to plant a seed of doubt in Eve's heart. He then challenged God's words and replaced them with a lie. Satan still tries to do this today. Do you have doubts or questions about God's Word? Write them down on a piece of paper and tape it to the back inside cover of this devotional. Be honest and tell God about your questions and/or hang-ups. Ask Him to help you with your doubts, then get ready for an exciting journey as you explore the Old Testament and learn about His truth.

salt and tar trade, constructs

How 'Bout a Sign or Two?
Taken from Genesis 6—9

Foundation

Take a moment to pray. Even though you may be familiar with the story of
Noah and the flood, ask God to help you see beyond what you already know
and teach you new things from His Word.

Focus

*Have you ever wished that God would give you a sign that He
really exists and is who He says He is?*

Noah felt sick. Everywhere he looked he saw selfishness, violence, and hatred. He
worried about the effects of this on his family. Sin had entered the world when
Adam and Eve disobeyed God, but since that time, it had spread like wildfire.
Instead of just being tempted by sinful things from the outside, people were being
tempted by the wickedness in their own hearts. For example, Cain—one of Adam's
sons—harbored jealousy in his heart and desired personal gain. As a result, he
killed his brother Abel, committing the first murder (Gen. 4). This was just the
beginning.

   Lamech, Cain's great-great-great-grandson (not the Lamech who was Noah's
father), didn't turn out so great. In his pride and arrogance, he married not just one
woman but two, violating God's original plan for marriage. He also bragged about
killing whoever displeased him. The poor example of Lamech and others like him
encouraged future generations to do the same and even worse, leading to the
wickedness of Noah's day.

16—ft high walls for protection from

Although Noah was thankful that he had found favor in God's eyes, he was bewildered. *Build an ark?* he wondered. *Every living thing on earth will be destroyed? A worldwide flood?* Noah pondered this as he made careful measurements and began working. The job would take over 100 years to complete.

During this time, people came to question Noah. Some shook their heads in pity for a man they thought was insane. "This box is going to float?" they laughed. "On what? Dry ground?"

Many came by to mock. Others simply ignored the years of warning. In spite of this, Noah faithfully went about his task, following God's blueprints exactly. He knew he had heard the Lord.

When God's perfect timing had arrived, He instructed Noah to prepare to enter the ark with his wife, sons, and daughters-in-law. They gathered every kind of food that could be eaten and stored it away for themselves and the animals. Noah then loaded the animals God brought to him—a male and female pair of every unclean animal, seven pairs of every clean animal, and seven pairs of every kind of bird. Then the Lord closed the door of the ark. At that point, the skies burst forth with rain, and water came flooding out from the depths of the earth. God kept His promise!

For forty days and nights, water flooded the earth, but that wasn't the end of it. The water rushing from underground springs and the rain pounding down from the heavens gradually covered the entire earth so that even the tallest mountains couldn't be seen. The swirling, violent

"Clean animals" (those declared acceptable by God and were without defect) were to be sacrificed to the Lord. After the flood, God gave His people permission to eat these animals. (Check out Lev. 11 and Deut. 14 to learn more about clean and unclean animals!)

Most cultures have legends of a worldwide flood. Some of these ancient legends, written on cuneiform clay tablets, describe the same event recorded in our Bible.

waters flooded the earth for 150 days—five months! But God hadn't forgotten Noah. He closed the underground springs and stopped the rain. He then brought a wind to make the waters diminish so the land could dry. After seven months of being in the ark, Noah felt it stop rocking. The ark had landed on Mount Ararat.

Three months later, the tops of other mountains appeared. But the time of waiting for the flood waters to recede was far from over. After another forty days, Noah sent out a raven and then a dove to see if the water had dried up, but the ground was still covered. Then a week later, Noah sent out another dove, and it returned with a freshly picked olive leaf in its beak. Noah waited yet another week, released the dove again, and this time it didn't return. Only then did he open the door and see that the ground was dry. A little over a year had passed from the time Noah and his family had entered the ark until now. God had kept His word.

After leaving the ark, Noah immediately worshipped the Lord by building an altar and sacrificing some of the clean birds and animals on it. God blessed Noah and promised never again to destroy the earth and its inhabitants with a flood. As a reminder of that, God placed a rainbow in the sky. It would stand as a reminder of the disaster and a sign of God's promise. That sign still appears in the sky today.

Footwork

Turn to Genesis 9:28-29 in your Bible. How long did Noah live after the flood? How long did he live altogether? Do you find that hard to believe? It's not so hard to believe if you understand that before the flood, the climate and atmosphere of the earth were very different from the way they are today. Life spans of people back then were much longer. After the flood, the environment changed drastically, and the amount of time people lived began to decrease. Interestingly, Adam's long life of 930 years meant that he could have possibly talked to Noah's father!

Fruit

The flood buried every living thing on the face of the earth in a watery, muddy grave. Everything perished, but not without leaving a record. To this day, fossils and rock layers show proof of a worldwide flood. Fossils of sea animals have been found on every major mountain range in the world, and trees (sometimes upside down) have been found crossing into several different rock layers. Evolutionists believe these layers took many millions of years to form, but the existence of the fossil remains offers compelling evidence that a worldwide flood took place. God not only gave His rainbow as a sign, but He also left fossils as a record of the actual event.

When you are wondering if God exists, will you accept His signs or reject them?

Trust Me
Taken from Genesis 12—17

Foundation

Take a few minutes to prepare your heart. Ask God to help you to know Him
more, so you can grow to understand how very much He cares for you.

Focus

Do you know people who make promises and never live up
to them?

Abram trembled. He knew the seriousness of the matter before him. Thoughts of
his past filled his mind. It seemed like only yesterday when God had called him to
leave the comforts of home and travel to an unknown place—a place God would
show him. With that call came a remarkable promise: I will make your descendants
great and through you all people on earth will be blessed.

God was going to raise up a nation to be His people—people who would live in such
a way that through them the world would come to know Yahweh, the one true God.
How well Abram remembered God's words, and yet how easily he had forgotten them!

Abram felt the depth of his own unworthiness as he remembered the scheme he had
devised while journeying to Egypt. He had heard that Egyptian rulers often killed the
husbands of beautiful women in order to take the wives as their own, so Abram, fearing
for his life, told Sarai to pose as his sister. This way Pharaoh would honor Abram as the
"brother" of a beautiful woman, treating him well and giving him gifts in hopes of striking
a good arrangement for Sarai. Having momentarily forgotten God's wonderful promises
and plan for him, Abram told Pharaoh a half-truth that Sarai was his sister. (He knew it

wasn't *totally* untrue, since they both had the same father but different mothers. But he also knew it wasn't entirely true either, since Sarai *was* his beloved wife!) When Pharaoh discovered the truth, he sent Abram and Sarai away, even though they could have easily been put to death. Abram's lying had needlessly put both their lives in danger.

Abram winced at the memory. Why had he doubted God's protection? Hadn't God promised him all nations would be blessed through his descendants? He should have known better than to fear for his life. Surely God was capable of doing what He promised! *Yet, how can I be sure I heard God correctly?* Abram wondered. *How can I know for certain that He will give me a son to be my heir and make my descendants more numerous than the stars?* Those questions jarred Abram's thoughts back to the present where he stood, trembling.

Abram had done everything according to God's instruction. He gathered together two birds—a turtledove and a pigeon, as well as a cow, goat, and a ram, each three years old. Then, cutting the cow, goat, and ram in half, he laid each half on opposite sides of a ditch. This was the custom for preparing to make a covenant—a life-and-death promise with someone else. It was the strongest binding agreement possible between two individuals or the representatives of two groups.

Abram knew that the next step in covenant making was to walk between the slain animals and say, "May what was done to these animals be done to me if I break my end of the agreement." By doing this, Abram would be agreeing to live a blameless life before God, and

God renamed Abram, Abraham. Hebrew names carried great significance and often described a person's character or specific circumstances in the person's life. In order to name someone, the one giving the name would have to have both an understanding of that person and authority over him.

Abraham didn't deserve to be chosen by God any more than we do, yet God reached out to him in love anyway—and in spite of Abraham's faults. In the New Testament this is known as God's grace.

Abram knew he couldn't possibly keep his end of the bargain. He had already messed up once. What if he failed at this? What if his descendants later chose a path independent of God? Great fear engulfed Abram.

When evening approached, Abram fell into a deep and troubled sleep, surrounded by a sense of dread and darkness. It was then that a most unusual thing happened! God, Himself, in the form of a smoking firepot and a flaming torch, passed between the animals! Abram wasn't required to walk through the ditch of blood. Yahweh God did it alone, taking full responsibility for both ends of the covenant! Through this one-sided act, He was saying to Abram, "I love you, and because I want to be in relationship with you, I will cover the consequences of your inability to keep your part of the agreement."

Abram would never forget what he had seen and experienced that night. It would change him forever. No longer would he be called *Abram* ("exalted father"). He soon learned his name would be *Abraham* ("father of many"). God was calling to Himself a people and a nation. Abraham was just the first of many to come....

Footwork

Turn to Genesis 15:6 in your Bible and read what was stated about Abram—even in spite of his earlier weaknesses! What does it say?

Fruit

Abraham is listed in the New Testament "Hall of Faith" (Heb. 11). It has been said that "faith is walking to the edge of all the light that you have—and taking one more step." Faith in God is not a blind leap. Rather, it's based upon knowing and understanding who God (Yahweh) is. Just as God wanted a relationship with Abraham, so He desires a relationship with us. He is "the same yesterday, and today and forever" (Heb. 13:8). Do you have a relationship with the one true creator God? Do you even know what that means? (If you aren't sure, turn to the back of this book. You'll find a special message there just for you.)

What You See Is What You . . .

Taken from Genesis 13—19

Foundation

Don't forget to pray! Allow God to search your heart and show you any weaknesses in your character. Take a moment to thank Him that He is the Designer and Completer of your life. He knows and desires what's best for you.

Focus

When given a choice, do you look out for your own needs first?

Lot couldn't believe it! The offer was too good to be true! Ever since his father died, Lot and his family had lived and traveled from place to place with his Uncle Abram (Abraham). But now Abram's and Lot's flocks, herds, tents, and possessions had grown too numerous. Their herdsmen began quarreling with one another, and Abram knew they could no longer stay together.

"Let's put a stop to all this quarreling and go our separate ways," Abram offered. "Look, the whole land lies before us! If you want the land to the right, I'll go to the left. Or if you want to go left, I'll take the land on the right. Either way, you choose first."

Lot looked eagerly over the vast land. Knowing the importance of having access to fresh water, he directed his attention to the Jordan River and its surrounding plain. From where he stood, Lot could see lush green vegetation growing along the banks. Surely this would be the best land! *How foolish of Abram to let me choose*

writing cuneiform (writing that look:

first! he thought. Lot pointed to the land he wanted for himself, the best land, and then both men parted ways.

As soon as Lot moved into the land he had selfishly chosen, he soon discovered it wasn't fertile at all, but actually barren! The seemingly lush, green banks along the Jordan River turned out to be filled with thickets, the part of the riverbed where his flocks could be watered was too small, and soil on the plains along the river was so poor, nothing was able to grow. Lot knew that his only solution was to travel south and settle near the Dead Sea. Little did he know the consequences he and his family would suffer because of his choice.

Although Lot knew that the people who lived in that area had no respect for God's laws, worshipped idols, and were known for being evil, he settled among them anyway and became a citizen of Sodom. He even rose to a position of leadership in the government and sat in the city gate! As time wore on, however, Lot grew accustomed to the evil influences around him— influences that soon affected not only him but his entire household.

One day, two angels appearing as men came to the city of Sodom. Lot was sitting at the city gate and noticed them.

"Come to my house," he offered the strangers. "You can clean up from your travel and get a good night's rest."

After some persuasion, the two men accompanied Lot to his home. Later that night, both old and young men from all over the city showed up and surrounded Lot's house, demanding the visitors come out. They had

Simply put, greed tempts me to:

G—Grasp
R—Rapidly at
E—Everything I
E—Envy and
D—Desire

A city gate wasn't just a door on the fortified walls surrounding a city. It was a large reinforced area containing several rooms and stalls where people could pay taxes, talk to officials, or buy from merchants. Sitting at the city gate meant that a person was a ruler, a judge, or an official.

31

wicked thoughts and burned with desires that were neither God honoring nor God-given.

Lot stood outside his front door trying to reason with them, but the angry mob wouldn't listen. Instead, the men almost crushed Lot in an attempt to break down the door. At that moment, the two visitors pulled Lot back inside the house and struck the mob with blindness. The two angels instructed Lot to gather his family and immediately leave the city, for God had sent them to destroy it.

Lot ran to warn his future sons-in-law. "You need to leave here at once!" he urged. "For this city is about to be destroyed by God!"

But they only laughed, thinking it was a joke. When Lot returned to his house and hesitated about leaving, the two visitors grabbed his hand and led him and his family safely out of the city.

"You must run for your lives," one of the angels instructed. "Whatever you do, don't stop—and don't look back."

Everyone in Lot's family heard the warning, but not all took it seriously. Lot's wife ignored it and looked back. The moment she did, she turned into a pillar of salt! Not only did Lot lose his wife and his home that day, but his daughters also lost their future husbands. Later they would defile their father to preserve the family line, and their offspring—the Moabites and Ammonites—would become the enemies of God's chosen people.

What started as a selfish choice and a greedy desire for the "best" only gave birth to a nightmare of consequences.

Footwork

Turn in your Bible to Genesis 19:16 and read it. What do the last few words of that verse say?
What was God showing to Lot when Lot hesitated? Now skip down to verse 29 and read it.
What do you learn about God from this verse?

Fruit

Throughout your life you'll be tempted to make decisions the same way Lot did. Don't! Lot thought only of himself first and his own greedy desires. He had little regard for others and even less regard for God's opinion. The result was a foolish choice that ended in painful consequences and disaster. What you see isn't *necessarily* what you get! Don't be fooled! Don't make decisions based upon what *appears* to be the best. Instead, ask God for His counsel. Lot learned this the hard way. How will *you* learn?

Thanks! I Needed That!
Taken from Genesis 22—24

— Foundation —

Take a moment to prepare your heart by praying. Ask God to open your eyes so you might discover what He would have you learn. Thank Him that He is a God who is always near, no matter how your circumstances may look to you.

Focus

Do you ever wonder whether God is paying attention to your needs or difficult circumstances?

As Isaac stood in the field near his home, thoughts of his rich family history flooded his mind. God had spoken to his father Abraham, promising an heir and descendants more numerous than the stars! Isaac knew he was that heir, even though he had a half brother named Ishmael. He knew his parents hadn't trusted God to provide them a son but had taken matters into their own hands. Ishmael was the result—a son born to Abraham through a maid named Hagar. Isaac was born later—just as God had promised.

Looking out over the horizon, Isaac remembered the long journey he took with his father when he was just a teenager. They had set out for the region of Moriah to worship the Lord. When they reached their destination, Abraham gave orders to his servants. "Wait here until my son and I return," he said with emotion in his voice. Then Abraham and Isaac began their journey up the mountain.

As they walked along, Isaac noticed that something was missing.

"Father," he said, "I'm carrying the wood, and you have the fire and the knife, but we have no animal to sacrifice!"

"God will provide what is needed for the sacrifice, my son," Abraham said softly.

When they reached the top of the mountain, Abraham built an altar and laid the wood on top. Isaac felt relieved to have the burden of wood off his back. Little did he know the heavy burden weighing on his father's heart. When everything had been prepared, Isaac saw a look of love and sadness in his father's eyes. Yet in those same eyes also shone a solid, unwavering obedience that spoke of deep trust and faith in God.

The next thing Isaac knew, his father was tying his hands and feet! Then he felt himself being lifted onto the altar. All of a sudden, panic rose up and lodged in Isaac's throat. What started as a good day of worship had quickly turned into a nightmare!

"The Lord will provide." Isaac kept hearing those words over and over in his mind, though the noise of his own pounding, anxious heart had nearly drowned them out. "The Lord will provide." Everything around Isaac seemed to be moving in slow motion. He saw his father raise the knife above his head. Glimmering in the sunlight, the knife was poised to come plunging down into Isaac's heart.

Hagar's son, Ishmael, gave birth to twelve sons who God said would become a mighty nation. Ishmael's sons are today's Arabs.

Abraham's chief servant, Eliezer, had sworn a solemn oath to find a wife for Isaac from Abraham's native land— a nine-hundred-mile journey round-trip!

Suddenly the silence was shattered—not by the knife, but by a heavenly voice.

"Stop Abraham! Don't harm Isaac! You have proved that you fear Me, for you have offered Me your only son."

With a great sigh of relief, Abraham let the knife fall limply from his hand. He grabbed and hugged Isaac, and they both wept. Looking up,

Abraham saw a ram struggling to free itself from a thicket where it had become caught by its horns. Isaac watched his father prepare the sacrifice and place it on the altar where he had lain only moments before. The Lord *did* provide.

Isaac smiled to himself. Even though he was now a man, those words still came to mind—sometimes in the most desperate of situations. "The Lord will provide."

Suddenly, Isaac's eyes caught movement on the horizon. Looking across the field, he spotted a small caravan coming toward him. It was his father's servant returning from a long journey to find a wife for him. He had left with the ten camels and many gifts, and was now returning with much less cargo—and apparently one special addition. Isaac walked through the field toward the caravan. As he drew nearer, he saw a young woman in a veil dismount from her camel. The servant had found him a wife. Isaac's heart rejoiced! As he watched her, he could tell Rebekah not only had outward beauty but inward beauty as well.

With great delight, the servant told Isaac about the special sign he had asked God to give him when he found the right woman: The woman would give him water from the spring and offer to water his camels as well. When Rebekah came to the spring and did just that—offering to water all ten of the servant's camels, he knew God had given him the sign he had asked for.

"And when I found out that her father was Sarah's brother's son," he continued, "I knew that God had answered my prayers. He has provided!"

Isaac was overjoyed as he took Rebekah to be his wife. Together they had twin sons, Jacob and Esau—and God's promises continued to unfold.

Footwork

Turn to Genesis 22 and read verses 7-8. Now skip down and read verses 13-14. Look closely at verse 14. What did Abraham do in this verse?

toes, corn, beans, squash, and manioc

Fruit

Yhwh-Jireh is a name for God that means "the Lord provides." Do you have a specific need, or are you facing a difficult situation? Take a moment and pray about it. After you've given it to God, write "Genesis 22:14—The Lord Will Provide" on a piece of paper and tape it someplace where you'll notice it. In times of doubt, ask God to help your unbelief; then thank Him in advance for what He plans to do. He knows best what you need most. Trust Him!

Trick or Treat!
Taken from Genesis 25—35

Foundation

Spend some time in prayer before you begin today's lesson. Quiet your thoughts before God and ask Him to help you understand the importance of honesty. Acknowledge that He is the Source of all truth.

Focus

Do you know people who trick others to get what they want?

"Jacob, I beg of you … give me some of that lentil soup you cooked," Esau pleaded.

Wanting to take advantage of the situation, Jacob cleverly replied, "Only if you give me your birthright in exchange for it!"

Before Jacob and his twin brother, Esau, were born, God had given their parents a prophecy that the older son would serve the younger one. If Jacob could exchange places with Esau in the family will, he would receive the benefits and inheritance normally given to the oldest child. Jacob smiled at the thought. Gaining Esau's birthright would make it all legal!

"Yes! Anything! Just give me some soup!" Esau hastily agreed. He cared little for his birthright and would gladly sell it for the price of a meal.

Since that time, everything had seemed to be going Jacob's way until his mother brought alarming news. "Your father is now old and nearing death. Just this morning he sent your brother Esau to hunt and prepare his favorite meal. When he returns, your father plans to give him the blessing due the firstborn—that blessing

ed and used for transporting water;

should be yours, Jacob! Listen to me and follow my directions carefully. This is what you must do while Esau is gone ..."

Jacob followed his mother's instructions, and as soon as he had finished preparing the meal, he entered the room where his father lay, having first disguised himself to look like his brother.

"Is that you, Esau?" Isaac asked.

Knowing that his father's eyesight was failing, Jacob lied, "Yes, Father. I have come with the meal you requested."

"You are back so soon, my son?" Isaac asked.

"Yes, Father. The Lord's hand was upon me," Jacob lied again.

Isaac called his son to him, and when he touched Jacob, he felt not the hairy arms of Esau but a cleverly placed goatskin to imitate them. Believing that Jacob was Esau, Isaac gave his blessing. Then Jacob brought the meal to his father and left the room feeling satisfied. But that feeling was short-lived.

A birthright was a special honor given to the oldest son, entitling him to a double portion of the family inheritance and a position of leadership. If he chose to sell his birthright or give it away, he would permanently lose those privileges.

Leah gave birth to Judah and Levi. From Judah came the kingly line (the line of Jesus the Messiah), and from Levi came the line of priests!

When Esau returned from the fields and discovered what Jacob had done, he was furious and sought to kill him. To put a safe distance between the brothers, Rebekah devised a plan, persuading Isaac to send Jacob away to find a wife for himself among her family in Haran. So with his father's blessing, Jacob left his homeland and traveled to Haran, where he eventually met up with Laban, his mother's brother.

Jacob worked for his father-in-law for several years just to earn the right to marry Laban's youngest daughter, Rachel. Now Jacob stood before his uncle in amazement. This couldn't be happening to him! Sure, he had tricked his brother and father, but that was entirely different. Or was it?

rrigation canals dug in Sumer.

"I worked seven long years for the privilege of marrying your youngest daughter, Rachel," Jacob said angrily. "And how do you repay me? You secretly substitute your oldest daughter for your youngest, and now I find that instead of marrying my beloved Rachel, I have married Leah!" Disgust rose in Jacob's voice, and rage burned in his heart.

Laban pretended innocence. "It's our custom for older daughters to marry first," he smugly replied. "But if you agree to keep Leah and finish this week of wedding celebrations, I will give you Rachel's hand in marriage as well—for another seven years of work."

Jacob realized that he had been tricked by one who was craftier than he. It was a hard lesson to learn, for during those seven years, Laban cheated and stole from Jacob, but Jacob continued to work hard to fulfill his commitment.

Upon completing his obligations, Jacob fled from Laban to his homeland in Canaan. In spite of Laban's schemes and stealing, God had blessed Jacob. Not only did he have many possessions and livestock, but he had also fathered eleven sons. Appearing to Jacob in a vision, God confirmed the covenant He had made with Abraham, his grandfather, and Isaac, his father. It was now Jacob's turn to carry God's plan onward—but not until he had learned his lesson fully.

Before entering the land of Canaan, Jacob received word that his brother, Esau, was coming to meet him with four hundred men. Jacob's heart was filled with fear. In desperation he divided his family into two camps, hoping that if one camp was attacked, the other would be spared. Then, hoping to buy his brother's forgiveness, Jacob sent messengers on ahead with gifts and livestock for Esau.

"Save me!" Jacob finally cried out to God, "even though I don't deserve any of the favor and consideration You have shown me, Lord."

When Jacob finally laid down his pride, God acted on his behalf. (You can find out how by reading Genesis 32-33.) But it had taken more than twenty years for him to learn that simple lesson.

Footwork

Open your Bible to Genesis chapter 32 and look at verses 27-28. What question did God ask Jacob? Do you think it caused Jacob to stop and think about his past? *Jacob* means "supplanter," or "trickster." The name *Israel* means "he fights with God," or "God fights." Because of Jacob's self-will, God fought against him. Jacob's twelve sons (Benjamin, the twelfth son, would be born not long after these events) were later called the sons of Israel, or the Israelites. They would experience victory only to the degree that they allowed God to fight for them.

Fruit

Doing things by our own efforts or in our own strength usually results in disappointment, because we don't have God's perspective to help us see the big picture. Rather than relying on God to work, we run ahead of Him with our own plans and schemes, often manipulating people or circumstances to get what we desire or believe we deserve. But God wants us to put things into His hands. If we try to work out the details ourselves, we'll either miss God's blessing or become disappointed by the results. God leaves the choice to us: Will we manipulate and deceive to get what we want, or will we let God work out His plan in our lives? Trick or treat? Which one will you choose?

epresent   words;   Hieroglyphic

Why Me?
Taken from Genesis 37—50

Foundation

Take a few minutes to search your heart and be quiet before the Lord. Ask Him to point out any people in your life you need to ask forgiveness from—or give forgiveness to. Thank Him for providing for your needs and forgiving you.

Focus

Do you ever find it difficult to forgive those who wrong you or cause you harm?

Joseph's heart skipped a beat as he recognized who was standing in front of him. What should he do? He thought about the loneliness, the suffering, and the painstaking labor that had marked his life since his brothers had sold him as a slave. That was twenty long years ago. Oh, how he missed his father! Was he still alive? Joseph remembered his father's last words to him, just as if he had spoken them yesterday....

"Joseph, my son," Jacob had said, "Please find the place where your brothers are grazing the flocks and see how they're doing. Then return to me with the news."

What started out as a simple errand ended up a nightmare!

When Joseph's brothers saw him approaching, anger and resentment burned in their hearts. They despised him for being the favorite son and hated his nonsensical dreams.

"Imagine!" they scoffed. "Us bowing down before our little baby brother? Never!"

Wanting to rid themselves of Joseph forever, they threw him into a pit and planned to leave him there to die. When a caravan of merchants drew near, their plans changed, and they sold Joseph to them as a slave. After watching the caravan disappear in the distance, the brothers returned home with Joseph's robe in hand and reported their brother had been killed by a wild beast. As evidence, they held up his robe, which they had torn and dipped in goat's blood. In their eyes, Joseph was as good as dead. Jacob was grief-stricken.

Now, sitting on a polished throne, Joseph swallowed hard, trying to keep his emotions under control. Obviously, his brothers didn't recognize him. Why should they? The Joseph *they* knew had been a teenager when they sold him into slavery. But now, twenty years later, Joseph was the second most powerful man in all of Egypt! And it hadn't been easy getting there.

Joseph was sold to Midianite merchants for twenty shekels of silver. The Midianites were descendants of Ishmael, Isaac's half brother.

The ring Pharaoh gave to Joseph authorized him to act in the name of the king. Joseph's new title—"Second Only to Pharaoh"—required everyone but the king to bow before him!

When he had first arrived in Egypt, Joseph was sold to Pharaoh's captain of the guard, Potiphar. It didn't take long for Potiphar to notice that the Lord was with Joseph and granted him success at every turn. As a result, Joseph found favor in the eyes of his master, and Potiphar put him in charge of his entire household.

Unfortunately, Joseph also found favor in the eyes of his master's wife, who thought he was handsome and desirable. One day she cornered Joseph while her husband was away, but he escaped from her advances. Furious, she devised a scheme and told her husband that Joseph had attacked her. Potiphar's anger burned, and Joseph was thrown into prison—even though he was innocent.

While in prison, Joseph interpreted the dreams of Pharaoh's cupbearer and baker, who were also prisoners. The cupbearer promised to present Joseph's case before Pharaoh when he was released, but it wasn't until

Pharaoh had a disturbing dream—two years later!—that the cupbearer finally remembered. Brought before the ruler at last, Joseph interpreted Pharaoh's dream, predicting seven years of bountiful harvest in the land followed by seven years of famine.

"Let Pharaoh take action and appoint a wise and discerning man as an overseer of the land," Joseph advised.

Recognizing the wisdom God had granted Joseph, Pharaoh gave him the job, placing an official ring on Joseph's finger and a royal robe on his back. Dressed in this manner, he now stood before his brothers, who had no idea to whom they were bowing!

Joseph weighed his options. Should he treat his brothers harshly as they had treated him? Should he reveal himself with an "I told you so" attitude, reminding them of the dreams they often ridiculed? Perhaps he would simply deny their request for grain and send them home empty-handed to suffer just as he had suffered.

Overwhelmed with emotion, Joseph could no longer contain himself. "I am Joseph—the brother you sold into slavery," he exclaimed.

His brothers stood there speechless, terror and guilt etched on their faces. But Joseph's next words shocked them even more, for they weren't full of anger and bitterness, as his brothers expected. They were words full of forgiveness!

Footwork

Through Joseph, a whole family line was preserved. Pharaoh even gave the best land in Egypt (an area called Goshen) to Joseph's brothers and father as a place to settle and raise their livestock. Joseph's forgiveness of his brothers had far-reaching effects. And yet, an unusual thing happened when their father died. Turn to the last chapter of Genesis (chapter 50) and read verses 15-21. Do you think Joseph's brothers understood what true forgiveness really was?

Fruit

When someone hurts you (either deliberately or accidentally), you'll be tempted to get even. Don't. Anger and bitterness don't make you the winner; they make you the victim. That's why God commands us to forgive one another: "Bear with each other and forgive whatever grievances you may have against one another. Forgive as the Lord forgave you" (Col. 3:13).

Asking for and giving forgiveness goes deeper than just saying "Sorry" or "That's okay" or "No problem!" It involves saying (and meaning) the words "I forgive you." Those words are hard to say unless you truly mean them. (That's why we usually say, "That's okay" and "No problem!") True forgiveness is impossible without God's help. So the next time someone offends you, put these simple steps into practice:

1. Give your anger over to God;
2. Check your heart to make sure you aren't falling prey to bitterness; and
3. Say the words "I forgive you" as soon as possible.

Exodus

Exodus is the second book in what we call the Pentateuch. (*Penta* means "five" and *teuchos* means "scroll.") It's also the second book out of the five books Moses wrote, and part two of Genesis.

As you explore Exodus, notice an immediate change in the terrain. Genesis ended with Jacob's family of seventy moving to Egypt and living favorably under Pharaoh's rule and protection for many years. Exodus opens 350 years later with the Hebrews living not as guests of Pharaoh but as his slaves! In Genesis we saw families; in Exodus we see the beginning of a nation.

Keep alert as you make your way through this book, and don't assume you already know what's ahead. Exodus is loaded with surprises and a fresh look at who God is. Are you daring enough to step out and explore? Then read on!

For an interesting lesson on a picture of God's great plan, check out "Blueprints? For What?" (taken from Exodus 25—31). You can find it online at www.cookministries.com/FaithFactor.

tomb structures called mastabas (pred-

I Pledge Allegiance . . .
Taken from Exodus 1—2

Foundation

Before you begin today's lesson, pause and ask God to direct your thoughts and your heart. He is all-knowing and wise. Everything you encounter in this life must first pass through His hands.

Focus

Have you ever struggled with obeying God when someone in authority tells you to do something wrong?

"We can't control all these Israelites," the new Pharaoh stated one day.

More than three hundred and fifty years had passed since Joseph's family had settled in Egypt. During Joseph's lifetime, Egypt was ruled by a group of people called the *Hyksos,* who were descendants of Shem. Since they were not fully Egyptians, they accepted foreigners in their land. Now, however, the Egyptians had regained control of the land. Joseph and his brothers were no longer alive, and the Hebrews living in Egypt were almost two million strong! Political powers had changed, and so would the Israelites' lives.

"If I don't do something about these Hebrews," Pharaoh muttered, "they could easily rise up against us and side with our enemies in a time of war."

Pharaoh knew the danger of enemies trying to take the land. He also knew the Hebrews had enjoyed peaceful living under the Hyksos people. The more Pharaoh looked around him, the more insecure he felt. Fearful

Watertight baskets were made with bundles of papyrus reeds overlapped in three layers and covered with pitch. The same materials and method were used in making small Egyptian boats.

The name Moses sounded similar in both the Egyptian and Hebrew languages. The name in Egyptian meant "son" or "is born." In Hebrew, it meant "to draw out," a constant reminder that God had rescued Moses from the Nile.

of the ever-expanding Hebrew nation, he came up with a wicked plan to stop its growth. Summoning two of the head midwives (Shiphrah and Puah), who helped deliver babies in Egypt, he ordered, "When the Hebrew women are giving birth, check to see if the baby is a boy or a girl. If it's a girl, let the baby live. If it's a boy, kill it."

Pharaoh's lips curled into a fiendish smile. Feeling quite pleased with himself, he muttered under his breath, "That will put a quick stop to these detestable Hebrews!"

But Shiphrah and Puah feared God and didn't carry out Pharaoh's wicked command. When Pharaoh noticed that the number of Hebrews wasn't decreasing, he questioned the two midwives.

"The Israelite women are so strong, they give birth before we can get there to help!" they lied.

The king was furious when he heard this. Now his secret plan would have to go public, and would come by way of a decree.

"Every newborn Hebrew boy must be thrown into the Nile River," he commanded. "Only the girls may live."

This time it would be law, and it would be *enforced!*

Upon hearing this decree, a Hebrew couple named Amram and Jochebed hid their newborn son. Choosing to follow a higher law—God's Law—they could not and would not follow the law of the land. But after three months of hiding their son, it became difficult to conceal him in their home. Not knowing what else to do, Jochebed made a watertight basket from the reeds that grew along the Nile River. With loving hands and a breaking heart, she placed her son in the basket and left him there among the reeds. Her daughter, Miriam, stood watch to make sure no harm came to the baby.

When Pharaoh's daughter went down to the river to bathe, she saw the basket floating in the reeds and had one of her attendants fetch it. Seeing it was a Hebrew boy, the princess had pity on the baby.

"The baby seems hungry," Miriam said, stepping out from among the reeds. "Would you like me to find a Hebrew woman to nurse him?"

When the princess nodded yes, Miriam hurried off to find her mother. She couldn't wait to tell her that her baby brother had found favor in the eyes of Egyptian royalty!

Pharaoh immediately saw his daughter's attachment to the baby and had little choice but to allow the boy to grow up within the royal courts. It went against his better judgment, but he couldn't say no to his daughter. Little did he know what the future would bring!

As the years passed, Moses grew from a little baby boy into an attractive young man. Although he had the best education possible and enjoyed all the benefits of Egyptian royalty, Moses' heart grew heavier every day. Looking around him, he noticed how poorly the Hebrews were treated and how much they suffered at the hands of the Egyptians. Although he was Egyptian raised, Moses never forgot he was Hebrew-born. Perhaps someday, in some way, he could help his people. Moses looked for that opportunity.

Footwork

Open your Bible to Exodus 1 and read verses 20-21. Does what you read strike you as unusual? Do you think God was rewarding the midwives for not telling the truth? Take a closer look, especially at the first half of verse 21. Shiphrah and Puah had things in their proper order—they feared (and obeyed) God first—regardless of the personal cost to themselves. The Lord saw their hearts and rewarded them.

nd domes in construction; engineers

Fruit

In our society, the "law of the land" sometimes conflicts with the laws of God. Just because something is legal doesn't mean it's moral or right. God often allows challenges to come across our path so that we might have opportunities to stand up for Him. The next time you're faced with a decision that forces you to choose between obeying people or God, where will your allegiance be?

You Mean, *Me?*
Taken from Exodus 2—4

Foundation

Your life is not a mistake! The God who created you has a purpose and plan for your life—and also wants to have a relationship with you. Take a moment to thank Him for that fact. Ask Him to help you discover what He wants you to learn through your time with Him today.

Focus

Do you ever not do something because you feel you aren't good enough, or you might fail?

Moses looked down and couldn't believe what he had done! His hands trembled, and he nervously looked around him to see if anyone had noticed. The sight of an Egyptian beating an Israelite—one of his own people—had filled Moses with rage, and he had reacted violently. Now, the lifeless body of the Egyptian lay at his feet. Moses glanced around again and quickly covered the Egyptian's body with sand.

The next day Moses saw two Hebrew men fighting.

"Why are you beating up your Hebrew brother?" he asked the man who was in the wrong.

The man sneered angrily, "Look who's talking! Do you plan to kill me like you killed the Egyptian the other day?"

Like a sharp dagger, the words cut deep into Moses' conscience.

pipes of baked brick.   •   3000s

News of the crime Moses had committed in a moment of anger began spreading all over. When word reached the ears of Pharaoh, he sought to kill Moses. He had never liked this Hebrew in the first place and now had a good excuse to do away with him.

Fleeing for his life, Moses left Pharaoh's court for the desert dunes three hundred miles east of Egypt. When he arrived in Midian, he sat down near a well to rest. Drops of perspiration rolled off his brow as he looked around him, noticing how harsh the desert was compared to the fertile land of Egypt. Where would he go? How would he eat? What would he do? Even though Moses was Hebrew born, he was raised as an Egyptian and knew nothing about the Hebrew shepherd's lifestyle. As he pondered his options, seven girls came to the well to water their father's flock. But when a group of shepherds arrived and pushed the girls away, Moses stepped up and watered their sheep for them.

Mount Horeb is another name for Mount Sinai, the place where God would later give Moses the Ten Commandments.

"A kind Egyptian came to our rescue!" the girls breathlessly reported to their father, Jethro, who was a Midianite priest.

After hearing his daughters' report, Jethro invited Moses to stay with them as a guest, and a friendship built upon trust and respect grew between the two men. Before long, Jethro gave Moses his daughter Zipporah in marriage, and Moses spent the next forty years of his life as a shepherd. As Moses became increasingly familiar with the desert terrain of the Sinai Peninsula, he was unaware that God would one day appoint him to lead more than just sheep through that barren land.

One day while journeying to the far side of the desert with Jethro's flocks, Moses saw something strange on Mount Horeb, where the sheep were grazing. A bush was on fire, but it wasn't being burnt up—or even scorched! So Moses drew near for a closer look.

"Moses! Stop right where you are!" a voice called from the flames. "Remove your sandals, for the ground beneath your feet is holy ground! "I am the God of Abraham, Isaac, and Jacob," the Lord said, identifying Himself.

When he heard these words, Moses was overcome with awe and fear. With his face to the ground, he listened carefully to every word God said.

God had seen the suffering of the enslaved Hebrews at the hands of the Egyptians, and He had a plan. Moses would return to Egypt, go to Pharaoh, and demand the release of the Hebrews. Then he would lead them to the land God had promised to give them.

Panic rose in Moses' throat. "You mean, *me*?" he managed to choke out.

Painfully aware of his past failures, Moses began listing the reasons why he would fail at the task God had given him.

"What makes you think Pharaoh would ever listen to me and release the Israelites, that I might lead them out of Egypt?" Moses added, calling attention to his own unworthiness.

God simply replied, "My presence will be with you." Then He gave Moses a future sign that would prove that fact.

"What if the Hebrews ask who sent me?" Moses countered.

God answered, "Tell them I AM has sent you."

Moses grew quiet. Never before had the Lord identified Himself with a name that spoke of His character. Moses began to grow restless and desperate. When he brought up other reasons why he wasn't qualified to go—his feelings of incompetence, his poor public–speaking ability, even his own cowardice—the Lord answered each objection. God would give him the ability to perform signs and wonders so people would know that he was God's messenger. His brother, Aaron, would speak for him. Above and beyond everything else, God Himself promised to be with Moses.

When Moses cried, "You mean *me*?" God simply replied, "Yes, and I also mean *Me.*"

Footwork

Turn in your Bible to Exodus 4:10-13, and read it. What was Moses' problem? Notice what he says in verse 13. Have you ever felt this way? Now skip down to verse 17. What did God tell Moses to do? Notice the word *miraculous* (NIV). God takes us as we are, and *He* will work the miracles in and through us.

Fruit

When Moses gave his list of excuses, God responded by revealing a part of His own character: "I am." In effect, God was saying, "I am the One who designed you. I am the One who gives you life. I am the One who wants to use your life in a significant way. I am all you need. I am God, and there is no other. I am that I am. Any questions?"

In your own life, think of three reasons why you feel you can't serve or obey God. Now give those excuses or weaknesses to Him. Start by saying, "Lord, You know that I'm ... (Tell him your weakness.) I know You are ... (Say the opposite of that weakness.) Please help others to see Your power in my life because of my weaknesses. Let them see You as the One they truly need. Amen."

Is This Really Necessary?

Taken from Exodus 5—14

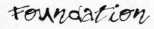

Stop and pray. Ask God to open your eyes and heart so you might discover what He wants to show you today. He is never far off or unconcerned about you.

Have you ever been blamed for the trouble someone else is having?

As a dark shadow moved down the streets and passed over each home, cries of pain and anguish rose up from some of the houses. It was a terrible night and one that would be remembered forever. God had sent His last plague, and final message—a message of deliverance for some, a message of destruction for others.

Moses stayed in his home as God had instructed, watching and waiting. The stillness of the night seemed heavy and quiet, only to be interrupted by sudden screams and crying outside. Moses stood in silence as experiences of the past few weeks and months flooded his mind. He knew God had sent him to rescue the Israelites from their slavery in Egypt, but it hadn't been an easy task.

"The Lord is concerned about us and has seen our misery!" the Hebrews rejoiced when Moses came with God' message of deliverance. They waited in eager anticipation as Moses pleaded their case before Pharaoh, but their excitement would quickly fade.

"Who is this God, that I should obey Him and let my slaves go?" Pharaoh answered arrogantly. He had little interest in hearing about the God of Israel. After all, he served all the gods of Egypt! "If these slaves have time to think about worshipping their God," he spat, "they must not have enough work to do!"

> *Each of the ten plagues targeted one of the many false gods of Egypt!*
>
> ---
>
> *Placing lamb's blood on the top, sides, and bottom of a doorframe symbolized more than obedience to God's command. A line drawn between the spots formed the shape of a cross and pointed to a future perfect sacrifice through Jesus. You can read about it in Faith Factor NT.*

So Pharaoh gave orders to make the work much harder for the Israelites while still demanding the same results. Instead of rescuing his people, Moses had only increased their suffering. In despair, the people revolted and would no longer listen to him.

"Why are you bringing more suffering on Your people? Why don't You deliver them as You promised?" Moses asked the Lord in frustration.

In response, God explained His plan to Moses and told him what would happen.

Suddenly, a scream echoed through the streets and caught Moses' attention. Another firstborn child had died—as would many more, along with firstborn cattle. It had been a long road up to this point in time, and God had given Pharaoh many signs and warnings. In the beginning, the plagues only caused discomfort for the Egyptians. The water throughout the land had turned to blood and killed the fish, creating a terrible stench. After this, the frogs came, and the gnats and swarms of flies. Then the plagues increased in intensity. All the livestock of the Egyptians died, while the Israelites' livestock remained untouched. Painful boils came upon the Egyptians, and hail destroyed most of their crops. What little remained was totally consumed by a plague of locusts. All of Egypt was devastated—except for Goshen, where the Hebrews lived.

Time and again Moses appeared before Pharaoh, but Pharaoh remained unwilling to release the Israelites, and turned a deaf ear to the warnings—at least until tonight. This final plague, yet another sign of God's awesome power, would cut deeply into Pharaoh's heart. Moses had warned Pharaoh and had helped the Israelites prepare for this night when they would finally see God's deliverance.

More wails rose from the valley. Moses knew that the angel of death had visited another Egyptian home and taken the life of every firstborn male within. But those who had obeyed God's command, sacrificing a lamb in exchange for the life of their firstborn and placing the blood on the doorframes of their homes, were not harmed. The angel saw the blood and passed over their homes.

In the middle of the night, Moses heard a rap on the door and the voice of a messenger summoning him to the palace. As Moses stepped out into the night air and hurried through the streets, the only tell-tale sign that the angel of death had come and gone was the trail of sorrow and despair left behind. Pharaoh was one of those despairing. He, too, had lost his firstborn—his only son and heir to the throne.

"Go! Leave my land and my people!" Pharaoh whispered through clenched teeth as Moses stood before him.

Because of the plagues, the people in Egypt now feared the God of the Hebrews and stood in awe of Him. Because of this, they gave the Israelites whatever they requested. So the Israelites plundered Egypt, taking with them clothing as well as articles of gold and silver. They were finally leaving Egypt and their worries behind—or so they thought.

Footwork

Do you know what happened at the height of the Israelites' victory? Turn in your Bible to Exodus 14. It's the exciting conclusion of today's lesson, and is worth reading on your own. For now though, skip down and read verses 10-12. Then compare these verses to verse 31. Who were the ones suffering this time? Do you think it was necessary? Now go back and read the whole chapter. You'll be glad you did!

Fruit

When hardship or difficult circumstances come into our lives, we often become discouraged. Sometimes we blame others, and sometimes we're the ones being blamed! When we point fingers at others and blame them for our troubles, we often miss the valuable lessons God wants to teach us. As a result, we fail to see Him at work in our daily lives. He might want to do a miracle in and through us, or He might allow our suffering so we can point others to Him. The next time you face a difficult situation, how will you respond?

Ti orders first fire drill; China

Is This a Test?
Taken from Exodus 15—18

Foundation

Take a moment to prepare your heart for today's lesson. Examine your heart, and ask God to show you areas in your life that are not honoring to Him.

Focus

Do you need to know all the "whys" before you obey certain rules?

Fear. Excitement. Relief. Curiosity. So many emotions filled the hearts of the Hebrews as they set out on their journey with Moses.

"Free at last!" they exclaimed joyfully, eyes aglow with the promise of a better future and a new land they could call their own.

Knowing the fragile condition of their hearts, God didn't lead them by the shortest route to the Promised Land, for traveling along the Mediterranean coastline would only have put the Israelites in possible danger of war with the Philistines. And they were not ready for that. Instead, God took them the longer route to the southeast, past Mount Sinai. They had many lessons yet to learn, and the three-month journey would provide ample opportunities for God to both teach and test His people.

"There are no gods who can even compare to Your awesome glory, Lord! You alone work magnificent wonders and Your holiness is filled with splendor!" the Israelites shouted with joy.

egins making rope from hemp.

The word **manna** comes from the Hebrew words **man hu** (pronounced **man-huh**), which mean "What is it?" This bread came down from heaven in white, thin flakes, that looked like seeds and tasted like honey wafers.

The women celebrated, dancing and shaking their tambourines. Even the very young and very old danced in celebration, for they had all seen God miraculously deliver them from Pharaoh and the army he had sent to pursue them. Hemmed in by the mountains on one side and the Red Sea on the other, the Israelites had faced certain death. But God delivered them, parting the Red Sea and allowing them to pass through on dry ground—nearly two million of them! As soon as the Israelites had safely crossed over, the Egyptians charged ahead, only to be drowned in a watery grave. It was a time of great rejoicing for the Israelites. The young nation knew that God was with them!

After their great victory at the Red Sea, the Israelites traveled three days in the desert without finding any water. When they finally came to an oasis at Marah, they found the water totally undrinkable and bitter. So the Israelites complained to Moses, and God instructed him to throw a piece of wood into the water, and the water would become drinkable. Even though this didn't make sense, Moses obeyed, and instantly the water turned sweet and was safe for the people to drink.

At that point, God gave the Israelites a command. "You must listen carefully to Me and do what is right and good. Pay close attention to what I say and keep the rules I give you."

Filled with the sweetness of the water, the Israelites easily agreed—and readily forgot.

As days passed into weeks, God faithfully led the Israelites from oasis to oasis. He guided them with a pillar of cloud by day and a pillar of fire by night. When the cloud stopped, the Israelites would stop and set up camp. When it began moving, they did too. Now, however, it had been a month and a half since they had left Egypt, and the excitement of the adventure had worn off. The people became hungry and irritable.

"It would have been better if we had stayed in Egypt and died as slaves," many complained. "At least *there* we had food to eat!"

Soon all the people were grumbling and blaming Moses for their discomfort. "Your grumbling isn't against me but against the Lord," Moses chided. "God has heard your complaining and will show you that *He* is the One who brought you out of the land of Egypt. He will give you meat in the evening and bread in the morning. Then you will know that He is the Lord your God."

Moses then relayed the specific rules God wanted the people to follow. "You are to go out each morning and collect what God provides," he stated. "Do not save any for the next day. But on the sixth day you must collect a double portion, for the next day is the Sabbath—a day of rest— and there will be no manna to collect." Although the rules were simple and easily understood, they weren't completely followed by everyone.

"That's a strange rule! Why should I collect only for today? There's plenty here, and who knows what tomorrow may bring!" some Israelites muttered to themselves.

They paid little attention to God's rules and stored away extra manna. But the next morning they discovered their manna spoiled and overflowing with maggots! Others forgot God's words of instruction and went out on the Sabbath hoping to collect manna, but found none. Returning to their tents with empty arms, the Israelites had to face the truth of God's words. If they listened to Him closely and obeyed what He said, they would be blessed. If they didn't, they would experience His judgment. Life in the desert would prove to be a testing and training ground for their careful obedience to God and His rules.

Footwork

God wanted the Israelites to depend on Him daily—a reason He commanded them not to store up manna. But in Exodus 16:4, God tells Moses another reason for His rule. What does He say? (Look this up in your Bible and find out!)

Fruit

As you go through life, you will encounter some rules that seem to make no sense at all. Be very careful how you react! You will be tempted to obey the rule only after it has met with your personal approval. Such an attitude is arrogant and sets you up for a fall. God wants us to be dependent on Him, and that includes allowing Him to be the source of our strength to help us obey rules we might feel are unnecessary. Sometimes rules are there as a test of our obedience. When faced with rules, don't give in to the temptation to challenge them—instead, accept them as a challenge.

Pleased to Meet You!
Taken from Exodus 19—24

Foundation

Take a moment to quiet your heart and be still before God. Think about His power. Think about His creation and everything you see around you. Ask Him to open your heart and eyes to His greatness and to help you appreciate Him more.

Focus

Do you ever feel that the Ten Commandments are just a list of dos and don'ts?

It had been three months—three long months—since the Hebrews had left Egypt and entered the desert. Already they had seen God's faithfulness and had been tested by His simple instructions. Now they were about to witness an awesome demonstration of His power and love.

Standing at the foot of Mount Sinai, the Israelites were filled with fear and awe as the ground trembled beneath them. They had spent three days preparing their hearts and cleansing themselves for this day, but nothing could prepare them for all they would see and feel.

Looking up at the mountain, they knew that touching it would mean certain death, for God had given specific instructions that no one was to come near. Barricades had even been set up to keep both people and animals at a safe distance. The Israelites stood by, ready to meet God.

ay India; Egyptians use papyrus

Lightning ripped across the sky, and thunder rumbled in the valley below. A thick cloud of smoke covered the top of the mountain as God came down from heaven in fire. The earth shook and smoke billowed from the mountain like a furnace, and a loud trumpet blast sounded. All the Israelites stood in silence, gripped by what they saw.

"Moses, your word is good enough for us and we promise to listen to your instruction! But if God speaks to us, we're afraid we might all die!"

They knew they were seeing only a glimpse of God's power and majesty. As they watched, Moses approached the thick darkness where God was, for God had a message He wanted to deliver.

A covenant is a life-and-death agreement between a greater party (such as a king) and a lesser party (his subjects) about how they can live in relationship with one another. Only the greater authority has the right to initiate it. The other has the opportunity to either accept or reject it.

"Tell this to the Israelites: I am the Lord your God, who brought you out of Egypt and out of your slavery," the Lord spoke to Moses. "You shall worship no other gods except Me. You shall not make for yourselves any idols or show dishonor to the name of the Lord. Keep the Sabbath day separated as a special and holy day. Honor your parents, so that you may live long as a nation in a covenant relationship with Me. Do not take another person's life by murder. Find delight only in the husband or wife who is yours. Do not steal. Do not ruin someone else's reputation with lies, and do not long for, or desire, anything that belongs to another person."

Moses listened as God continued listing His ground rules for how the people could live in a covenant relationship with Him.

When the Lord finished, Moses came down from the mountain and gave his report to the people. "This is what the Lord says …," he began, and carefully detailed all that God had spoken to him. He not only gave them the Ten Commandments, but he also described many other commands and instructions for how they were to live and govern themselves as a nation.

Standing in the shadow of Mount Sinai, the people heard God's conditions and readily accepted them. "We will do everything God says!" they proclaimed with a loud voice.

The Israelites were to be God's holy people, and God wanted their lives to be different. Surrounding nations worshipped false gods and lived in continual uncertainty. How would they know if they had pleased or angered their gods? But the Lord God of Israel lovingly drew His people into a special relationship with Him. They would not be left guessing about where they stood with God but would know exactly what He required of them. God, the Creator of the universe, had revealed His power and holiness and the conditions necessary for keeping His covenant. To be in relationship with Him was an awesome and unique privilege that would enable the Israelites to experience both security and trust.

Footwork

In your Bible, turn to Exodus 20:20. What was God's purpose in displaying His power to the Israelites? Notice Moses' first words, "Do not be afraid." Being afraid is based on a lack of trust in a person or situation. But the "fear of God" is based on respect for His power and a true understanding of who He is. This lays a foundation for trust and confidence in Him.

Fruit

God desires to be in relationship with you. Because of who He is, He has given you guidelines so you will know what pleases and displeases Him. Because such a great chasm exists between His holiness and our sinfulness, we immediately see where we fall short and "miss the mark." Even though the Ten Commandments were just a summary of the entire covenant with Israel, we find them impossible to keep. God gave them as a way of saying, "I love you and want you to know Me."

The fact that we can't keep them should cause us to respond, "I need You!"

Have you ever said those words to God—and meant them? If not—and if the desire of your heart is to know Him—bow your head right now and pray, "Lord, I see Your holiness and my sinfulness. Please forgive me for my sins and shortcomings. I want to be in a relationship with You, but I need your help. I can't live a good enough life on my own."

Now turn to the back of this book and read the special message God has for you!

How Could You?
Taken from Exodus 32

Foundation

You may be tempted to skip this part, but don't! Take the time to stop and pray before going any further. Tell God what's on your mind right now, and wait for Him to tell you what's on His.

Focus

When you trust somebody with a job, and he or she lets you down, do you find it hard to trust that person again?

More than a month had passed since Moses went up Mount Sinai to meet with God. *"What could be taking so long?"* Aaron wondered as he looked up at the mountain. From the valley below, the top of the mountain appeared to be on fire.

"Aaron! What do you think has happened to Moses?" the Israelites asked one day as they gathered around him.

Aaron could see that the people were becoming concerned and discontent. It had been hard for them to leave the comforts of Egypt (the comfort they'd known before they became slaves) and all that was familiar. Sure, they had seen God miraculously deliver them from Pharaoh's army when crossing the Red Sea. And He had also guided them through the wilderness, providing manna for them to eat and water to drink. Yet Moses was the only one who could communicate directly with the God they were just getting to know. He was their spokesman. Without him, the Israelites were filled with questions and doubts. At least in Egypt they were comforted by the images of gods they could see. *Perhaps that is what they need,* Aaron thought.

And soon enough, the people were asking him for that very thing.

"Make us gods we can see who will lead us!" they demanded, gathering around Aaron.

Aaron hesitated and then sighed as he gazed up at the mountain. No sign of Moses—still. *Will he even return? What am I to do with these people?* he thought. Aaron knew about as much as the people did, for although he could speak well, he himself had never spoken with God.

Aaron felt torn. He knew that the Israelites were working themselves up into a panic, and his own heart wasn't far behind! He glanced back up at the mountain and then slowly looked away. *There's no harm in giving the people what they want. After all, it's only a little thing,* he reasoned.

"Bring me all the gold jewelry you are wearing," Aaron announced.

The people did as he asked. Then Aaron took the gold they had given him and made an idol in the shape of a calf. When the people saw the idol, they rejoiced, for now they had a god they were familiar and comfortable with.

"Here are the gods who rescued us from the hand of Pharaoh!" they shouted in unison.

When Aaron saw the people celebrating, he built an altar in front of the calf and announced, "Tomorrow we will celebrate with a festival to the Lord!"

Everyone was in the mood for a good time, but things soon got out of control.

"To our gods!" the people cheered as they became drunk and danced about wildly. They didn't see Moses approaching from Mount Sinai, carrying the stone tablets containing the terms of God's covenant with them.

The closer Moses got, the angrier he became with Aaron. When he reached the camp, Moses' eyes caught sight of the golden idol. Filled with rage, he threw down the stone tablets. The pieces that lay at his feet represented Israel's broken covenant relationship with God.

Not much later, Moses found Aaron. "How could you *do* this?" he demanded. "Why would you lead these people into such great sin?"

Aaron remained quiet for a moment, realizing the seriousness of what he had done. He had led God's chosen people astray.

"Please don't be angry," Aaron stammered, hoping to cover his wrong. "It was the people—they demanded I do this. Since you weren't around, they insisted I make them a god they could see and talk to for themselves. All I did was collect their gold jewelry, toss it into the fire, and out popped this calf!"

Moses turned his attention from Aaron and looked at the scene before him. As a result of Aaron's bad leadership, the Israelites would become a laughingstock to their enemies.

"Everyone who is for the Lord come and stand by me," Moses yelled above the chaos.

All the Israelites from the tribe of Levi came forward, and Moses instructed them to go throughout the camp, killing all who claimed loyalty to the golden calf. Three thousand people were killed that day, and God killed the remaining rebels with a plague.

Footwork

It would be sad if the story ended here, but it doesn't. Moses took his disappointments to the Lord and prayed that God would forgive His people. Because of this, God gave the remaining Israelites—and Aaron—another chance. Turn in your Bible to the last chapter of Exodus (chapter 40). Now look at verses 12-13. What job did God give Aaron? What does that tell you about God's forgiveness?

Fruit

In this life, the people you trust will eventually let you down. When this happens, you could react with explosive anger: "How could you?" Or perhaps you could choose to ignore that person, giving him or her the silent treatment to show your disapproval. Or you could stuff your feelings and pretend that nothing ever happened. Even though these responses are very common, they're deadly. Moses didn't choose to hold a grudge but turned his disappointment over to God and even prayed for Aaron and the remaining Israelites. He knew that God could take something bad and turn it around. Only God could restore broken trust.

This week, be careful how you respond to those who might break *your* trust.

Leviticus

Feasts, festivals, offerings, sacrifices, and laws—all of these are described
in the book of Leviticus. At first glance, Leviticus seems strange and quite
boring to read. It's like reading a highly detailed instruction manual on a
subject you aren't even familiar with! But that's just the first glance. By
stepping back and looking at the *big* picture, we come away from this
book with some pretty important lessons for living.

All the instructions we find in Leviticus were given to Moses on Mount
Sinai. The tabernacle had been built, and God needed to teach the
Israelites how to worship Him. He got the Israelites out of Egypt, and now
He would have to "get Egypt out of the Israelites" and teach them a new
way of life! Many of the rules and regulations found in this book were
meant to keep the Israelites separate and different from the nations
around them. They were also safeguards to keep the people from sinking
back into the practices of the other godless nations.

As you explore Leviticus, remember that each law and regulation in this
book served a purpose. Many laws protected the Israelites' physical
health, such as the laws that prevented them from eating scavenger
animals, which often carried diseases. Other laws protected their spiritual
health by keeping them from slipping into their old lifestyles and forcing
them to depend on God for their forgiveness. Although we won't explore
all the rules and regulations in Leviticus, this book points loudly and
clearly to one thing: God's holiness and our need to respect it. ─────

Poof!

Taken from Leviticus 8—10

Foundation

Begin your time today in prayer. Be honest with God, expressing your desire to know Him better. Ask Him to give you a greater understanding of His power and holiness so you might learn to truly worship Him.

Focus

Do you know people who treat God casually?

It was a day of great rejoicing! The tabernacle had been built and dedicated according to God's specific instructions. Now Aaron, the high priest chosen by God Himself, would stand before God and represent the Israelites. His sons would serve as regular priests under his authority.

"This is what the Lord commands," Moses proclaimed loudly to the people. Aaron and his sons Nadab, Abihu, Eleazar, and Ithamar stood at Moses' side. Gathered before them at the entrance to the Tent of Meeting stood the entire assembly of Israel, waiting and watching with great expectation.

Moses had already washed Aaron and his sons with water, dressed them in their priestly garments, and anointed Aaron with oil. Now they stood silently watching as Moses skillfully prepared the animal to be sacrificed according to God's command. It was a solemn moment, for Aaron and his sons understood the symbolism of the bull taking their place and paying the penalty for their sins. They reached out and placed their hands upon the animal's head just before it was slain—totally identifying with that bull as their personal substitute.

After presenting the sacrifices and offerings to the Lord, Moses gave instructions to Aaron and his sons: "Stay here at the entrance of the tabernacle for seven days and do what the Lord tells you to do," Moses instructed.

For those seven days, Aaron and his sons carefully obeyed every command the Lord had given through Moses. On the eighth day, Aaron offered his first sacrifices as high priest on behalf of the people. When he had finished, the Lord sent fire down from heaven, and it burned up what remained of the sacrifice. Seeing this, the people shouted for joy and fell facedown in worship. Having only seen God's glory from a distance, they were now experiencing His presence close up!

As Aaron went about his priestly duties, he respected God's holiness and knew that it wasn't to be treated casually. Unfortunately, his two oldest sons lost sight of this.

Nadab and Abihu had a very important job. Their job was to take a piece of coal from the altar of the Lord and place it in the bottom of their incense burners. Only fire from this altar was considered holy. Special incense was then to be sprinkled on top of the hot coal, causing a pleasing aroma to go up before the Lord's presence. The burning of incense was only to happen at specific times in the morning and evening, all according to what God had commanded.

Nadab and Abihu knew these things, and yet, with incense burners in hand, they completely disregarded God's instructions. Casually entering the Holy Place, the brothers disobeyed God and offered Him a different kind of fire than He had commanded. *A fire is a fire,* they reasoned. To them it might not have mattered *where* they got the piece of coal, or the exact timing by which they carried out their duties—but to God it did. Coming before God was a privilege, not a right.

The second they offered their incense, a hot fire came out from the presence of the Lord and

> **Even though all of the Levites were dedicated to serve as priests, only descendants of Aaron could hold the office of high priest.**

consumed Nadab and Abihu. This wasn't the kind of fire God sent to show that he approved and accepted Aaron's sacrifices. Instead, it was an act of judgment and punishment. God put a quick end to such careless treatment of His holiness, and provided a warning for all who might be tempted to follow in Nadab and Abihu's steps.

God Himself had said, "I will be treated as holy by those who come near to Me. Before all people I will be honored." Nadab and Abihu had carelessly forgotten that fact and paid for it with their lives. What they did (and didn't do) stands as a lesson for all time: Treating God's holiness casually only results in casualties.

Footwork

Where did Nadab and Abihu first see a glimpse of God's holiness? Turn in your Bible to Exodus 24 and look at verse 1 and then verses 9-11. This was a special treat, not an ordinary occurrence! Note that they didn't see God face-to-face, for no one can see God face-to-face and live (see Exod. 33:20). Instead, God chose to reveal a part of Himself to them in a way they could picture and always remember. For Nadab and Abihu, there was no excuse.

Fruit

Right now, take a quick inventory of your life and ask yourself these questions:

- How big is God in my eyes?
- Have I reduced Him to something I can comfortably handle?
- Do I feel that He is here to serve me or that I am here to serve Him?
- Do I treat God's holiness lightly?
- Do I use His name in an empty, careless, or disrespectful way?

Over and over in Scripture, we're reminded of the holiness of God. Much like Nadab and Abihu, we, too, are without excuse. Spend a few minutes thinking about this and letting God speak to your heart. God is the same holy God now as He was back then. He is still to be highly respected. Want proof? Just remember how Nadab and Abihu went *poof.*

Lord, please forgive us for how casually we treat Your holiness. The miracle of a relationship with You is more than we can understand. Help us to know more clearly all that You are, that we might honor You better through our attitudes, our words, our actions, and our very lives. Amen.

Ho-Hum

Taken from Leviticus 23

Foundation

Stop! Don't just skip over this part. When you pray, be honest with God and commit this time to Him. Invite Him to show you that He is a God of purpose and that nothing in His Word is there by mistake.

Focus

Have you ever read something in the Bible that seemed boring, so you skipped over it?

When we read about the feasts God commanded the Israelites to celebrate, we may be tempted to skim the pages until we find something we feel has more meaning to us. If this is what you've been tempted to do, then read on. You're in for a great eye-opener!

"Tell the Israelites they are to worship Me and celebrate these seven feasts as a reminder of all I have done for them—and all that I will do," the Lord commanded Moses.

These weren't the kind of feasts we think of—like Thanksgiving—where families gather for a huge meal. They were times of celebration for remembering what God had done and drawing their hearts toward God. Each feast had an important meaning and message and was to be done exactly as God had commanded. Why? God would use these days not only as a reminder of what had happened but also as a picture of what was to come.

When God set up the feasts, He divided them into two seasons. The first four came in the spring, and the remaining three came in the fall:

later, Abraham is born in Ur.   ●   209

Spring Feasts

Passover

The Feast of Unleavened Bread

The Feast of Firstfruits

The Feasts of Weeks (Pentecost)

Fall Feasts

The Feast of Trumpets (*Rosh Hashanah*)

The Day of Atonement (*Yom Kippur*)

The Feast of Booths or Shelters (*Sukkot*)

Do the feasts still sound ho-hum? Remember: God is a God of purpose! Not only did the feasts help the Israelites remember all that God had done in the past, they also laid the groundwork for something He planned to do in the future. What God began, He Himself would bring to completion.

To fully understand this, let's jump ahead to New Testament times, around fourteen hundred years after Moses died. The time is the Passover season in the spring—Jesus' last days on earth. The place is Jerusalem. During this particular time, Passover fell on a Friday, the Festival of Unleavened Bread began on the next day (Saturday), and the Feast of Firstfruits, the day after that (Sunday).

On Friday, the day of Passover, the high priest sacrificed one lamb for the sins of the entire nation. In the middle of the afternoon, a priest would climb to the highest part of the temple, and at precisely 3:00 P.M., he would blow on a ram's-horn trumpet called a *shophar* (prounounced show-far). At the sound of this blast, everyone in the city would briefly stop what they were doing and look toward the temple, knowing at that exact moment one lamb was being offered up for the whole nation. This was also the exact time when Jesus, the Lamb of God, said, "It is finished," and offered up His life on the cross to redeem all mankind.

> *Jesus' very life and ministry fulfilled the springtime feasts that God established in Leviticus. According to Scripture, the complete fulfillment of the fall feasts will happen when Jesus returns.*

At sundown on Passover, the Feast of Unleavened Bread began. During this feast, the people recognized their dependence upon God to bless their wheat-growing season, which began at this time. They would seek God, asking Him to give them bread (or life) out of the ground.

It's significant that Jesus was buried during this feast. Only one week earlier, He had said, "Unless a grain of wheat is planted in the ground and dies, it cannot give life."

The Feast of Firstfruits came the next day to celebrate the barley harvest. During this feast, the people picked the first few barley grains beginning to ripen in their fields and brought them as an offering to the Lord. In doing this, they were saying to God, "Just as You have given us these firstfruits of the harvest, we trust You to bring about the rest of the harvest."

It was during this very feast that God raised Jesus from the dead. In 1 Corinthians 15:20, Jesus is called the "firstfruits" of all who die, meaning that He was the first one to rise from the dead, and through faith in Him, we will too! His resurrection is the proof and promise of eternal life for all who accept God's provision—a provision pictured in the feasts and fulfilled in Christ.

Footwork

When God does something, He does it with a purpose. His ways are so much higher than ours! Turn to Leviticus 23:4 and read what it says. What does the first part of that verse emphasize? Who came up with the idea of the feasts? Did it matter if the feasts followed a special schedule or appointed time?

Fruit

The next time you read something in Scripture that appears to be boring and of no purpose, will you simply skip it and say "ho-hum," or will you explore it and say "hmm"?

Numbers

Reading through the book of Numbers is like exploring the depths of a dark cavern, for in this book we see the nation of Israel at its worst. Of the many thousands of Israelites who left Egypt in the Exodus, Caleb and Joshua were the only men of their generation whom God allowed to enter the Promised Land. Even Moses was denied entry! What happened to everyone? That is what the book of Numbers is all about and it's something we'll explore together.

This book gets its name from "numbering" or taking a census of all Israelite men of military age (twenty years of age and older). A census occurs at the beginning of this book, and another was taken near the end—forty years later, just before the Israelites entered into the Promised Land. Although taking a census may seem unimportant to us, it had great significance for the Israelites. As you read through Numbers, you'll find out why. So let's get started. The book of Numbers is filled with surprises, so lose your way—and don't try to shortcut! You won't want to miss anything!

Be sure to check out www.cookministries.com/FaithFactor for three bonus stories, "If Only …" (taken from Numbers 11), "Step Aside, Please" (taken from Numbers 16—18), and "It's Close Enough" (taken from Numbers 32).

lesopotamia; ethyl alcohol, the

No Way!
Taken from Numbers 13—14

Foundation

Before beginning today's lesson, give your day to the Lord. Ask Him to help you see things from His perspective.

FOCUS

Do you ever feel discouraged or tempted to give up when others say you won't accomplish what you're trying to do?

"It's great! What a perfect opportunity!"

"No way! Are you crazy?"

It had been forty days—more than a month of anxious waiting—and now that word had finally come back, there were differing opinions. Who should the people believe? Only moments ago there had been excitement in the air as the returning Israelite spies appeared on the horizon. Their assignment had been to enter enemy territory (also known as Canaan, the Promised Land) to see what the land, the people, and the towns were like and to bring back a sample of the fruit in the land.

Everyone marveled over the size of the grape cluster they brought back, as well as the pomegranates and figs.

"What fertile soil!" some exclaimed. "What wonderful land! It really does flow with milk and honey as God said!"

"Just imagine! This is the land God has promised to give us!" others added with delight.

first drug, is used to help with pain

But the excitement and eagerness that filled the air slowly died out as one after another of the men gave their reports.

"We went into the land, and it *does* flow with milk and honey! Here is the fruit to prove it!" one spy reported before hesitating, searching for the right words to say next.

"But the people who live on this land are very powerful," another spy added, coming to his rescue. "Their cities are like large fortresses!"

One by one, ten of the twelve men gave negative reports. With each comment, the hearts of the Israelites grew heavy, and their discouragement pulled them away from their faith and trust in God.

Caleb and Joshua stood by, watching in amazement and disbelief. Both knew that the words the others spoke were true because they had seen the land with their own eyes. Yet the recommendations given by the others were all wrong. They were focusing on the wrong thing!

Finally, Caleb's voice rose over the confusion. "We should take the land! We can do it!" he urged.

"No way!" the others shot back, trying to silence him. "The land is full of large people—the descendants of Anak. We couldn't possibly defeat the Amalekites, the Hittites, the Jebusites, the Amorites, *and* the Canaanites! We'd all be killed!"

That night many of the people wept in despair. "Why did the Lord bring us to the border of this land only to let us die?"

Soon they began grumbling against Moses and Aaron, and their fear led them to rebellion. "Our women and children will be taken captive! It would be better if we went back to Egypt. Let's choose a leader and return!" they shouted.

Disregarding all that God had done for them and promised to do, the Israelites were ready to turn their backs on Him and walk away.

Knowing this, Caleb and Joshua urged again "This land is good land, and if God has led us to it, He will lead us safely through it! Don't be afraid of the people in the land; the Lord is with us. He will give us the land from the hands of our enemies!"

2066 BC — Isaac is born; Egypt

But the Israelites didn't see that the obstacles ahead were opportunities for God to show His power through them. No one would listen. In fact, the whole community even talked about stoning Caleb and Joshua to put an end to the nonsense. But at that moment, God appeared at the Tent of Meeting in all His glory and in front of all the Israelites.

"How long will it be before My people stop rebelling?" God said to Moses. "In spite of all the miraculous signs I have provided them, they still refuse to believe and trust in Me." The Lord's anger burned against the Israelites. "Those who saw My glory in the desert and the miraculous signs I performed on their behalf, yet chose to disobey and test Me—they will never enter the land. No one who treats Me with contempt will ever see the land I promised on oath to give your forefathers," God stated. "Instead, the very thing you stated will come true: your bodies will be left in the wilderness to die. No man over the age of twenty will live to enter the land— except for my servants Caleb and Joshua. Your children will enjoy the land you have chosen to reject, because their hearts seek to follow Me wholeheartedly."

> *"Flowing with milk and honey" is an expression that means the land was very rich and fertile, able to supply rich pasture for cattle (which would then produce an abundance of milk) and filled with a large variety of plants and flowers (a source of food for honey-making bees).*

God's punishment of the Israelites for their rebellion was severe. For forty years—one year for each day the spies explored the land—the Israelites would suffer for their sin and not be permitted to enter the land until the generation that had been in Egypt died off. As for the men who spread the bad report about the land and made their fellow Israelites turn against God, the Lord struck them with a plague and they died.

Footwork

Believe it or not, this wasn't the end of the story! Turn in your Bible to Numbers 14:39-45 and read it aloud. What were the Israelites trying to do here? Did God honor it? Why or why not? Now back up and read verse 24 and compare it to the verses you just read. God desires faithfulness and obedience the first time around.

Fruit

When you are faced with a difficulty, you'll be tempted to reason it out by looking first to your own abilities and resources—often leaving God completely out of the picture (or on standby in case all else fails). In so doing, you're actually turning your back on God and His faithfulness to carry you through difficult situations. That's what many of the Israelites did—and they missed out. Don't play that game. Instead, say "No way!" when your circumstances or friends begin to influence you not to trust God. Dare to be a Caleb.

Is This for Real?
Taken from Numbers 21—25

Foundation

Before reading on, quiet your heart before God. Simply take a moment (or several minutes) to pray and ask Him to still your thoughts and help you block out any distractions. Ask Him to help you understand what He wants you to learn today. (Don't read on until you've done this.)

Focus

Have you ever been around someone who turned out to be a completely different person than you first thought?

Balaam listened to the messengers who stood before him. They brought word of how King Sihon and all the Amorites attacked a nation called Israel and were soundly defeated. Now the Israelites were nearing the land of the Moabites, and King Balak knew they were too powerful to defeat. So he sent princes to Balaam, a soothsayer, with this message:

These people who have come out of Egypt and settled in the plains next to me seem to cover the entire land, and I fear they are growing too powerful. If you were to place a curse on them, I might then be able to defeat them and drive them from the land. For word has it that anyone you bless becomes blessed, and anyone you curse becomes cursed.

dogs, cats, geese, and monkeys.

Balaam studied the messengers who held out money to pay for his services. Of all the soothsayers in the land, he was the best. Because his reputation as a sorcerer was well known, he wasn't surprised that King Balak would send princes to pay him to work his magic and win the favor of the gods. Balaam knew that a people's own gods held the most power over them—for good or for bad—so he sought to make contact with the God of Israel. To him, this god was no different from any of the gods of the land. Little did he know....

Having instructed the messengers to spend the night, Balaam assured them he would have an answer for them in the morning.

That night, God spoke to Balaam and told him not to go with the men. "Do not curse the Israelites," the Lord said, "for they are blessed by Me."

Because of this, Balaam refused to go and sent the princes away. But King Balak wasn't one to be turned down, so he sent a larger and more distinguished group of princes. On behalf of the king, they offered to richly reward Balaam and do whatever he told them to do. Such an offer sounded good to Balaam, so he agreed to once again seek the God of the Israelites, but he warned the men, "Even if Balak were to give me his entire palace and fill it with silver and gold, I still could not go beyond what God commands."

That night God came to Balaam and said, "You may go with these men, but do only as I say."

Balaam was excited. Perhaps the Israelites' God was giving in! He would go with the intent of doing as King Balak asked. Maybe he would get that reward after all!

The next morning Balaam saddled up his donkey and went with the princes of Moab. On the way, however, his donkey began acting strangely. At first she turned off the road into a field; then she crushed Balaam's foot against a wall. When the donkey finally lay down in the road and refused to move, Balaam angrily beat her with his staff.

Then the Lord opened the donkey's mouth, and she said, "Why do you beat me? What wrong have I done?"

"You've made me look like a fool!" Balaam responded. "If I had a sword, you'd be as good as dead right now!"

It was then that the Lord enabled Balaam to see what his donkey could see: an angel standing with a sword in his hand, blocking the donkey's way.

"If it hadn't been for your donkey, you would be dead now. But I would have spared her life," the angel said.

> *Balaam has been compared to Judas in the New Testament. Both men came close enough to truth to seem sincere. Both seemed to serve God—for a time. But they eventually turned against God, motivated by their own ambitions and greed.*
>
> ---
>
> *King Balak's name means "destroyer" or "emptier" and describes the very thing he tried to do to the nation of Israel with the help of Balaam.*

Realizing the Lord had sent the angel to confront him, Balaam admitted his wrongful motives and sin, offering to turn back. The angel, however, stepped aside and instructed Balaam to continue onward, warning him to speak only what God would tell him to speak.

The next morning King Balak took Balaam to a high point where he could see part of the Israelite army. In a solemn ceremony, Balaam told the king to sacrifice seven bulls and seven rams, and then wait beside his offering. "Hopefully the Lord will come to meet with me—and if He does, I'll tell you whatever He says," Balaam said reassuringly over his shoulder as he made his way to a secluded place.

God did meet with Balaam and put a message in his mouth, but it wasn't what King Balak wanted to hear. Instead of cursing the nation of Israel, Balaam gave a blessing!

Unhappy with the results, the king whisked Balaam to another spot, hoping a change of scenery would inspire Balaam to curse the Israelites. Again, Balaam only blessed them. When this happened a third time, King Balak was angered.

"I brought you here to curse the Israelites, but you wouldn't! Now leave my sight and return home! I said I would richly reward you for your services, but because God has made you bless these people, you won't get a thing!" the king snapped.

Turning to leave, Balaam said, "Before I go, let me warn you of what the Israelites are going to do to you and your people in the coming days...."

Footwork

On the surface, it seems that Balaam had a change of heart and decided to follow the Lord. But appearances can be deceiving! In your Bible, turn to Numbers 22:18 and read it. How did Balaam refer to the Lord in this verse? Coming from the lips of a sorcerer, does this seem odd to you?

Fruit

The story of Balaam doesn't end with chapter 25, although that seems to be the last we hear from him. In Numbers 31:16, we learn that Balaam, after failing to manipulate God, later offered advice to the enemy on how the Israelites could be lured into sin. In spite of coming so close to the truth and even talking the talk, Balaam quickly returned to his treacherous old ways. He wasn't for real.

Throughout your life you'll come across "Balaams" who seem genuine on the outside but really aren't. Their motives aren't to serve God but to use Him to serve themselves. Watch out for them. Just because someone looks like a believer or talks like one doesn't mean that he or she truly is one.

Native Americans immigrate to

Deuteronomy

Deuteronomy is the last of the first five books of the Old Testament. It acts as a bridge between the five books of the Law, or the Pentateuch (*penta* meaning five) and the Historical Books (starting with the book of Joshua).

Deuteronomy is made up of three speeches Moses gave to the Israelites as they were poised to enter the Promised Land. In these three speeches, he did three things:

1. He gave a history of God's past dealings with the people.
2. He restated the rules for maintaining their relationship.
3. He gave a list of curses and blessings that depended on whether the Israelites broke or kept their covenant with God.

What Moses did in the book of Deuteronomy is very similar to how a covenant is laid out. For our purposes, however, we'll only look at a couple of the issues Moses addressed.

Before finishing your journey through Deuteronomy, be sure to check out www.cookministries.com/FaithFactor *for a bonus story titled "What Are My Options?" (based on Deuteronomy 30).*

North America from northern Asia.

Who?
Taken from Deuteronomy 7—11

Foundation

Stop for a moment and pray. Ask God to open your eyes to areas in your life that draw your heart away from Him or cause you to lose your focus.

Focus

Do you find it easy to forget about God—especially when things are going well in your life?

The Israelites looked up and followed Moses' gaze out toward the horizon. How easy it was to think they were better than others, to think they deserved what God was going to give them, to think they had somehow earned it.

"After the Lord drives out your enemies and you take possession of the land, don't say, 'Look what I've done for myself!' Don't let the success you experience turn your head from God," Moses warned. He knew all too well the Israelites' tendency to forget the Lord their God. "Walk closely with God, that it might go well with you," he advised.

Moses paused, thinking of the right words to express what was on his heart. He knew that his life would soon end, for God told him that he would not enter the Promised Land on the other side of the Jordan River. Moses looked at the sea of faces before him. Because of their parents' disbelief and rebellion against the Lord, they had been forced to wander in the desert for forty years. Now that God had raised up this new generation of Israelites, would they follow in the footsteps of their forefathers? Would they disobey God and forget Him and His promises as their parents had? Would they turn their backs on Him, or would they worship and honor Him?

An idol is anything you cherish in your heart more than God. It's something that knocks Him from His place of honor and importance in your life.

Moses spelled out the key to the Israelites' success in Deuteronomy 11:22-23. By observing God's commands and loving Him, by walking in His ways, and by holding fast to Him, the Israelites would experience a success that would come from the hand of God, not from their own efforts.

Moses watched as everyone nodded agreement to the fact that God had worked wonderful miracles and signs on their behalf. They all cheered as they remembered how He had divided the waters of the Red Sea so they could pass safely through, and then closed them on top of Pharaoh and his army. The people smiled at how God fed them with manna and provided water for them in the desert. And they couldn't deny the fact that He had just helped them defeat the Amorites and the Midianites, giving them the land they were now standing upon.

"Moses, don't worry! We'll have faith in the Lord. Haven't we trusted Him in the past?" the Israelites responded confidently.

Moses continued, reminding the Israelites about the dangers ahead and their tendency to turn away from the Lord. Their smiles of triumph faded as they remembered some of their past actions and the painful consequences. One by one, Moses brought each incident to mind so the people might never forget. One by one, the words hit home, like carefully placed nails hammered into wood: "making a golden calf and worshipping it," "complaining and murdering," "lacking faith in God," "rebelling against His command for you to go and possess the land He promised to give you."

Several in the crowd shuffled their feet uncomfortably. Others simply glanced down at the ground, embarrassed at the truth of Moses' words. As a nation, they hadn't been the most obedient group of people. Success in the new land would come only because God was faithful to carry out what He said He would do for them. It wouldn't come because of their own great accomplishments.

"O Israel," Moses challenged, "the Lord your God only asks this of you: that you never lose sight of His awesome and mighty power, that you walk in covenant relationship with Him and love Him with your whole heart, and that you obey His commands. No matter how well it goes in the land, never forget the Lord your God."

Moses knew that his days with the Israelites were drawing to a close. He would soon hand the mantle of leadership to Joshua, who had proven himself faithful and wholehearted in serving the Lord. *The people will be in good hands, Lord,* Moses thought, *as long as they never forget about You.*

Footwork

Open your Bible to Deuteronomy 11:16. What does it say? It's interesting to note that the gods the Canaanites worshipped all symbolized success. (For example, there was a god of rain so that farming might be successful and produce plenty of crops.) Next, take a look at the very next verse (verse 17). Knowing what you know about the false gods in the land, what do you think is the significance of what God says He will do? Finally, read verses 18-21. (Go ahead! Reading God's Word for yourself is vital for your spiritual growth.) What does God tell the Israelites to do? What do you think was the reason behind these instructions?

Fruit

Moses warned the Israelites to be careful or they would be enticed to turn away from the Lord and worship the false gods of the land. To be *enticed* means "to be lured into something," much like a fish that's drawn to a hook with bait dangling on it. By getting too close to the bait or even sampling a taste, the fish finds itself hooked. So it is with us. Our culture tries to entice us away from God by using bait like success in life, approval from others, wealth, recognition, materialism, pride, and even activities that keep us constantly moving so we don't have time for God. These are the "gods" of our land. Beware of them and don't be fooled when they come dangling into your life.

joshua

The book of Joshua is the first of the Historical Books in the Old Testament. This doesn't mean that everything up to now wasn't historical or didn't really happen. It simply means that the focus will shift to the Israelites as a new nation in a new land. As we explore this book, we'll read about their amazing victories and their deadly mistakes.

Joshua is an exciting book, but it's not without its difficulties. Reading through this book often raises the question of why God would have the Israelites wipe out entire cities—even killing innocent women, children, and animals—when He Himself said in the Ten Commandments, "You shall not kill." Because of this question, we are tempted to overlook what doesn't feel comfortable to us and never come to understand the purpose behind it all. If you've struggled with this, brace yourself and read on! This is an area we're going to explore together.

Before we venture into Joshua, you need to know that God had already given His Law to the people, and everything was in place. Moses and Aaron were no longer alive, and Joshua was now in charge. Aaron's son, Eleazar, is high priest. You also need to know something about God's character. Even though God brings judgment upon people and nations, He also gives them ample opportunity to turn from their wickedness. Those living in Canaan, with the exception of Rahab, continued living in wickedness and because of that choice, they would suffer God's judgment at the hands of the Israelites. So, what about the commandment not to kill? Didn't God cause the Israelites to break one of His rules? When God gave the command, "Thou shalt not kill," (Exod. 20:13) as it's commonly quoted from the *King James Version*, what he actually meant was, "You shall not commit *murder*." There is a difference. Murdering is killing for your own selfish and sinful reasons.

By journeying through the book of Joshua, you'll have other opportunities to learn about God's character. See how He answers the people's cries for help and changes someone's life around. Learn how He shows His power and love and makes His wisdom available, even when it is ignored.

As you can see, Joshua is far from being a ho-hum history book! It's packed with life lessons just waiting to be discovered. Now go and explore the land before you!

Be sure to check out www.cookministries.com/FaithFactor and read the lessons titled, "Ouch" (taken from Joshua 7) on how your sin affects others, and "But I Thought …" (taken from Joshua 9). It deals with operating in our own wisdom!

Help

Taken from Joshua 1—2

Foundation

As you begin exploring the book of Joshua, ask God to search your heart and help you change how you view others. Thank Him that He never gives up on you—or anyone else who truly wants to know Him.

Focus

Have you ever looked at certain people and assumed they would never be interested in God?

The towering walls of Jericho loomed ahead, daring anyone to be foolish enough to attack. Cautiously, the two Israelite spies entered the city and looked for a place where they could gather information with no questions asked. Their eyes were drawn to a house on the city wall. Judging by the people going in and out of the home, it looked as if it belonged to a woman who had little honor.

"No one will ever think of asking for us there!" they agreed. "Not with the whole town used to seeing strange men coming and going from that place!"

The spies knew the importance of the mission Joshua had sent them on, and the need for information drove them forward. They would go to this woman's house.

When the king of Jericho heard that Israelite spies were in the city to discover the best way to attack, he sent orders for Rahab to hand over the men who were reportedly seen entering her home.

ge of 175 and is buried in the

Linen clothes were made from flax plants. Bundles of three- to four-foot lengths of flax were soaked in stagnant water to separate the fibers, and then hung on rooftops to dry. Because the flax gave off an unpleasant odor, the rooftop provided an ideal hiding place for the spies!

As the spies promised, Rahab and her family were spared and lived among the Israelites. In Matthew 1:5 we learn that Rahab married an Israelite named Salmon, and they had a son named Boaz. It was through this family line that King David, and later, Christ, would come.

"Yes, the men were here, but I didn't know who they were or where they came from," Rahab lied. "They left at sunset, but I don't know where they went. If you hurry, though, you might be able to catch them!"

Rahab closed the door and let out a sigh of relief. It was good the soldiers hadn't searched her home, for she had hidden the two men on the rooftop under bundles of drying flax. Assuming that a woman like her wouldn't have any interest in the God of Israel, the soldiers left in hot pursuit of two men they would never find.

Climbing to the roof, Rahab yearned to talk with the two men she had risked her life to save. She knew they were Israelites who served the one true God.

"I know that your God has given our land into your hands. We know that He parted the Red Sea so you might pass through and that He has given you victory over your enemies. Because of what God has done for you, all who live in this country are melting with fear," Rahab confided. Then, in a moment of quiet reflection, she stated what she knew in her heart to be true: "The Lord your God is the only true God in heaven and on earth."

The two spies looked at each other, shocked at what they heard.

"Please," Rahab continued, "promise me that when you attack our city, you will return the kindness I have shown you and spare my life as well as that of my family.

The spies assured her that because she'd risked her life for a God she barely knew, they would spare her life as well as the lives of her entire family so that she might come to know Him better.

family burial plot at Machpelah.

"Please give me a trustworthy sign that what you say will come to pass," Rahab asked of them.

"The fact that you've spared our lives is proof we will spare yours," the men assured her.

With that, Rahab let the men down by a rope through a window. Since her house was on the city wall, it would make their escape easier. "Hide in the hills so those pursuing you won't find you. Wait there three days until the soldiers return to the city. Then it will be safe for you to leave," she advised.

Before slipping over the edge of the window, the two spies cautioned Rahab. "The promise we have made to you will only be fulfilled if this scarlet cord remains in this window. If you or anyone in your family leaves this house during the time of our attack, you will not be spared."

Rahab agreed and sent the spies on their way. "May it happen just as you say," she whispered as she watched the two men disappear over the horizon. Rahab secured the red cord in the window. She would watch and wait.

Footwork

Turn to Joshua 2:11 in your Bible and look at the second half of that verse. What did Rahab say? Coming from the source they did, these words were totally unexpected! Rahab was able to make that statement because she knew what God had done on behalf of the Israelites. Even though Rahab had a bad past, she didn't let that stop her from personally coming to God.

Fruit

Take a moment to think about the people in your life. Do you know someone who seems unlikely to ever come to know the one true God? Put that person's name on an index card and write Joshua 2:11 across the top. Keep this in your Bible and use it as a reminder to pray for that person. Then live your life in such a way that it points others to God. Don't assume people aren't interested in Him. The cry for help is often heard in the least expected place.

steals his birthright; Jacob flees t

What's the Meaning of This?

Taken from Joshua 3—4

Foundation

Before reading today's devotion, stop and pray. Ask the Lord to help you conquer any fears or concerns you have that keep you from following Him wholeheartedly.

Focus

Do you sometimes find it difficult to make a total commitment to God or to other things in your life?

The water roared swiftly past, slamming against rocks in a frothy foam and crashing against the riverbanks. The fast-moving Jordan River was at its peak during flood stage. Just beyond it lay the fortress-like city of Jericho, secure and imposing. The people there worshipped Baal, a god they believed controlled the wind, storms, rain, and the depth of the river. Knowing the Jordan was at flood stage, they felt protected and shielded by their god. They had nothing to worry about—or so they thought.

"Come and listen to what the Lord your God says," Joshua yelled to the Israelites over the noise of the river.

For three days they had camped along the banks of the Jordan, watching its sheer power carve through the gorge. The river stood in the way of the mission God was calling them to. They could go no farther until they crossed that barrier.

"What you are about to do will prove to you that God is with you and will help you accomplish what He has for you to do," Joshua continued.

Looking at the priests, he signaled them to carry the ark and go ahead of the people. "The ark of the covenant of the Lord—the Lord of all the earth—will go before you into the Jordan. The moment the priests step foot into the river, its waters will stop flowing." The Israelites became quiet when they heard Joshua's words. Only the thundering water could be heard, threatening to swallow up anything crossing its path. This would be an extreme test of their faith. The Israelites all watched as the priests neared the banks of the river.

"Standing stones" were used as memorials to help people remember an important event. Travelers passing by would stop and ask, "What happened here? What's the meaning of this?" In some ways, they were like the Lincoln Memorial in Washington DC or the war memorials in Russia. Seven different times in the book of Joshua they were set up to point the attention of the world to God's power.

As soon as they had positioned themselves directly in front of where they were to cross, the priests carrying the ark stopped. There was no gentle slope where they could stick their feet in to test the waters and see if God would do as He promised. This would be an all-or-nothing commitment. Once they stepped off the bank, the priests would either be in water over their heads or on dry ground as God had promised. With a lurch, the ark moved forward as they took their first step—a step of faith that God was waiting for them to take.

Suddenly everything fell silent. The mighty roar that challenged the Israelites' faith had vanished. There, in the middle of the riverbed stood the priests—completely dry and standing on firm ground! With excitement and newfound faith, the Israelites passed in front of the ark, ever mindful of God's presence with them.

Joshua then gave specific orders to twelve men God had told him to choose, each representing one of the twelve tribes of Israel. "Each of you go over to where the ark of God is in the middle of the Jordan and select a large stone. Carry this stone on your shoulder to the place we will camp," he commanded. "These stones will serve as a sign. When your children ask, 'What happened here? What's the meaning of these rocks?' tell them the great thing God has done on your behalf and how He stopped the flow of the Jordan River, a large obstacle that stood before you," he explained.

Once the Israelites had accomplished all God had instructed them to do, Joshua commanded the priests to come up out of the Jordan. The moment they set their feet on the land, the waters returned and raged at full flood level. Taking the stones that the men had carried from the middle of the river, Joshua stacked them together as a standing memorial to God's power in their lives. There the stones would remain for all the world to see.

The Jordan River (which means "to descend" or "to go down") was named because of how rapidly it drops in elevation. Being only fifty to seventy-five feet across in most places, the Jordan runs along a ridge in the earth's crust. The place the Israelites crossed was very near to where Jesus was later baptized.

Footwork

In your Bible, turn to Joshua 4:23-24. What does it say? There were two reasons God did what He did. What were they? [*Hint:* The first reason was something for all humankind to see, and the second reason was for every Israelite to do.]

Fruit

God's promise to the people of Israel wouldn't be fulfilled until they were willing to trust Him and take the first step. Once they did, God worked powerfully on their behalf. What barriers do you face that keep you from the mission God has called you to? (If you're not sure what that mission might be, ask Him to show you.) Take a moment and search your heart. God wants to use your life as a "standing stone" or memorial to His power and love, but He won't do anything until you're willing to make a total commitment to Him. When you're faced with challenging obstacles, remember they are only opportunities for Joshua 4:24 to be fulfilled in your life. Memorize this verse and keep it handy.

River; spoked wheels are invented in

Let This Be a Lesson to You!

Taken from Joshua 5—6

Foundation

Find a quiet spot and take a moment to reflect on all God has done for you and provided in your life. Ask forgiveness for the times you've taken Him for granted or neglected to thank Him.

Focus

Does it ever bother you when people take credit for a job they didn't do?

Joshua looked out toward the horizon at the fortified walls of Jericho. Because word had gone out about the miraculous crossing of the Jordan, fear of the Israelites and their God reigned in the hearts of those living in the land. As a result, Jericho was tightly closed up, allowing no one to enter or exit. *This will make attacking the city all the more difficult,* Joshua thought as he drew closer to the fortress for a better view. He looked back over his shoulder to where the Israelites were encamped at Gilgal. During the past forty years of wandering in the wilderness, the people had observed neither the celebration of Passover nor the rite of circumcision—not until now. Now the Israelites could walk obediently before their God as a nation. They were an army poised for battle.

A movement suddenly caught Joshua's eyes and caused him to look up. Standing before him was a soldier with a drawn sword in his hand. *If this is an Israelite,* Joshua thought to himself, *he is out-of-bounds. If this is the enemy, I'm ready to fight!*

> *God instructed the Israelites not to take any plunder from Jericho, as the destroyed city was to be dedicated to God as a "firstfruits" offering. It was the first of more promised victories the Israelites would need to trust God for.*
>
> ---
>
> *Joshua's curse in Joshua 6:26 was fulfilled in 1 Kings 16:34 when a man named Hiel tried to rebuild Jericho in the days of King Ahab. Hiel lost both his oldest and his youngest sons in the process.*

"Who are you?" Joshua demanded. "Friend or foe?"

"Neither one," came the powerful reply. "I am commander of the Lord's army."

The meaning of those words struck Joshua, and he fell facedown to the ground out of respect.

"I am at your command," he replied, shaken. Realizing the battle plan had little to do with the Israelites and everything to do with God, he humbly asked, "What do you want your servant to do?"

"Take off your shoes, for the ground you are standing on is holy," the soldier answered.

Joshua did as he was told, then listened carefully to all the instructions the Lord had for him. When he returned to the men who were armed and ready for battle, he shouted, "God has promised to fight for us and deliver Jericho into our hands!"

The soldiers and priests listened intently, waiting to hear Joshua's words of wisdom and his plan of attack. They weren't prepared for what they heard next! "This is what we are to do," Joshua told them. "Take up the ark of the Lord and have seven priests in front carry their ram's horns, blowing them as we march. An armed guard will go in front of the ark, and one behind. We'll march around Jericho once, then return to camp."

When Joshua finished giving instructions, no one said a word. *What kind of battle plan is that?* they wondered.

The Israelite army did as it was told and marched around Jericho once before returning to camp. The whole process took no more than about thirty minutes. The next day, the Israelites rose at dawn and repeated what they had done before.

Each day for six days straight, the Israelites did this—just as God commanded. Each day they carried the ark before them and circled Jericho one time while the priests blew on the ram's-horn trumpets.

When the seventh day came, however, the orders changed. "Today we will march not just once, but seven times around the city!" Joshua proclaimed. "After the seventh time around, the priests will sound a long blast on the horn, and you are to shout, for the Lord has given you the city!" (See 6:5.)

Obediently, the Israelites picked up the ark and marched. In their hearts they knew such an act would never deliver the city into their hands—not unless God was behind it. For every lap they marched, the Israelites endured the ridicule of the soldiers on the wall above. It seemed to take forever to march around seven times.

Suddenly the Israelites heard the long blast on the ram's horn, and lifting their voices to the heavens, they gave a great shout. Panic suddenly replaced the laughter they had heard from their enemies. With a loud rumbling sound, the walls began to crumble and explode outward! Screams and cries of terror rang out as the Israelites ran in. According to God's instructions, they were to completely destroy anyone and everything that remained, sparing only Rahab and her family.

"Take nothing for yourselves," Joshua warned, "for this city is to be totally devoted to the Lord!"

Joshua knew the victory had come from the Lord alone; therefore, the Lord alone deserved the rewards and the credit.

Footwork

Turn to Joshua 6:26 and read what it says. Does this make sense to you? Why do you think Joshua said this? The destruction of Jericho was God's way of saying, "Let this be a lesson to you." For the people of the land, it would stand as a monument of God's power so that the world might know He is God. To the Israelites, it would also stand as a promise of more victories to come.

evelop the undecipherable Linear

Fruit

When the Lord gives you success, do you give the credit to Him, or do you bask in the rewards as if you accomplished it by yourself? How do you acknowledge the "Jerichos" of your life?

Give Me a Chance to Explain!

Taken from Joshua 22

Foundation

Come to this time of exploration today with a heart that's ready and willing to learn. Ask God to remove any distractions or thoughts that battle for your attention, including wrong thoughts or attitudes you have toward others. Dedicate this time to Him.

Focus

Does it ever frustrate you when others assume they know what you're thinking—and they're wrong?

Joshua let out a sigh of satisfaction. With the Lord's help, the Israelites had conquered thirty-one kings and their cities! The battles were over, the land had been divided up, and each tribe had received the inheritance God had promised. *Thank you, Lord,* Joshua breathed, and then turned his attention to the tribes of Reuben and Gad, and half the tribe of Manasseh.

"You have been mighty warriors, faithful to help us conquer the land of Canaan," he commended. "You've done everything you promised to do and completed the mission the Lord gave you. Now that the battles are over and the land has been divided, you are free to return to the land you

t Knossos is constructed and the

Shiloh was in a central location for all the tribes in the land of Canaan. By having the tabernacle and the altar of the Lord there, it became the primary place of worship for the Israelites.

According to Leviticus 17:8-9, if an Israelite offered a sacrifice on any altar other than the one at the tabernacle (Tent of Meeting), that person had to be cut off from the community. Building an altar was also something only a priest could do.

requested as your inheritance, the land just outside Canaan on the opposite side of the Jordan River."

The soldiers looked at Joshua with equal satisfaction. Seven long years of fighting had finally ended. Now they would return to their families with great wealth—large herds of livestock, silver, gold, bronze, and iron, and a great quantity of clothing. All this God had provided from the cities they had helped to conquer. Finally able to return to their families, they would divide up the wealth among themselves.

Joshua met their gaze and blessed them before sending them away. "Take great care to keep the Law of the Lord. Love Him and walk in His ways," he reminded them. "Obey God's commands and hold tightly to Him—serve Him with all your heart and soul."

Each of the men knew the importance of Joshua's words and vowed to do just that. With a heartfelt good-bye, they left Joshua and the other tribes in Canaan and headed east to Gilead.

At the banks of the Jordan, the men remembered how God miraculously parted the waters so the Israelites could cross over and how He gave them victories in the land of Canaan. Looking up, they saw the mountain ranges—more than two thousand feet high—on either side of the Jordan River. Between these mountains lay the Jordan Valley like a large trench with the river running through it. The separation between their tribes and the rest of the Israelites suddenly hit them. "Someday, the ten-and-a-half tribes may say to us, 'You have nothing to do with the Lord our God. See, the Jordan stands as a boundary line between us.' What will happen then?" the men asked one another.

"Let's build an altar on the border of the land of Canaan," one of them suggested, "that will remind us of the God we share with all the tribes of Israel."

The men agreed that this was a good solution and built a huge altar that could be seen from a great distance.

The Israelites on the other side of the Jordan saw the altar and became enraged. Why had the eastern tribes built an altar when they were supposed to offer sacrifices only at the tabernacle in Shiloh?

"How could they do this?" they asked. "How could they forget the Lord so easily and build their own altar?"

"They are rebelling against God!" someone shouted.

"Are they taunting us by placing this altar on our side of the Jordan, tempting us to bow down to idols?" another added.

Gathering together at Shiloh, the whole assembly made plans to go to war against the eastern tribes of Gad and Reuben, and the half-tribe of Manasseh. The Israelites appointed Phinehas (son of Eleazar the high priest) and a delegation of ten leaders—one man to represent each tribe—and they quickly left Shiloh to confront the matter. Anger drove them forward.

When they arrived at Gilead, the ten leaders fired their accusations at the men who had built the altar.

"How could you break your covenant with God?" they demanded. "Don't you know that your rebellion will bring God's anger down upon us all?"

Reuben, Gad, and the half-tribe of Manasseh listened in stunned silence. "May that never be!" they quickly answered. "We didn't build this altar for worship or offering sacrifices. It is to stand only as a reminder of our right to offer sacrifices at the one true altar of the Lord in Shiloh. We feared that one day your descendants would say to ours, 'You have no right to share in the Lord with us,'" the men explained.

When Phinehas and the leaders heard what the men had to say, they no longer talked about going to war against them. Instead, they rejoiced and praised God.

Footwork

Take a look at Joshua 22:28 in your Bible. The eastern tribes had an explanation for their actions. Now, skip down and read verse 30. Notice the words "when" and "heard" (or similar words)? They are critical! Listening can make all the difference in the world.

Fruit

When we get into a conflict with someone, we're often tempted to react before we hear the whole story. Sometimes we assume we know what the other person is thinking and don't take time to listen to or understand his or her side of the issue. Busy trying to prove our point, we often misunderstand what the other person has said or done. God isn't honored by this. Everyone deserves a chance to explain and be heard. The next time you come in conflict with someone, make a point to practice the art of listening! Use this as your guide:

L – Let the other person express himself or herself.

I – Ignore the urge to interrupt or cut in.

S – Seek to understand what the other person is saying.

T – "Tune in" to what's being said.

E – Examine the facts.

N – Never assume you know what's going on in the other person's heart.

Judges

When we hear the word judge, the idea of a courtroom usually comes to mind. But this isn't what Judges is about. Many people look at this book and think of heroes like Gideon, Deborah, and Samson, who came to rescue the Israelites. Even *that* isn't what Judges is all about. So, exactly what *is* it about? The book of Judges (which spans approximately 350 years) is all about what happens when people turn from God and make their own rules for living. It graphically shows the lowest levels to which people can sink when they neglect the Lord. The last verse of Judges sadly states that every man did what was right in his own eyes. Having just experienced the victories and rewards of obedience in the book of Joshua, how could the Israelites change so drastically? What happened? That's what you'll discover as you go through Judges.

As you explore this book, look for a pattern in the Israelites' behavior. Their sin caused them great suffering at the hands of their enemies. When they called out to God, He sent someone to rescue them. As time passed, the nation forgot about its relationship with God and started sinning again. So the cycle continued: sinning, suffering, asking, receiving, forgetting, sinning.... This sad cycle was repeated not just once or twice, but over and over.

Even though this book is filled with dark times, one bright light penetrates the darkness: God's patience. God never gives up on His people or abandons them, in spite of major flaws in the character of

ater, becomes a ruler of Egypt.

His people and the mistakes they make. Instead, He patiently worked with them, desiring to draw them back to Himself. Judges is a book of second chances and opportunities for new beginnings.

Be sure to check out www.cookministries.com/FaithFactor for two bonus lessons titled "You're Sure You're Sure?" (taken from Judges 3—7) and "Give Me Leadership ... or Give Me Death!" (taken from Judges 8—9). These lessons deal with doubting God and the dangers of seeking to be number one.

That's Good Enough for Me!

Taken from Judges 1—2

Foundation

Before you explore today's lesson, ask God to help you be more willing to obey Him all the way (rather than halfway). Ask Him to speak to your heart and show you areas in your life that need to change.

Focus

When faced with a hard task, do you quit early?

Joshua had died, and now it was up to each tribe to finish driving out the enemy from their own territory. Although only pockets of Canaanites lived here and there, the task of entirely conquering the enemy remained incomplete. "Remember, God will fight for you," Joshua had said. The people remembered what Joshua had said to them some time before, "As you rely on Him, He will help you accomplish the task. Only be very careful not to associate with those living in the land. You must drive them out completely, or they will become a snare to you."

Joshua then reminded the Israelites of God's rules, spoken through Moses. While Joshua was still living, the Israelites had obeyed those rules. When he died, however, the people quickly forgot them. One compromise led to another, and instead of completing the job God had given them to

In Deuteronomy 7:2-6, God gave the Israelites three rules for when they entered the Promised Land: (1) Totally destroy the enemy; (2) Don't marry the inhabitants of the land; and (3) Don't follow after their false gods. The Israelites ignored all three rules.

The Canaanites lived in city-states governed by separate kings. This made conquering the land more difficult, for a captured king could not surrender on behalf of the other kings. Each city had to be conquered individually.

do, the Israelites looked for easier alternatives, following the path of least resistance.

"Come up to our territory and help us battle the Canaanites," those in the tribe of Judah asked the tribe of Simeon. "In turn, we will help you with your battles."

So the two tribes made a deal and fought side by side. When they conquered the city of Bezek, however, they didn't kill the king. Instead, they made sport of him by cutting off his thumbs and big toes so he could no longer hold a weapon or lead his troops in combat. As God had told them at other times, this was something He neither commanded nor approved of.

Continuing on in battle, the two tribes gained control of Judah's hill country but stopped short of gaining control over the valley because the Canaanites were using iron chariots.

"We're no match for such weapons!" they cried out in fear as the chariots bore down on them. Backing away from the challenge of completing the job, the Israelites limited their fighting to where the chariots couldn't go.

While all this was happening, the tribes of Joseph (Ephraim and the half-tribe of Manasseh) were making compromises of their own. "If you show us the way into your city," they bargained with a man from the Canaanite city of Bethel, "we'll make sure no harm will come to you."

The Canaanite man agreed, and even though the entire city was destroyed, he and his family were allowed to live. This was only the beginning. Ephraim and Manasseh soon found it difficult to drive the Canaanites out of the land, for they were a strong and stubborn people.

"Why should we get rid of them," they began to reason in their hearts, "when we can force them to serve us and benefit from their skills and trade?"

So rather than struggling to conquer the land and finish driving out the Canaanites, the tribes of Joseph decided to simply live alongside them. It wasn't long before the other tribes did the same.

The very thing Moses and Joshua warned the Israelites about doing had finally happened. Rather than loving and following God with their whole hearts, the Israelites were influenced by their enemies and began to bow down to pagan idols. Because they hadn't fully obeyed the Lord's rules, their compromising actions would lead to their own downfall.

Footwork

In your Bible, look up Judges 3, and read verses 5-6. (Don't worry about pronouncing all the "ites" in verse 5 correctly. The main point is in verse 6.) According to these verses, what did the Israelites do next? Did you see this coming?

Hammurabi reigns over Babylon for

Fruit

Many of us are no different from the Israelites. Instead of obeying God fully, we come to the halfway mark in wrestling with sin. Feeling like we've done a good enough job, we look for an easier standard to reach, or a partial compromise. Because we've come partway, we say, "That's good enough for me!" and pat ourselves on the back. Unfortunately, "That's good enough for me!" isn't good enough for God. In His eyes, doing something halfway is just as bad as not doing it at all.

Take a moment and think about your own life. What difficult task has God called you to do that you've given up on? Tell Him about it right now. Ask for His forgiveness, then make a point to make it right. Use today as a starting point to live wholeheartedly for Him.

Lord, I've only followed You halfway and have grown comfortable living with my sin. I want that to change. Right here, right now, I dedicate my life to following You wholeheartedly. Give me a heart that seeks to obey You completely so I'll have no retreats and no regrets.

Signed_____   Date_____

Can We Erase That?
Taken from Judges 10—12

Foundation

Stop and pray, asking God to help you deal with old habits and hasty actions that tend to get you into trouble. Thank Him that He is able to give you the power and ability to change.

Focus

Have you ever gotten so caught up in the moment that you made rash statements without really thinking?

"You stole our land!"

"Did not!"

"Did too! Now give it back peacefully—or else!"

Jephthah knew he had a decision to make. For three hundred years the Israelites had lived in Gilead, and there had never been a dispute over the land—until now. Suddenly claiming that the land was his, the Ammonite king threatened to attack. When the people of Gilead heard this, they were terrified and came to Jephthah asking for help.

How strange, Jephthah thought to himself, *my own brothers living in Gilead drove me away saying that I wasn't worthy to have an inheritance with them. Now, when there's trouble, they come to me for help!*

Jephthah's father was the one for whom Gilead was named. Unlike his brothers, Jephthah wasn't born through Gilead's wife, but rather through a Canaanite woman of little honor. Regardless, Jephthah was still one of

Hammurabi, the first legal code

The Amorites were the original inhabitants of the land of Canaan. Amorite means "westerner." The Ammonites were a race that descended from Lot's youngest daughter and often teamed up with other nations against Israel.

Here's a simple definition of acting on impulse:

I
Mistakenly
Plunge ahead,
Underestimating
Long-term
Side effects on
Everyone and everything
in my life.

Gilead's sons, and that had caused problems with the rest of the family. For years they had considered their half Israelite and half Canaanite brother worthless. But now his help was needed, and they offered to make him leader over all of Gilead if he would help fight the Ammonites. Jephthah agreed and considered his options.

Hoping to solve the problem peacefully, he sent a message to the Ammonite king.

"Gilead was never yours in the first place," Jephthah stated. "It was taken from the Amorites, not the Ammonites. Furthermore, God gave this land into our hands, and we have the right to possess it—just as you have the right to possess any land your god gives to you." Jephthah smiled at that thought. "Finally, no one has ever challenged Israel's ownership of this land since it was conquered three hundred years ago! We haven't wronged you, but you are wronging us by waging war against us."

But the king of Ammon ignored Jephthah's message and continued preparing for war. It was then that God empowered Jephthah to lead his army against the Ammonites.

While marching his troops across the land, Jephthah reflected on his life. *I was cast off as worthless, and now I hold command over an Israelite army,* he thought with wonder. Living outside of Gilead as he did, Jephthah knew he had gained valuable leadership experience by heading up a band of adventure-seeking men. This, however, was totally different—and the stakes were much higher. Jephthah felt the heavy weight of responsibility on his shoulders. The people of Gilead were counting on him to pull this off.

In a moment of emotion, Jephthah spontaneously blurted out, "Lord, if You give me the victory and I return home triumphantly, I will gladly sacrifice to You as a burnt offering whatever first comes out of my door to greet me!"

Jephthah felt better that he had included God in his plans, and he went on to defeat the Ammonites, conquering twenty towns. What a victory it had been!

Word of Jephthah's success quickly reached Gilead, and everyone began celebrating, especially Jephthah's household. As Jephthah strode up the path to his home, the door flew open, and Jephthah's daughter ran out to meet him, dancing to the sound of tambourines. Jephthah froze in his tracks. At that moment he realized what a rash and unwise vow he had made. His face suddenly changed from celebration to grief. *Oh, that I could go back and erase what I vowed*, he thought. Jephthah's daughter, his only child, sensed something was drastically wrong. How would he explain it to her?

Footwork

Open your Bible to Judges 11 and read verse 30. (Even though verse 31 completes the thought, stop after you read verse 30.) Now closely look at the first few words Jephthah says to the Lord. What are they? [Hint: Look for the word *if* or a similar word (depending on the version of the Bible you are using).] Have you ever spoken those kinds of words to God?

Fruit

Many struggle with this event in the Bible. (Although some commentators think the term *sacrifice* might have meant something other than death.) How could God allow Jephthah to make such a vow when He knew Jephthah's daughter would be the first to greet him? The real point is, how could Jephthah make such a vow in the first place? God isn't impressed or honored when we act impulsively without stopping to think about our actions. By His mercy, we do have an "eraser"—His forgiveness—to use when we make mistakes, but in spite of this, we often suffer the consequences of our actions. In the emotion of the moment, Jephthah acted impulsively and made a foolish vow before God.

Gotcha!
Taken from Judges 13—16

Foundation

Spend some time talking with the Lord. Confess to Him those areas in which you're prone to temptation. He already knows them and is simply waiting for you to agree. Thank Him that He is available to rescue you from temptation—if you let Him.

Focus

Have you ever been tempted to play around with temptation?

No problem, Samson thought with a smile. *It's not that big a deal. I'm still in control, and I'm big enough and strong enough to handle just about anything. After all, didn't I kill a lion with my bare hands?*

Samson reflected on his life and how easily he had gained whatever he wanted. When he saw a beautiful Philistine woman he desired to marry, his parents had given in to his demands even though they hoped he would marry an Israelite. When he discovered bees making a hive in the carcass of the lion he had killed, he made up a clever riddle about it, and bet that the Philistines would be unable to solve it:

Out of the eater, something to eat;
Out of the strong, something sweet.

oot in use in Babylon; beginning

If his bride hadn't nagged him for the answer and secretly told her people, they would never have guessed it. *Even so,* Samson recalled, *I easily killed thirty men, stripping them of their possessions to gain my reward for the bet I lost. Is there anything that can ensnare me or keep me down?*

Samson remembered his Philistine bride and how angry he had been with her for causing him to lose his bet. In fact, he was so furious that he left the wedding party and went to live with his parents. Believing Samson had rejected his daughter, the girl's father gave her as a wife to Samson's best man. When Samson discovered this, he took revenge on the Philistines and played a damaging prank on them that they would feel the effects of for a long time. Catching 150 pairs of foxes, Samson tied them together by their tails and fastened a torch to each. Then he lit the torches and set the foxes loose in the Philistines' fields, destroying not only their grain but their vineyards and olive groves as well. When the townspeople saw what Samson had done, they killed his former bride and her family. In return, Samson attacked them viciously.

No one has the last word against Samson! he thought with rage.

Samson's actions greatly concerned the Israelites, who wanted to avoid trouble with the Philistines. So a large group of men from the tribe of Judah went to the cave where Samson was staying.

"Why have you caused problems for us with the Philistines, Samson," they asked.

Looking at the men, Samson replied, "I only paid them back for the harm they did to me."

"We're here to take you captive," they replied, "and hand you over to the Philistines. We promise not to kill you ourselves but will tie you up and deliver you to them as they demand."

Samson allowed himself to be bound, knowing he'd be able to escape—one way or another. As he approached the Philistine camp with the men from Judah, Samson felt the Lord's strength come over him, and he easily snapped the ropes that had held him fast. Then, picking up the jawbone of a donkey, he used it to strike down and kill a thousand Philistine soldiers.

"With a donkey's jawbone, I have made donkeys of them. With a donkey's jawbone, I have killed a thousand men!" Samson boasted triumphantly. He felt confident about his ability to escape danger, not knowing that one day it would lead to his destruction.

Samson was strong, brave, unstoppable, in control, and full of power, but he wasn't always full of wisdom. For twenty years he fought against the Philistines and rescued Israel from their oppressive rule, but he couldn't fight his own desire to play around with temptation!

One day while in the Philistine town of Gaza, Samson visited a woman of little honor. When word spread that Samson was there, the Philistines surrounded the city gate and planned to attack him. But Samson had already left, surprising the Philistines by removing the city gates and carrying them off with him. Because of this, the Philistines wanted to do away with Samson even more. Aware of his weakness for Philistine women, they knew it would only be a matter of time before they would capture him....

Delilah stroked Samson's head, and for the fourth time asked him to tell her the secret of his strength. Samson had already lied three times about how his strength could be taken away. Knowing that Philistine soldiers waited in the next room, Delilah was determined to be successful this time.

"If you really loved me, you'd tell me," she whined.

Unable to resist Delilah's charms and her continual nagging, Samson told his secret. Then, while he rested in her lap, Delilah cut Samson's hair, breaking the Nazirite vow he had made before God.

"Samson, quick! The Philistines are here to capture you!" she repeated once more.

As he had done three times before, Samson shot up, trying to break the

Most Nazirite vows were temporary, but Samson's was lifelong. A person who took this vow wasn't permitted to touch anything dead, to drink wine, or to cut his hair. One by one, Samson broke all three restrictions.

Grain, grapes, and olives were major crops for people living in the land of the Philistines.

ammurabi dies.   *   1700 BC   —

ropes binding him. But this time he couldn't escape. As his enemies gloated over him, a sick feeling hit the pit of Samson's stomach. He finally had been "gotten".

Footwork

Turn to Judges 16:20 in your Bible. Read what it says and then read it again. It's a sad commentary on the lure of temptation—and the consequences! Thankfully, this wasn't the end of Samson's story. In verses 21-30, we see God's mercy and a second chance for Samson. It makes for some exciting reading!

Fruit

Temptation comes in many forms and disguises. Even the strongest man in the world couldn't handle the snare of temptation. Like Samson, if we relax our standards—playing with temptation and falsely believing that we're in control—we, too, will fall victim. Take a moment to reflect on your life. What temptations do you face? Do you find yourself running from them, or are you playing with them? Watch out! You just might get burned!

Ruth

After the book of Judges, Ruth is a breath of fresh air and gives us a glimmer of hope! Interestingly, the story of Ruth takes place during the time of the judges—most likely around the time of Gideon—and shows us a beautiful picture of God's love and faithfulness.

Another interesting thing to keep in mind while exploring Ruth is to understand that Ruth wasn't from the nation of Israel—yet she becomes the great-grandparent of King David! How does all this happen? You'll just have to read on to find out!

I'm with You
Taken from Ruth 1—4

Foundation

As you begin your time with God today, start with prayer. Thank Him for what you've seen Him do in your life and for how He's provided for you—not just the big things but also the small.

Do you ever feel anxious about the future?

"Please don't keep me from going with you," Ruth pleaded. "Wherever you go, I have determined to go. Your people, the Israelites, will become my people; your God will become my God," she stated.

Seeing that Ruth would not back down, Naomi could think only of their uncertain future together.

"Is that Naomi?" the women from Bethlehem whispered to one another as Ruth and Naomi entered town. "What happened to you? And who is that with you?" they asked.

Naomi simply replied, "I left Bethlehem full—with a husband and two sons—but now I'm returning empty-handed. Don't call me Naomi anymore; (which means "pleasant"), but call me Mara, (which means "bitter"), because God has made my life very bitter."

Naomi grew quiet. Her mind flooded with memories of leaving Judah because of a famine in the land and moving to the land of Moab east of the Jordan River. Her husband wanted to stay there only until the famine had passed, but he ended up dying in that foreign land—and not only him but her two sons as well. Now, ten years later, she was returning without them.

Naomi looked silently around her, noticing how full the fields were with grain and barley. She could tell it was the beginning of the barley harvest. *Such a difference from when we left,* she observed quietly.

Ruth looked into the sorrowful eyes of her mother-in-law and followed her gaze out into the fields. What would the future hold? Would they be able to survive without husbands to provide for them?

"Please permit me to go into the fields and gather the leftover grain behind anyone who will allow me," Ruth asked Naomi.

"Go, and may your efforts be blessed," Naomi replied, watching Ruth go out the door. How thankful she was for God's Law that permitted the poor to glean in the fields after the workers. *Even if Ruth returns with little,* she told herself, *at least it will be something—and that something could mean the difference between life and death.*

Little did she know what Ruth would bring back …

"Who is that young woman?" Boaz asked his foreman as he noticed Ruth hard at work, gleaning behind the harvesters.

"She's Naomi's widowed daughter-in-law who returned with Naomi." the foreman replied. "She's been working hard since morning, except for taking a brief rest," he added.

A kinsman-redeemer was a close relative (a brother or cousin) who would buy or "redeem" a piece of property that his brother or cousin's family was selling due to poverty. By redeeming it, the property would be kept in the family. If a widow came with the property, he was to marry her and raise a son so that his brother's name might live on.

Boaz was the son of Salmon, the husband of Rahab (from Jericho). When Boaz married Ruth, they had a son named Obed who later became the grandfather of King David!

Boaz pondered the foreman's words, and approached Ruth to speak with her. "You may stay here and glean in my field," he offered kindly. "Follow along after my servant girls, and whenever you become thirsty, help yourself to the water that is in my water jars."

Ruth looked up into Boaz's eyes. "Why are you being so kind to me, a foreigner?" she asked.

"Because I've heard all that you have done for your mother-in-law, Naomi, and how you willingly left the familiar things of your people and country in order to remain by her side," he answered. "May the God of Israel richly bless you because of it."

With those words, Boaz invited Ruth to eat with his workers. He then secretly instructed his men to purposefully leave behind stalks of grain for her to pick up. By the time evening came, Ruth had more than enough grain to last several days—almost thirty pounds!

When she returned home, Ruth showed Naomi all she had gathered and told her about Boaz's kindness.

"Boaz?" Naomi repeated, hardly able to believe her ears. "Boaz is one of our close relatives—a kinsman-redeemer!" Delighted to see how God was already providing, Naomi began to feel hopeful. Perhaps their future wasn't so dim after all.

Footwork

Do you want to know what happens next? Then turn to Ruth 4:13-17. You won't want to miss it! Clearly, God was watching out for Ruth and Naomi's future—and much more.

Fruit

Think for a moment about some of the fears you have concerning your future. Perhaps it's a great opportunity you're afraid you'll miss or a task you think you might fail at—especially when it counts the most. Whatever it is, stop right now and tell God about your concerns. Allow yourself to be comforted by the fact that He says, "I am with you" (Isa. 41:10; Matt. 28:20). God is a God who is in control—even over the little things in life.

Deuteronomy 31:8 states, "The LORD himself goes before you and will be with you; he will never leave you nor forsake you. Do not be afraid; do not be discouraged." Memorize this promise, or copy it down on something you can easily carry with you this week. Use it as a daily reminder to trust God with your future.

1 Samuel

Faith facts

The book of 1 Samuel is full of exciting adventures, sharp corners, and stark contrasts. As you explore this book, you will notice three main people: Samuel (for whom this book is named), Saul, and David. Samuel was the last of the judges who came after Samson. He was also one of the first prophets and a priest who had the privilege of anointing Israel's first king. (No wonder he had a book named after him!) It has been thought that Samuel wrote most of this book, but the last seven chapters were finished by the prophets Nathan and Gad.

Saul was the first king over the nation of Israel. Though he started out well, he finished poorly. As you read about his life, see if you can discover where he went wrong. David is introduced in this book as the king-to-be, whom God would use to replace Saul. Follow David's life and crawl with him into the dark corners and difficult situations he faced. Would you have made the choices he did?

Originally, 1 and 2 Samuel were written as one book, but in our Bible they're divided up into two. As you explore 1 Samuel, you'll see that little things really do matter. If you're careful, as you're reading about the lives of the people within these pages, you'll pick up on at least seven things not to do. There are also a few bright spots here and there, which provide terrific examples to follow. See if you can find them. Enjoy your walk through this book!

For two bonus lessons check out "It's My Duty" (taken from 1 Samuel 18—20) and "Let Me at 'Em!" (taken from 1 Samuel 25—26). You can find them online at www.cookministries.com/FaithFactor.

to Amram, a Levite, and Jochebed, makir

It's Just a Little Thing
Taken from 1 Samuel 1—3

Foundation

As you begin your time in 1 Samuel, start with prayer. Ask God to show you what He would have you learn. Ask Him to help you be more faithful in the little things.

Focus

Have you ever gotten tired of doing ordinary tasks, thinking no one really notices anyway?

Samuel looked around him. Day in and day out he did the same thing: opening the tabernacle doors each morning, cleaning the furniture, sweeping the floors. Even though they were ordinary tasks, he knew he needed to be faithful in them. Eventually he would be able to help Eli the high priest perform some of the sacrifices, but for now this was his job. Lost in thought, Samuel remembered how his mother said she prayed for him—even before he was born …

"Oh, Lord," Hannah wept bitterly, whispering the words through clenched teeth and parched lips. Her heart grieved, for she loved her husband but wasn't able to bear him a child. Although Elkanah was understanding and loved Hannah in spite of this, Hannah couldn't bear it. In her heart she felt that her inability to have a child announced to everyone that she was a failure—and it was a social embarrassment to her husband as well! The jeers and snide remarks of Peninnah, Elkanah's other wife, only made matters worse. *No,* Hannah said in her heart, *I won't give in to bitterness. Instead, I will ask the Lord to grant me a son—and that son will be brought up to serve Him all the days of his life.* With that, Hannah laid her prayer out before the Lord.

Eli, who was sitting by the temple door watching, saw Hannah's lips moving but heard no sound. Thinking she was drunk, he reprimanded her at first, but then realized that she was pouring out her heart to the Lord.

"May the God of Israel grant you the request you ask of Him!" he told her kindly.

Elkanah had two wives, and this caused only grief and conflict in his family. Peninnah was Elkanah's other wife.

Because God didn't give land to the Levites (the priests), He met their needs through the offerings people brought to the tabernacle. It was a common practice to allow a priest to stick his fork into the pot of boiling meat and keep for himself whatever his fork speared. Eli's sons took advantage of this by using a special meat hook rather than a fork.

God in His mercy did grant Hannah's request, and she gave birth to a son.

When he was three years old, Samuel was brought to the temple and presented to Eli. "Remember the prayer I prayed several years ago?" Hannah asked. "God answered and gave me a son. I am now going to keep my promise to the Lord by dedicating Samuel to His service."

Eli looked down at the young boy. He remembered Hannah and would honor her vow to the Lord. From that day on, Samuel lived with Eli in order to be trained in the ways of a priest.

A loud noise startled Samuel and brought him back to the present. *What's going on in there?* he wondered. Finishing his task, he went to investigate and found Eli's sons, Hophni and Phinehas, threatening one of the worshippers.

"Give us the portion of the sacrifice we deserve," they demanded, "or we'll take it by force!"

Daily, Eli's sons showed disrespect for the Lord and His offerings. They would demand their cut of meat before it was sacrificed to the Lord, taking the best for themselves and leaving the leftovers for God. This made a mockery of the worshipper's offering and brought disgrace upon the office of priest. Hophni and

Phinehas had no regard for God or for others. They thought that what they did was a little thing, and little things didn't matter.

Samuel watched their actions but didn't allow them to influence his own behavior. He was dedicated to God's service—not just by his parents but also by his own choice. He would do his best to live for the Lord and not selfishly for himself. He determined in his heart to be faithful to whatever task God called him to do, even if it meant doing simple, ordinary things for now. God would soon show him the great plans He had for Samuel's life.

"Did you call me, sir?" Samuel asked one evening.

Eli looked at Samuel in surprise. He hadn't called Samuel's name all night, yet this was the third time Samuel had gotten out of bed and come to him! *Could it be God calling him?* Eli wondered.

"Go back to bed, and if you hear a voice calling your name again, say, "Speak to your servant, Lord. I am listening," Eli instructed.

So Samuel went back to bed and did exactly as he was told.

The next morning Eli called for Samuel, but Samuel didn't have good news. The message the Lord had given him was about Eli and his sons. God was going to judge Eli for not correcting his sons' bad behavior, stripping the priesthood from his descendants forever. As proof of this, both of Eli's sons would die on the same day. Eli's heart was grieved. He had allowed his sons to act unfaithfully in what they thought were little things, and soon they became unfaithful in bigger things. All those "little things" added up to bad character—and that's a big thing in God's eyes.

Footwork

Open your Bible to 1 Samuel 3:19-20 and read it. Does what you read here sound different from the descriptions of Eli's sons you read about earlier? What do you think made the difference?

Fruit

Little things add up and shape our character. Samuel must have known that, for he remained faithful in the "daily stuff" of life. Interestingly, what we consider a "little thing" is often a big thing to God. Eli's sons had no respect for the Lord or for their duties as priests. Being faithful in the little things is often a test to see if we will be faithful in the big things in life. (It's much easier to be faithful with the big things than the small!) God evaluates both our actions and our motives. Little actions do speak louder than words! This week, what will your actions say about you?

This Is *Not* Working
Taken from 1 Samuel 4—7

Foundation

Stop and pray. Take a moment to really talk *with* God—not just *at* Him. God wants a relationship with you; thank Him for that and ask Him to teach you what that really means.

Focus

Do you know anyone who carries (or wears) something, thinking it will bring him or her luck?

"The Philistines are destroying us!" the Israelite leader panicked. "Run!"

It had been a terrible day in battle for the Israelites. The Philistines had attacked, and now four thousand Israelite soldiers lay dead on the ground.

"What happened?" many of the survivors asked one another. "Why were we defeated? Where was the Lord?"

Because the Israelites had slowly adopted the wicked practices of surrounding nations, they didn't realize how far they had strayed from the Lord or why He wasn't helping them now.

"I know!" someone shouted in a moment of inspiration. "It's because we don't have the ark of the Lord with us! If we take it into battle, it will bring us great victory over the Philistines!"

Everyone agreed, and men were quickly sent to Shiloh to get the ark from the tabernacle while the rest of the Israelite soldiers prepared for

large population of people is

135

another battle. Soon, the sons of Eli the high priest, Hophni and Phinehas, appeared in the distance along with the ark. When they entered the Israelite camp, a great cheer rang out. "We have the ark!" the people shouted excitedly, gaining a sudden sense of confidence.

"What's going on? Why are the Hebrews shouting?" the Philistine commander asked his soldiers.

"They have brought a god into their camp!" came the fearful reply. "It's the same god who destroyed the Egyptians with plagues!"

Looking over into the Hebrew camp and seeing the ark, the Philistine commander grew fearful and ordered his men to fight even harder than before. "If you don't," he warned them, "we'll become the Hebrews' slaves, just as they have been ours!"

That was all the Philistines needed to hear. The battle was on, and they fought fiercely.

"This isn't working!" some of the Israelite soldiers shouted in fear. "The Philistines are still too powerful for us and are slaughtering our whole army!" Others shouted, "This shouldn't be happening—we have the ark of the covenant with us!"

One by one the Israelite soldiers fell to the ground dying as the Philistines drove hard at them. By the time the battle was over, the Israelites had suffered an even greater loss than the day before. Thirty thousand Israelite soldiers lay dead, and the ark of God had been captured by the Philistines. Without the ark, the Israelites felt that God was no longer with them.

A messenger from the tribe of Benjamin ran back to Shiloh to report the terrible news. When Eli heard that the ark had been captured and his two sons had died that day he fell into a state of shock. At that moment, he tumbled backward off his chair, broke his neck, and died.

Meanwhile, the Philistines were celebrating over the spoils of war. To them, capturing the ark meant they had captured Israel's god, for pagan gods could easily be captured and taken into exile. The Philistines took the ark and placed it in their temple beside their god Dagon so everyone would know that Dagon was the victor and the Lord was his prisoner. Or so they thought!

The next day the Philistines were surprised to see the figure of Dagon lying facedown in front of the ark, and they quickly set the idol back on its pedestal. But the next day they found it lying facedown again. And this time the statue had lost its head and hands, which lay shattered in front of the ark. The Philistines feared that something was terribly wrong—and they were right! When a plague broke out against the people of the town, the Philistines sent the ark on to the next town. When a plague broke out there as well, they knew they were in trouble. "The Israelite god is angry," they cried. "We must send him back to his people!"

So they loaded the ark of God onto a cart and sent it back to the Israelites. When the ark arrived in Israelite territory, the people rejoiced. But when some of the Israelites casually lifted the lid of the ark to see if the Law of Moses was still inside, seventy were struck down by the Lord and died. The ark was then sent to the Israelite city of Kiriath Jearim for safekeeping, since Shiloh had been destroyed. There, Eleazar, the Levite, was placed in charge of guarding the ark, and there it remained for twenty years. And all of Israel mourned, for it seemed that the Lord had abandoned them.

After Shiloh was destroyed, Mizpah became the central place of assembly for Israel.

The Philistines believed that the Israelites' god lived in the ark, while the Israelites treated the ark almost as a god. Both were wrong.

By that time, Samuel had grown into a young man. Not only was he a judge and a priest, but he was also a prophet. "If you're really sorry for turning away from the Lord and want to experience His hand of blessing, get rid of your idols and return to Him," Samuel challenged.

The people did just that. Gathering at Mizpah to confess their sins, they had Samuel pray to God for them. When the Philistines heard that the Israelites were meeting in one place, they attacked. But the Lord intervened and protected His people, showing His presence among them—ark or no ark.

C — The Exodus from Egypt begins

Footwork

Turn in your Bible to 1 Samuel 4:3. What does it say? Read it again. What mistake were the Israelites making?

Fruit

Many people today use symbols of God as their "good-luck charms." They believe that by having these, they will experience God's blessing. Their religion is based on relating to a lifeless object instead of having a relationship with the living God. Once this happens, they open themselves to all kinds of false teachings and ideas, of many kinds—including New Age beliefs and the teachings of Eastern religions and cults. These philosophies promise much but deliver nothing. Don't substitute a copy for the real thing!

That Was Then . . . This Is Now
Taken from 1 Samuel 10—15

Foundation

Take a moment to ready your heart. If you don't feel like praying, that means you really need to! Ask God to forgive you for those things you've done that push Him away or keep Him at a distance.

FOCUS

Have you felt closer to God in the past than you do now?

Samuel sighed as he looked into Saul's eyes. *How different Saul seems now from when he first started out,* Samuel thought to himself. Samuel remembered first meeting Saul and anointing him as king. He was a young man full of promise who stood head and shoulders above the rest of the Israelites. "Here is your king!" Samuel had proclaimed as a great cheer rose from the Israelites. Now they would have a king of their own—and now they would be just like the other nations. Or so they thought!

Even though most of the Israelites were pleased with Saul as king, some wicked men refused to submit to his leadership. After King Saul won his first battle, his supporters rose up and shouted, "Now where are those who said Saul shouldn't rule us? Bring them here so we can kill them!"

But Saul humbly stopped them, saying, "No one will be executed, for the Lord is the One who rescued Israel today!"

Saul had rightly given credit to God for the Israelites' victory over their enemies. Killing those who didn't honor Saul as king would only be a waste and a sin. God was the King, and Saul was His servant. Saul had started out well, but….

In 1 Samuel 8:5, 20, the Israelites gave three reasons why they wanted a king: (1) Samuel's sons (who were judges) were unfit to rule them; (2) a king would unify all the tribes of Israel; and (3) a king would make them just like all the other nations.

Why did God want the Amalekites destroyed? You can read about it in Exodus 17:8-16 and Deuteronomy 25:17-19. Saul's refusal to obey God's instructions was a bigger deal than Saul thought.

How things have changed! Samuel marveled as he thought about how Saul had grown not only in power but also in pride.

Not only was Saul king over Israel, but he was also king in his own eyes and had little regard for things of the Lord. He had even disregarded Samuel's specific instructions for dedicating his troops to God before going into battle with the Philistines. Then when his men began to lose their nerve to fight, Saul went ahead without Samuel and sacrificed a burnt offering—a job God specifically said only a priest could do.

"You didn't arrive when you said you would," Saul had given as his excuse.

But his excuses wouldn't work with Samuel—or God. Saul's foolish disobedience to God would cost him his crown. "Your dynasty will end," Samuel had stated, "for the Lord has found a man to replace you who has a heart for Him."

The words had hit Saul like a cold slap in the face. And from that time on, Saul did things his way, fiercely guarding himself and not letting anything threaten his kingship. He even ran his troops hard while pursuing an enemy—forbidding his soldiers to eat any food for nourishment. When his son,

Jonathan, ate some honey (for he hadn't heard Saul's decree), Saul had been ready to put his own son to death!

Clearing his head of these memories, Samuel returned to the present moment and began to speak. God had sent him to deliver a message to Saul.

"I anointed you king over Israel because the Lord told me to do so. Now then, listen to what the Lord commands you to do," he said, eyeing Saul doubtfully. "Because the Amalekites attacked the Israelites when they came up out of Egypt, you are now to carry out God's judgment upon them. Go, therefore, and attack them—only be sure not to leave a single person or animal alive."

Saul followed God's instructions and slaughtered the Amalekites. However, instead of killing every living thing as God had commanded, Saul took Agag, king of the Amalekites, as prisoner. He also spared the lives of the best sheep, cattle, calves, and lambs—everything that seemed of value to him. He then set up a monument to himself in honor of his victory. But in the end it would prove to be a monument to his losses.

"Why didn't you obey the Lord?" Samuel later challenged him.

"But I did!" came Saul's surprised reaction.

"Then what is that noise I hear?" Samuel asked as he heard the bleating of sheep.

Saul hesitated a moment, then answered, "I carried out the mission God gave me. I spared the best of the livestock so that I might sacrifice it to the Lord ... and I captured Agag, but everything else I destroyed!"

Saul had done things his way, hoping that God would somehow say it was okay. He had slipped away from serving the Lord to serving only himself. As a result, the kingdom of Israel would slip from his hands. Instead of receiving God's blessings, Saul would receive His judgment—that's how far he had strayed from the Lord. In his earlier days, Saul had been God's servant—but that was then ... this is now.

ppointed leader; Hebrews enter

Footwork

Open your Bible to 1 Samuel 15:22-23 and read what it says. What does Samuel say to Saul? From Saul's perspective, he was doing a good thing for God (even though he disobeyed God by doing it). How does God view this? (See the last part of verse 22.)

Fruit

Little by little, Saul slipped away from his relationship with God. Each act of disobedience took him a step further away from the Lord, and it wasn't long before Saul began operating on automatic pilot, leaving God completely out of the cockpit of his life! Saul started well, but he didn't end that way.

Take a moment to think about your life. Where are you now in your walk with the Lord? If you feel further away from God than you did at the beginning, then something you've done may be creating a barrier between you and God. Talk to Him right now and ask Him to show you if there's anything you need to set right with Him. If He reveals something in your life, don't think that just because you've messed up, things can't be restored. If you confess your sin, it's in the past. Don't dwell on it, but rather learn from it. In 1 John 1:9 in the New Testament, we're told that "if we confess our sins, [God] is faithful and just and will forgive us our sins and purify us from all unrighteousness." This is made possible only because of what Jesus did for you on the cross. (If you'd like to know more about this, then turn to the back of this book. There's a special message just for you.)

Pay No Attention to Him
Taken from 1 Samuel 16—17

Foundation

Commit this time to the Lord, asking Him to speak to your heart. Tell God your desire to become all He wants you to be—even if that might mean stepping out of your comfort zone.

Focus

Do you sometimes rate people's worth based on the way they look?

"No."

"Hmm. Okay, then, what about that one?"

"He won't do either."

"All right. Then how about him?"

"Nope."

"How's this one?"

"Sorry."

"This is the last one—surely!"

Samuel didn't know what to think. God sent him to the household of Jesse to anoint one of Jesse's sons as the future king over Israel. When he arrived, Samuel saw the oldest son, Eliab, who was tall and handsome in appearance. *His name even means "God is Father"* Samuel smiled to himself. *Surely he is to be the next king!*

But God had other plans.

cinnamon to Egypt; Highly devel—

Goliath stood over nine feet tall (most house ceilings are ten feet tall). He carried armor that weighed 125 pounds, and the iron tip on his spear weighed about 15 pounds! He was a trained warrior—and a large one!

One by one, seven of Jesse's eight sons were brought before Samuel. And one by one, God rejected them. *Each of these men would make a fine leader,* Samuel thought to himself. *They are all handsome, tall, and strong—some even standing head and shoulders above the rest! Surely God's chosen replacement for Saul has to be one of these!*

Samuel grew quiet as he looked at the hopeful young men, then into the surprised eyes of Jesse. "Are you sure I've seen all of your sons? You don't have any others?" Samuel asked.

Jesse shifted his weight uncomfortably, almost embarrassed by the question. "I do have one more son, but he's my youngest and is out tending my sheep ..." Jesse's voice trailed off.

Wondering what God was up to, Samuel asked, "Could you please send for him?"

Soon David appeared in front of Samuel.

"Anoint him," the Lord spoke to Samuel. "He is the one I've chosen to be king in place of Saul."

Samuel looked doubtfully at David because of his size but did as he was told. He questioned in his heart why God had chosen David above the others. "I am not looking for the same qualities you are," God answered Samuel. "Humans judge by how things look on the outside, but I look at the heart." So in front of his father and brothers, David was anointed as Israel's next king.

During this time, Saul began feeling troubled and tormented in his spirit, unable to find relief. He knew that God's presence was no longer with him and that his days as king were numbered. His attendants noticed this and convinced Saul that some soothing music might help ease his mind and emotions.

"We know of just the musician!" they suggested. "It's one of Jesse's sons who not only knows how to play the harp but is also a brave warrior! He's a good-looking man, and the Lord is with him!"

Saul grunted and waved his attendants off to fetch the one they were talking about. When David arrived, he cautiously entered the king's presence, took out his harp, and began playing. Comforted, Saul asked if David could remain in his service. Little did Saul know that one day David would sit in his place on the throne! David, the promising "king to be" was serving Saul, the "king who should have been."

One day David's father sent his son to the battle lines to bring back word on how his brothers were doing. Like other valiant soldiers, they had joined Saul's troops to help fight the Philistines. When David arrived at their camp, what he saw surprised him. Silent and fearful, the Israelite soldiers were standing on their side of the battle line, unable to answer the challenge of a gigantic Philistine soldier who was daring someone to fight him. David knew that it was a common practice to select one champion soldier to fight the enemy's champion soldier. The results of that fight would then determine which side won the battle. Since it was thought that the soldiers' gods controlled the outcome, David grew especially concerned. God's honor was at stake.

"Who is this man who stands against the Lord's army?" David asked the Israelite soldiers. "Why doesn't someone fight him? Pay no attention to him or his size, God will give the victory!"

Many of the men glanced away in fear—even Saul had lost his confidence. Goliath looked like a strong and successful warrior. Seeing this, David himself went out to fight Goliath.

"I challenge you in the name of the Lord! May people everywhere know that the God of Israel alone is the one and only true God!" he said.

With God's help, David miraculously struck down and killed Goliath with a stone from his sling. David knew there were certain things in life—like the outward appearance of people or circumstances—you just didn't pay attention to.

Earthquake destroys Palace of

Footwork

Look up 1 Samuel 16:7 in your Bible. This is a classic verse that goes against the way we normally think. What does it say?

It's interesting to note that God chose David *in spite of* his size, and the Israelites feared Goliath *on account of* his size.

Fruit

Too often we evaluate people's worth based on their appearance. How they look, dress, and who they hang around influences what we think of them. Even though we're easily fooled, God isn't. We look at the outward stuff, but God looks at the heart. What do you pay the most attention to? On the line below, write down the name of one person you know you could reach out to (someone you wouldn't normally befriend because of the way he or she looks). Pray for that person this week, and then step out and get to know him or her.

_____

(person's name)

Think Nothing of It
Taken from 1 Samuel 18—19

- *Foundation*

As you begin your time with the Lord today, take a few moments to stop and pray. Recognize that all you need is found in Him—and in Him alone.

FOCUS

Do you sometimes feel jealous when others get special recognition?

Everyone was celebrating! David had slain Goliath! Because of this brave deed, David was quickly promoted to commander in Saul's army, delighting all the Israelite soldiers and officers. They knew that David had acted bravely and spared them an embarrassing defeat. Before he had come along, they had all been melting with fear, hopelessly held captive by one huge Philistine warrior. David recognized that Goliath's taunting was against the Lord God Almighty, and he knew it must be silenced. With his sling in hand and his faith in the Lord, David put a quick end to Goliath's boasts and turned everyone's eyes back to God's greatness. His bravery brought the praise of many, and won him a spot of favor in Saul's eyes. But that favor would soon fade.

"Saul has killed thousands!" the people sang and danced for joy in the streets. "But David has killed *tens* of thousands!" Over and over Saul heard this message, and it began to sound like a broken record. Each time he heard it, he grew angrier.

"What is this?" Saul finally said in disgust. "The people credit David with tens of thousands and me with only thousands? I suppose next they'll want him to be king!"

> *"An evil spirit from God"? How could God, who isn't evil, send an evil spirit to torment someone? In the book of Job, we learn that Satan must first ask God's permission before harming anyone who belongs to Him. This also happened in the New Testament. In Luke 22:31-32, Jesus told Peter that Satan had asked permission to sift Peter like wheat, then He added: "But I have prayed for you ... that your faith may not fail."*

From that point on, Saul kept a close eye on David.

The next day God sent an evil spirit to torment Saul, and David began to play his harp to calm Saul down. All of a sudden, Saul took a spear in his hand and hurled it at David with the intent of pinning him to the wall. Jumping aside, David managed to escape—not just once but twice! Saul acted out of fear and jealousy because the Lord was with David and no longer with him. As a result, he banned David from his presence and stripped him of his command over such a large army. Now David would be in charge of only a thousand men.

Much to Saul's dismay, David faithfully led his troops into battle and succeeded in everything he did. This made Saul panic all the more. *I've got to think of a way to get rid of David!* Saul plotted. *Ah! I'll offer him my oldest daughter, Merab, as a wife but first require him to prove himself a real warrior by fighting the Lord's battles!*

Saul secretly hoped that David would be killed in battle. His plan seemed perfect. But when David humbly declined Saul's offer, stating that he wasn't worthy of the honor of being called the king's son-in-law, Saul's plans were destroyed. It wasn't until his younger daughter, Michal, fell in love with David that Saul tried again.

"The king really likes you, and so do we," Saul's men falsely told David. "Why don't you accept the king's offer and become his son-in-law?" they urged.

"I can't, for I am poor and come from a humble family," David replied. "How could I afford the bride-price?"

When this word got back to Saul, he instructed his men to tell David that all he required for a bride-price was revenge on two hundred Philistines. Saul once again planned for David to be killed by the Philistines and was greatly surprised when David brought back the evidence that he had killed them instead. With reluctance, he gave Michal to David as his wife.

Not long after this, Michal warned David in a panicked voice "I heard my father is planning to send his men to kill you in the morning! You must escape tonight, or you will be dead!" Hearing these words, David thanked his wife as she helped him climb out of the window and escape into the night.

The next morning Saul's men came to capture David, but Michal lied and said her husband was sick in bed. When the men left and reported this to Saul, he became very angry.

"Then bring him to me in his bed!" he shouted, sending his men back to Michal.

The men returned and demanded to see David. When they went into the back room, they found David lying in bed—or so they thought. Michal had tricked the men by placing an idol in the bed with goat's hair on top. David had escaped safely, and she was thankful.

Night and day Saul was consumed with fear and jealousy toward David. Because David's name had become famous in the land, Saul was determined in his heart to spend the rest of his life hunting him down. Jealousy had so taken over Saul's heart, he could think of nothing else but destroying David.

Footwork

Open your Bible to 1 Samuel 18:28. According to this verse, what two things did Saul realize? Now look at verse 29. What was Saul's response? (Note Saul's feelings, which led to his actions. It's a sad commentary on jealousy and fear.)

proclaims himself god, Egyptian

Fruit

Jealousy is a silent killer, often taking victims before they realize they're under its control. The first stage of jealousy is comparing ourselves with others. When we do this, we either feel better about ourselves (which leads to pride) or worse (which leads to jealousy because someone else has it better than we do). Both are deadly and lead to self-destruction. Don't imitate Saul's actions. When other people are praised, rejoice with them, then think nothing more of it.

rigid art forms change to more natura

You'll Get What You Deserve!
Taken from 1 Samuel 21—24

Foundation

Begin today's lesson with prayer. Ask God to speak to your heart through His Word and help you learn to trust Him with all the circumstances in your life. His ways are just, and His timing is perfect.

Focus

Do you have a hard time respecting those in authority—especially when you don't think they deserve it?

"What brings you hear by yourself? Where is everyone else?" Ahimelech the priest asked David fearfully.

"The king sent me on a special mission," David lied, "and told me not to tell anyone why I'm here. I've told my men where they can meet me later."

David looked around. Having gone without food for days, he was extremely hungry. "Do you have five loaves of bread you could spare me?" he asked.

"All I have is the holy bread that has just been replaced with fresh bread," Ahimelech answered. "Although it is normally only to be eaten by the priests, you are welcome to it, as long as you and your men aren't ceremonially unclean," he added.

David eagerly took the bread, assuring the priest they weren't. "Do you also have a sword or spear?" he asked. "The king's business was so urgent, I didn't even have time to grab my weapon!"

The only sword here is the one you took from Goliath the day you killed him," Ahimelech said. "You are welcome to it—it's all I have."

After the Philistines captured (and returned) the ark of the covenant, the tabernacle was set up at Nob. Nob means "city of the priests."

David ran from Saul for about ten years, learning many lessons in the process and pouring out his heart to God. David wrote Psalm 52 after learning that Doeg had turned in Ahimelech the priest for helping him. He wrote Psalm 57 when he was living in a cave, hiding from Saul.

"And it is one of the best!" David replied enthusiastically.

As Ahimelech went to get the sword, David noticed one of Saul's servants was there. Their eyes met briefly, and David recognized the man to be Doeg, Saul's head shepherd. Quickly gathering his supplies, David left, hoping to put as much distance as possible between Saul's servant and himself.

Saul will never think to look for me among the hated Philistines! David thought. He knew he would be safe from Saul in the city of Gath, the very city Goliath had come from. David's plan worked—but only for a brief time.

"Hey! Isn't that David, the Israelite king?" one of the Philistine servants said, pointing at him.

Realizing that he was in danger, David began drooling and scratching at the doors, pretending to be insane.

"Let him alone. He's harmless!" another man responded.

Knowing he couldn't stay in Gath, David left the city and found a cave to live in. There his brothers and some relatives came to join him. Soon others began coming who had debts they couldn't pay or were simply discontent with Saul as king. Before long, David found himself leader of nearly four hundred men! These men would eventually become his mightiest warriors.

Not long after this, David returned to the land of Judah. When Saul learned that he was back in the area, he wasn't at all pleased.

"Don't any of you care about me?" Saul whined while resting under a tree with his officials. "Has David promised you things I haven't? Has he promised to make you commanders in his army or to give you fields or vineyards?" he demanded. "Is this the reason you're plotting against me? Whose side are you on, anyway?"

Saul's officials became quiet. Then Doeg, Saul's head shepherd, cleared his throat and began to speak. "I saw David not long ago in Nob. Ahimelech the priest gave him food—and even Goliath's sword!"

Saul's anger began to boil. *So,* he thought to himself, *even the priests are working against me! We'll just see about that!* In a fit of rage, Saul ordered all the priests to be killed, and eighty-five lost their lives that day. Only Abiathar, one of Ahimelech's sons, escaped and fled to David to report the tragic loss.

After this, Saul continued to pursue David. Day after day he hunted him, and day after day David ran. Saul was so obsessed with killing David that he only let up his search once when a Philistine attack called him away. Upon returning, he finally found out where David and his men were hiding. He went straight there. *I'll get you yet, David!* Saul sneered. When he arrived, he went into a cave to relieve himself—the same cave where David and his men were hiding.

"Now's your chance!" David's men whispered. "God has delivered Saul into your hands this very day!"

Listening to his men's words, David slowly lifted his sword. With a quick flip of his wrist, he cut off a corner of Saul's robe.

"You should have killed him and given him what he deserves!" David's men challenged as David rejoined them in the back corner of the cave.

"He is the Lord's anointed—the one God selected to be leader at this time," David replied. "I cannot kill the king—and I did give him what he deserves: respect."

Taking the piece of robe, David ran outside and called after Saul while bowing low.

At the sound of David's voice, Saul turned around. "David?" he asked.

en years and dies prematurely.

Before Saul could think twice, David held up the corner of Saul's robe for him to see. It was then that Saul realized not how close he had been to finally killing David—but how close David had been to killing him, and didn't.

Footwork

Find 1 Samuel 24:17 in your Bible and read it. What does it say? Do you think David's actions made an impression on anyone? Who? Is that all?

Fruit

Showing honor to a leader who doesn't deserve it takes real character. It's much easier to make jokes about that person or help spread lies about him or her. Even when it seems that the opportunity is right to attack, God calls us to a higher standard. Take a moment now to think about those in leadership over you—parents, teachers, city officials, members of congress—even the president. What is your heart attitude toward them? Pray for them right now and ask God to help them in their positions of responsibility.

2 Samuel

Faith facts

The book of 2 Samuel focuses on David's life as a king—the good, the bad, and the ugly! Within its pages you'll explore the tragic results of hiding behind lies and the blessings of following through on your word. You'll also encounter great victory as well as defeat. Even though David was considered a godly man, you'll soon see that he wasn't perfect.

Take your time exploring this book. Spend time looking around, observing the obvious and the not-so-obvious. When you finish, you'll understand more deeply why God called David a man after His own heart.

Be sure to check out www.cookministries.com/FaithFactor for a bonus lesson from this book, titled "You, I Can Trust," taken from 2 Samuel 24. It's about having confidence in God. Enjoy your journey through 2 Samuel!

You, You're the One!
Taken from 2 Samuel 5—7

Foundation

As you prepare your heart for today's lesson, spend a few moments in prayer. Tell God how much you love Him. Thank Him for what He has done and for what He promises to do for you. Thank Him for who He is.

Focus

Are you tempted to take credit for your successes?

David glanced around him. What he saw filled his heart with thankfulness. How different this was from the years he spent in the wilderness hiding in caves to escape Saul. No longer would he live as an outlaw. Now he was king, something he had patiently waited for since Samuel had anointed him as a youth nearly twenty years before. God had fulfilled His promise, and now David would fulfill his. He would be a man after God's own heart and would remember God as the true King.

Already David had experienced great success and the people's admiration. His first mission as king over all Israel was to capture the city of Jerusalem from the Jebusites and make it Israel's new capital. He then sent for the ark and had it brought to Jerusalem, once again establishing a place of national worship. As David made wise choices and grew in power, it was clear to all that God was with him. Even a king from the distant land of Tyre sent messengers with cedar logs, carpenters, and stonemasons to build a palace for David. This was the palace he now sat in, overwhelmed at God's goodness.

BC — Ehud becomes Israel's second judg

"Nathan," David finally spoke, glancing over at the prophet, "This doesn't seem right. While I sit here in this beautiful palace, the ark of the Lord is being housed in a tent!"

Nathan looked at the beauty of the palace and then at David. "You should do what is in your heart to do, for God is with you," he replied.

But that night God spoke to Nathan. "Tell David, 'This is what the Lord says: You desire to build a house for Me, and a house will be built— but not through your hands. For many years I have made My dwelling among the Israelites as they have moved from place to place—with only a tent as My house. Remember how I took you from herding sheep and placed you on a throne as king? My presence has been with you wherever you have gone. As I have faithfully delivered you from before all your enemies. So I will establish your household.'"

Nathan listened carefully as the Lord described how He would establish the Israelites and plant them so they might live without wicked nations oppressing them. "Tell David that when his days are over, I will raise up his son to succeed him, and he will be the one to build a house for My name. I will be like a Father to him, and he will be like a son to Me. Even though I will discipline him when he does wrong, I will never remove My love from him as I removed it from Saul. David's throne will be established forever, for he is a man after My own heart."

The next morning Nathan reported to David all that God had spoken to him, and upon hearing this, David went in and sat before the Lord. "O Lord, I am undeserving of all You have done for me," David whispered from the depths of his heart. He knew that his successes came from

Jebusites were warriors who lived in the hill country in the land of Canaan. The city of Jerusalem, built on an uneven, rocky plateau, was their fortress. It was strategically located where three different valleys came together.

This is the first time the prophet Nathan is mentioned, but not the last. It's interesting to note that God raised up a prophet during the reign of each of the kings of Israel.

God's hand, not his own. "And if all this weren't enough," David spoke in awe, "You've even spoken about favor upon my offspring! I am almost speechless! How great You are, God. There is no one like You."

David paused a moment in quiet gratitude, then continued. "Out of all the nations on the earth, You chose the Israelites to be Your people—that through us the whole world might know You are the one true God. You are the One who has performed miraculous signs and wonders, driving out nations before us. It is You who delivered us from troubles and brought us to this point. You are the One, Lord...."

David's voice trailed off as he recognized all that God had done for him personally and all that He promised to do in the future. Just as God had been with the nation, so He would be with David. For David, there would be no confusing just who was King.

Footwork

Although David wanted to be the one to build a temple for the Lord, God said no. Turn ahead in your Bible and look up 1 Chronicles 28:3. (After 2 Samuel comes 1 and 2 Kings, then 1 and 2 Chronicles.) According to this verse, why wasn't David allowed to build the temple? (*Note:* It *wasn't* because he had disobeyed God or turned from Him, and it *wasn't* because he was being punished, either!)

Fruit

David recognized that his success had everything to do with God fulfilling His plan in and through David's life. God deserved the credit, and David made sure to always remember that fact. God was the One who would be King.

Take a moment and think about your own life. How often do you recognize God as King? When you have a plan and God says no to it, do you accept that? When others praise you for a success you've had, do you offer that praise up to God as a gift? This week ponder these questions and see how well you put them into practice.

Paid in Full
Taken from 2 Samuel 8—9

Foundation

Begin your time today with prayer. Tell God about your struggles when it comes to keeping your word, and ask Him to help you in this area. Then take a moment to praise Him for His faithfulness. He is a God you can count on, and He always keeps His word!

Focus

Do you have a hard time following through on your promises?

Mephibosheth froze in fear. Messengers from the king stood at his front door, wanting to take him with them. *What have I done wrong? Why have they come to take me away?* he wondered, panicking. His thoughts were racing and his heart pounded wildly in his chest. *Why can't they just leave me alone?*

Over and over Mephibosheth relived that terrible day in his memory—the day word came from Jezreel that both his grandfather and father had been killed in battle. "King Saul and his son Jonathan are dead!" came the shocking news. What would happen next? Who would take the throne? Would the new king kill off the remainder of Saul's descendants in order to guarantee loyalty to himself? Fearing the answers to these questions, Mephibosheth's nurse had picked him up and fled. Unfortunately, she stumbled, and Mephibosheth was thrown from her arms and became crippled in both feet. He was only five years old at the time. Now grown,

Mephibosheth had a young son of his own named Mica. *What will happen to me?* he wondered. *Hasn't there been enough hate between my grandfather and David?* Mephibosheth had no idea of King David's real intentions.

"Are there any family members of Saul's household left?" David had asked one day. "I made a promise to my friend Jonathan when we were younger, saying that I would show kindness to his family. I plan to keep that vow, but I don't know if anyone remains alive!"

David's servants knew that a man named Ziba, a servant under Saul, was still alive. So they summoned him to appear before the king.

"Is there no one left in Saul's household that I can show God's grace and favor to?" David asked.

Ziba answered, telling about Jonathan's son, who had been crippled. "He lives in Lo Debar, in the household of a man named Makir."

David was delighted to hear such news and sent his messengers to get Mephibosheth.

"Mephibosheth!" David whispered with emotion.

Mephibosheth couldn't see David's face, for he had bowed down to pay David honor. "I am your servant," he said, trying to choke back the rising sense of anxiety in his heart. His words already sounded weak, and he wished he could just disappear. Standing before the king was a terrifying experience. Mephibosheth swallowed hard, then slowly raised his eyes to meet the gaze of David. *Oh, that this day had never come!* Mephibosheth panicked. *I have to pay the punishment for being born in the household of Saul!*

"Don't worry," David said gently, noticing that Mephibosheth was trembling. "I plan to show you kindness. This is something I promised your father, Jonathan, that I would do for all his descendants, for he was my friend."

> **Mephibo-who?** Believe it or not, there were two Mephibosheths! One was the son of Saul's concubine. The other was Jonathan's son. Second Samuel 21:7-9 lists them both and tells what happened to them.

Mephibosheth looked up uncertainly as David continued. "All the land that was once your grandfather, Saul's, will be given back to you. Not only that, but you may come and live with me here at the palace."

Upon hearing these words, Mephibosheth's heart filled with gratitude. *Instead of harm, I am being shown favor?* he wondered in amazement. *After all these years, David has hunted me down not to harm me but to fulfill a vow he made to my father—a vow no one would have known whether he fulfilled or not!* Mephibosheth knew that years ago his father had seen this loyalty in David and had chosen him as a friend.

Ziba was summoned once again to come before David.

"I have given Mephibosheth everything that belonged to your master and his family. You are to farm the land with your sons and servants and harvest the crops, bringing them in, so Mephibosheth can be provided for," David instructed. "Mephibosheth will always have a place at my table," he added.

Ziba heard David's words and bowed before him. "I will do whatever you command me to," he said willingly.

David's heart was pleased, for he could now consider his debt to Jonathan finally paid in full.

Footwork

Keeping a vow is important. Turn to 2 Samuel 21:1 and read what it says. What happened here? Long before, Joshua made a covenant with the Gibeonites (Josh. 9) that the Israelites would never destroy them. But when Saul was king, he didn't keep that vow. How different Saul was from David! Now skip down and read verses 3-7. Even though punishment had to occur in the situation described by these verses, what did David do (verse 7)? What does this tell you about his character?

Fruit

It's very easy to make a promise or vow and not fulfill it. Sometimes we falsely believe that if a great deal of time passes since we first made our promise, it automatically "erases" our commitment. *Out of sight, out of mind!* we mistakenly think. But this is a dangerous and deadly action that quickly grows into a lifelong habit. Don't let it! Take your cue from David and fulfill all your commitments. The blessing for doing so is incredible—for both you and others.

This Isn't Lookin' So Good
Taken from 2 Samuel 11—12

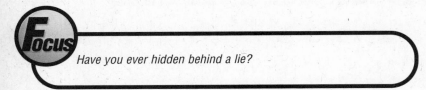

Foundation

Before starting today's lesson, take a moment to be honest with God. Ask His forgiveness for the times you "mess up" in your relationship with Him or with others. Thank Him for His mercy and the forgiveness He extends to you.

Focus

Have you ever hidden behind a lie?

David stretched as he got up from his bed. Normally he would be out leading Joab and the army into battle, but he decided against going this time. While the Israelites were off destroying the Ammonites in Rabbah, David chose to remain at home. It was a quiet, uneventful day, and he felt restless and unable to continue with his nap. Strolling out onto the roof, it didn't take long for his eyes to find something of interest. There on the rooftop of a nearby home was a beautiful woman taking a bath. David glanced at her, then looked away. Then he glanced back at her again.

I must find out who this woman is, for she is very pleasing to look at, he thought. When he discovered that she was Bathsheba, the wife of Uriah, who was off fighting the Ammonites, David was pleased. *This is looking good!* he thought.

As king, David knew he could command a person to come into his presence, and no one would think twice about it. *I'll send for Bathsheba so I can enjoy her beauty for myself,* he schemed in his heart. Then he did just that—without thinking of the consequences.

Thebes; Chinese dictionary developed

Some time later, David received a message from Bathsheba with alarming news. She was expecting a baby, and everything pointed to David as the father! David knew he needed to do something about the situation—and fast!

"Tell Uriah the Hittite I desire to see him" he wrote on a message addressed to Joab, the commander of his army.

It wasn't long before Uriah was removed from the battleground and brought to stand before David. After Uriah gives me his report, David schemed, *I'll send him home to be with his wife for the evening. Then Uriah will believe (as will everyone else) that he is the father of Bathsheba's baby!* David felt pleased with his plan. *This is looking good!* He smiled to himself, relieved that matters could be taken care of so quickly and painlessly.

Unfortunately, David hadn't counted on Uriah being such a man of honor. Instead of sleeping at home in the comfort of his bed with his beautiful wife, Uriah stayed that night at the palace entrance with some of the king's other servants. When David heard this, he became angry. "What's the matter with you, Uriah? Why didn't you go home to your wife?" he asked, trying to hide his panic.

"How could I go home to the luxury and beauty of my wife when my comrades are sleeping in tents and camping in the open fields? I would never do such a thing!" Uriah stated.

"Very well," David replied, "stay here tonight, and tomorrow you may

Why did Bathsheba's baby have to die? In Old Testament times, the birth of a son was recognized as a sign of God's approval and blessing. God couldn't allow this. But He still forgave David, and Bathsheba later gave birth to another son— Solomon.

The prophet Nathan told David what the consequences for his sin would be. All of them came to pass: The baby would die (2 Sam. 12:18), violence and murder would follow his family (2 Sam. 13:28-32; 1 Kings 2:23-25), and his household would rebel against him (2 Sam. 15:13).

return to the battlefield." *Perhaps if I invite Uriah to dinner and get him drunk, then he'll go home to his wife,* David plotted.

But in spite of this, Uriah showed his dedication and slept at the palace entrance again that night. David's scheme had been ruined, and he was now afraid of being discovered. In one last effort to cover his sin, David sent Uriah back to the battlefield with a written message for Joab. "Send Uriah to the front lines where the battle is the fiercest, then pull back so that Uriah will be killed."

Joab did as instructed, and innocent Uriah, an honorable man, was killed to cover up David's dishonorable actions.

After the time of mourning was over, David married Bathsheba, and she gave birth to a son. But God was displeased with what David had done, and He sent David a message through Nathan the prophet. The message wouldn't be one of encouragement for the king—but rather a rebuke.

Nathan eyed David carefully and prayed for the best way to deliver his message. Knowing David was a passionate man, Nathan told a story he knew would stir up David's anger.

"Once there was a poor man who owned just one lamb, which he tenderly cared for and nurtured in his arms. Living nearby was a rich man who owned hundreds of sheep. One day a guest came to the rich man's house for dinner. But instead of killing one of his own lambs, the rich man took the poor man's lamb and killed it." Nathan paused to let his words sink in, but David cut him off before he could finish the story.

"As God is my witness, David burst out, "anyone who would do this deserves to be put to death! He should pay four times the value of that lamb because he did such a terrible crime! Even though David was now king, he hadn't forgotten his years as a shepherd. Stealing from another person was inexcusable!

Although David thought he understood the meaning of the story, he was about to have a point driven home to him.

Nathan looked David squarely in the eyes and challenged, "That man is you!"

Footwork

How did David respond to Nathan's challenge? Turn to 2 Samuel 12:13 in your Bible to find out. Notice David's words. What did he say? Now turn to Psalm 51:10-13. David wrote this Psalm after Nathan confronted him. What does this tell you about David's heart?

Fruit

David had gotten himself into a deep mess and looked for ways to blame others, hoping to wiggle out of it. But it didn't work. It never does! Yet when his sin was pointed out to him, David then publicly admitted his wrongdoing and asked God's forgiveness. Although David's relationship with the Lord was restored, he still suffered the consequences of his actions. One of those consequences included the death of his first child by Bathsheba. What once looked like a pleasurable moment suddenly wasn't looking so good. What is in *your* life that doesn't look so good?

Na-Na Na-Na Na-Na
Taken from 2 Samuel 15—19

Foundation

Begin your time today with a moment of prayer. Prayer is simply talking with God and allowing Him to speak to your heart. Commit your day into His hands, and ask Him to help you live in a way that honors Him.

Focus

Do people ever annoy you?

"Hey, king!" *Heh heh.* "Nobody wants you anymore! Go on, run! Run like a baby!" *Heh heh.*

The words pounded in David's ears, grating his nerves and causing him to grit his teeth. He looked up at the man standing on the hillside and recognized him as Shimei, from the same clan as Saul's family. Shimei bent down and picked up stones, then began pelting David and his officials with them. "Get out! Get out you scoundrel! The Lord is repaying you for taking the throne from Saul! Now He has handed over the kingdom to your son Absalom!" Shimei kept following David along the top of the ridge, kicking dirt down and pelting him with stones and insults.

David continued on silently. He knew that Shimei's words weren't true. David never once raised his hand against Saul; instead, he had waited patiently for God to give him the throne. Now David's own son Absalom had plotted a revolt against him! For four years Absalom had secretly worked on the people, sowing discontent among them while promoting his own cause. Then, taking two hundred men with him, Absalom left for Hebron, saying he was going to fulfill a vow. But in reality, he left to set himself up as king there. By the time word had reached David, the rebellion was widespread. Not wanting to see Jerusalem destroyed, David decided to flee with those who were loyal to him rather than face off with his son. His heart was torn and deeply grieved. He knew there was a time to fight and a time to back down.

"Hey, king-o. I'm *talking* to yoooouuuu!" Shimei mocked, pointing at the king and spitting on the ground.

David's men had had enough. "Why do you let this worthless man curse you?" Abishai finally asked. "Just give me the word and I'll cut off his head! That'll put an end to his taunting!"

But David simply looked at Abishai and said no. He knew there were things of greater concern, such as his son Absalom trying to kill him and take the throne. Shimei was just a small nuisance along the way.

"Let him alone," David continued. "Perhaps God will see how I'm being wronged and bless me because of it."

David and his men continued down the road, and Shimei continued following them along the hillside, cursing and pelting them with stones and a shower of dirt. Finally, David and his followers reached their destination completely exhausted.

> *Even though Shimei's life had been spared, David had suspicions about his sincerity and warned Solomon about him. You can read about Shimei's tragic end in 1 Kings 2:8-9, 36-46.*

Soon, war broke out and word came that Absalom had been killed. Once again David was filled with grief, for although Absalom was treacherous, he was still his son. *Now I have one less son,* David lamented, *and a kingdom that has been torn apart by strife.*

Journeying back to Jerusalem with his loyal men, David was faced with the enormous task of setting the nation back in order. He was still grieving Absalom's death and wishing the whole event had never taken place.

When David arrived at the Jordan River, he noticed a large group rushing down to help them across. "We're here to help you cross and to do whatever you wish!" the large mass of people offered. Then David looked up and saw a man running to greet him. It was Shimei!

"Please, please O king," Shimei begged, falling facedown to the ground in sudden respect, "Don't hold my actions against me! Please forget my wrongful taunting of you when you were leaving Jerusalem!" he said with a whimper, fearing for his own life now that David was king again. "I know I've done wrong, but see? I'm one of the first down here to greet you and welcome you back!" Shimei groveled at David's feet. Once arrogant and full of insults, he now spoke in an entirely different tone of voice as he begged for David's mercy.

Abishai, one of David's men, saw what Shimei was doing and approached David in disgust. "Shouldn't Shimei be killed for cursing the Lord's anointed?" he asked, eyeing Shimei with contempt.

David looked at Shimei and knew that Abishai spoke the truth. Death was the usual punishment for anyone who slandered a king. Yet David refused to take that course of action.

"This isn't a day of execution but a day of celebration," he said, "for I am once again the king of Israel!" Then, looking directly at Shimei, he added, "Your life will be spared."

Abishai was stunned, and Shimei was greatly relieved. Shimei didn't get what he deserved—instead, he had been shown mercy.

Footwork

Open your Bible to 2 Samuel 17 and read verses 27-29. (Don't get stuck on the names in verse 27, but read on to see what happened in the verses following it.) It's interesting to note that one of the men who joined David was Makir, the same man who had taken care of Mephibosheth when Saul was killed. (See 2 Sam. 9.) Mephibosheth was still living in Makir's household when David sent for him to live in the palace. According to these verses, what did Makir and these other men do for David? What impact do you think that had on David?

Fruit

Although Shimei leveled a constant attack on David's character, David refused to give in to hatred. Because he chose not to fight back and cut Shimei down to size, David experienced God's blessing. For it was then that God sent Makir and the others to meet David's physical and emotional needs. Think about it. God's timing is perfect. The next time someone insults you and tries to cut you down, will you return the insults and be pulled into that person's hatred, or will you remain above it and move forward, knowing that God will be faithful to provide what you need emotionally and physically?

1 Kings

The book of 1 and 2 Kings were originally written on one scroll in the Hebrew language. When this scroll was translated from Hebrew (a language first written with no vowels) into Greek (a language requiring vowels), it became too long and was divided into two books: 1 Kings and 2 Kings.

As you journey through 1 Kings, you'll read about the wisdom of Solomon and the glory of his kingdom. But darker times for Israel would soon follow. One thing you'll notice is that the nation of Israel comes to a huge fork in the road and splits into two separate kingdoms. Ten tribes call themselves "Israel" and reign in the north, while the remaining two tribes call themselves "Judah" and establish themselves in the south. Why did the nation split, and what happens next? Read on to find out!

In 1 Kings you'll come face-to-face with honor and dishonor, the corrupting influence (and lure) of power, the emotional highs of victory, and the depressing lows of defeat. Most of all, you'll see people making choices and experiencing the consequences. This is what 1 Kings is all about. Although the terrain can get bumpy, you'll enjoy a few smooth spots along the way. Enjoy the journey! There's much to be discovered....

Be sure to check out www.cookministries.com/FaithFactor for two additional lessons from 1 Kings. "Oops!" is taken from chapters 1—2 and deals with contentment. "Woe Is Me!" is taken from chapter 19 and addresses ... well, you'll just have to read it for yourself and find out!

1050 BC — Saul elected Israel's firs

And That, Too? Wow!
Taken from 1 Kings 3—4

Foundation

Take time to prepare your heart before you begin. Having your heart
in the right place will make your time with the Lord more meaningful. Spend a few minutes just praising Him for who He is. Thank Him
for His faithfulness, His love, His holiness and mercy, His unending
power, and the fact that He knows the deepest secrets of your heart
and still loves you anyway.

Focus

*Do you sometimes have a problem with wanting the best only
for yourself?*

Now that Solomon was king, Israel enjoyed a great time of peace. The
nation was no longer engaged in civil war or battles with surrounding
nations. All signs of internal strife had ceased, and Solomon's kingdom
had been firmly established. Yet Solomon knew he needed help—God's
help—in order to govern the nation.

"What do you want? Ask, and I will give it to you," God spoke to
Solomon one night in a dream.

Such an offer was overwhelming! The very same God who had
miraculously parted the Red Sea for the Israelites and sent plagues
upon their enemies was now promising to give Solomon whatever he

asked! Solomon thought quietly. He had many options.

If I ask for success, I won't have to worry about the threat of my kingdom being taken from me as my father experienced, he thought. *On the other hand, if I ask for honor or wealth, I could live securely and have all that I need.* Solomon knew all of these were tempting choices, but not any he would choose.

"O Lord, You were wonderfully kind to my father because he had been honest, true, and faithful to You. Your kindness to him continues because You have allowed his son to sit on the throne." Solomon paused a moment before continuing. "I am Your servant, Lord," Solomon whispered. "Now I sit as king among Your people, but I am like a child who doesn't know my way around. The nation You have given me to govern is so vast! There are too many people to even begin to count!" Solomon added, feeling the weight of his responsibilities. "Please give me an understanding mind that I might know the difference between right and wrong and be able to govern Your people well," he asked. *Yes, this is my request of You,* he said in his heart. *I need wisdom.*

Not long after this, Solomon was faced with an opportunity to display the wisdom God had given him. Two women of little honor had come to Solomon to settle a dispute.

"We live together in the same house," one woman began. "I had a baby—a son— and three days later she had a son as well. During the night her baby died, so she switched her son with mine while I slept! I know this because when I woke up, the baby I cradled in my arms wasn't mine!"

"Liar!" the other woman snapped. "She's making this up because her son is dead and she's jealous that my son lives!"

Solomon took a deep breath and looked closely at each woman. He knew that on his own he could never determine who was telling the truth and who was lying. But at that very moment, the Lord delivered on His promise and gave Solomon amazing wisdom.

"You each stand before me, arguing that the child is yours," Solomon stated. "Each person's claim is as strong as the other's. Because of this, I order that the baby be cut in two, and each of you can have half! Bring me a sword!" he ordered. Solomon did this as a test, for he knew that the real mother would want to save the life of her son at all costs—even at the risk of losing him to the other woman.

"Stop!" the first woman shouted. "Don't kill the child! Please spare his life and let her have him."

"No!" the other shouted, "Neither of us will get him! Cut him in half!"

Solomon then knew immediately who the real mother was and returned the baby to her, unharmed. As a result of this, word about Solomon's great wisdom began to spread throughout the entire kingdom.

God answered Solomon's prayer for wisdom and then went a step further. "Because you didn't ask for riches, a long life, or the destruction of your enemies, but rather unselfishly asked for wisdom, I am greatly pleased," the Lord told Solomon. "Because of this, I have given what you asked for—wisdom and discernment. But I will also give you riches and honor—something you didn't ask for. In your lifetime, Solomon, no king will be equal to you."

Solomon was rewarded for first seeking what was best for the nation, not what he wanted for himself. God allowed him to enjoy both.

Footwork

Open your Bible to 1 Kings 3:13. What does it say? How sweet these words must have sounded to Solomon! Is the first half of this verse something God has ever said to you?

Fruit

Asking God for things that benefit you personally is very common, but it's not the most rewarding. Stop for a moment and think about your prayer life. What is it like? Do you mainly ask God for things for yourself, or do you look beyond your own desires? If God looked over your prayer "wish list," what would He see—the desires of a selfish person or the heart attitude of a servant? Take a few moments to compare your requests to Solomon's, and then make any necessary changes today.

It's Not Easy ... Being King

Taken from 1 Kings 8—11

Foundation

Spend a moment to pray for those who hold leadership positions over you (parents, teachers, coaches, bosses). Ask God to protect them from the temptations they face in their roles. Then ask Him to help you handle power appropriately whenever it comes your way.

Focus

Have you ever tried to bend the rules a little?

Solomon was pleased with all that surrounded him. *It's been seven years,* he sighed, *the temple is now completed, and the ark of God has a permanent resting place—a place my father, King David, dreamed of building.*

The temple stood as a marvel for all to see and a reminder of God's magnificence. This pleased Solomon greatly, and at the dedication ceremony, he led all the Israelites in worshipping and recommitting their hearts to the Lord.

"O Lord, there is no god anywhere who can match your faithful love.

BC — Kite invented in China;

Your splendor and majesty are so great, not even the highest heavens can contain You—and certainly not this temple I have built!" Solomon prayed, recognizing God's vastness, power, and holiness. "Please show mercy to the foreigners who desire to worship You, that all may know that You are the one true God. And forgive us, Your people, for the times we sin against You. Please don't ever turn Your face from us ..."

Solomon continued praying and when he finished, he got up and addressed the Israelites. "May the Lord turn our hearts toward Him, and may we always have the desire to do His will in everything—carefully obeying the commands, laws, and regulations He gave our ancestors!" It would later turn out that the very charge Solomon gave the Israelites, he himself would have trouble keeping.

Solomon was not only the wisest man who ever lived, but he was also a master builder. Besides the temple, he directed the building of three fortresses along the Mediterranean Coast, a protective wall around the city of Jerusalem, and a palace for himself (as well as other buildings). Solomon grew in riches and honor, and his kingdom continued to expand. By building fleets of ships, he soon began to trade with foreign countries. Every three years, ships returned loaded with gold, silver, and ivory, adding to Solomon's growing wealth and power. It wasn't long before word of Solomon's kingdom spread to faraway lands.

When the Queen of Sheba heard about Solomon's fame, she traveled twelve hundred miles just to see him! After seeing his great wealth and testing his power and knowledge, she was amazed and said, "Your wealth and wisdom are far greater than I ever imagined!"

> *The three fortress cities Solomon built were strategically located and offered the best defense against enemies. Hazor protected the northern kingdom, Megiddo protected the central lands and the valley of Jezreel, and Gezer protected the southern lands.*
>
> *Solomon's ships brought back more than gold, silver, and ivory. They also carried apes, baboons, and peacocks! (See 1 Kings 10:22.)*

She also brought Solomon many expensive gifts—tons of gold, large amounts of spices, and precious stones. The queen knew it was important to be on favorable terms with such a powerful king as Solomon.

Kings from other lands and lesser kingdoms also came to visit Solomon, acknowledging the power and glory of his kingdom and seeking his favor. Often they would give their daughters to him in marriage in hopes of making stronger political ties. Although Solomon knew God's command for Israelites not to marry foreigners (because of their false gods) or accumulate wives, he did so anyway, bending God's rules. Before long, Solomon had seven hundred wives, three hundred concubines, and a heart that began to stray from God's commands.

As time wore on, bending God's rules became more natural for Solomon. Even though his wealth and power continued to increase, he began making unwise choices as he strayed even further from God's commands. In spite of God forbidding Israelite kings to collect large amounts of gold or silver, Solomon continued to do so. He also controlled the major trade route that connected Egypt to the rest of the world and began collecting taxes as payment for traders passing through. This brought him even more gold and riches, which he then used to purchase fourteen hundred chariots and twelve thousand horses.

This will greatly improve my kingdom and establish our security against enemies who might attack! Solomon rationalized. Once again he had bent God's rules. According to the Law handed down through Moses, Israelite kings were not permitted to acquire great numbers of horses for themselves. This was so that God's people would depend on Him for protection rather than on people or things that would give them a false sense of security. Because Solomon wasn't fully devoted to the Lord in his later years and didn't follow Him completely, the hearts of the Israelites slowly began to turn away from God as well.

Footwork

Open your Bible to 1 Kings 4:32–34. What do these verses say? Do you find this odd in light of the unwise choices Solomon began making? According to 1 Kings 9:4–5, God said He would establish Solomon's throne if Solomon was careful to do three things: (1) walk before God in uprightness and integrity of heart; (2) do everything God commanded; and (3) observe and obey God's rules. Now turn ahead a few chapters and read 1 Kings 11:9–12. This is God's "report card" on Solomon's leadership. What did God say?

Fruit

With power and leadership comes the temptation to stretch the rules just a little here and there. No matter how wise leaders may seem, if they bend the rules, they will soon find themselves way off course, and in some cases, ruined. If God allows you to be in a leadership position, be careful! It's not easy being "king." Learn from Solomon's example.

That'll Do It
Taken from 1 Kings 11—12

Foundation

Don't forget to pray as you begin your time with the Lord today.
Quiet your thoughts before Him, and then come expectantly, ready to
hear what He has to show you in His Word.

Focus

Are you easily distracted?

Jeroboam met Ahijah's gaze as he clutched the ten pieces of fabric the
prophet had given him. Ahijah had taken off his new cloak, torn it into twelve
pieces (each piece representing one of the twelve tribes of Israel), and
handed ten pieces to Jeroboam.

"These ten pieces are for you, for God has spoken and said He is going
to give you ten tribes when He tears the kingdom out of Solomon's
hands," Ahijah announced.

Jeroboam looked around him just to be sure Ahijah hadn't made a
mistake. No one else was in sight. Only he and the prophet stood on that
deserted road.

"For the sake of David, God won't take the whole kingdom from
Solomon but will allow him one tribe, that there might always be a
descendant of David to reign in Jerusalem," Ahijah added.

Jeroboam knew that the one tribe referred to Judah and included the
smaller tribe of Benjamin. They were represented by the two pieces of

`n China (later known as Beijing);`

The Sidonians worshipped Ashtoreth. Followers of this goddess engaged in gross immoral deeds and the worship of stars. The Ammonites and Moabites, who worshipped Molech and Chemosh, offered their children as human sacrifices!

1 Kings 13:1–3 gives a remarkable prophecy! God sent a prophet to Jeroboam naming a king (Josiah from the house of David) who would rise up and destroy Jeroboam's high places—a king who wouldn't appear for 290 years! The prophecy was fulfilled in 2 Kings 23:15–20! Check it out!

cloth remaining in Ahijah's hands. According to the prophet's words, God was sending His judgment upon Solomon and the nation of Israel because they hadn't obeyed God's laws and statutes. Instead, they worshipped the false gods of the Sidonians, the Moabites, and the Ammonites. Even King Solomon had been led astray by his many wives and embraced these false gods.

Ahijah continued, "I will not tear the kingdom from Solomon's hands until after he dies because of the promise I made to David. Rather, I will take the kingdom from his son, Rehoboam, giving the ten northern tribes to you. Just as I split this cloak, so will Solomon's kingdom be split. Solomon's son, Rehoboam, will have Judah. You, Jeroboam, will have the northern tribes of Israel."

The words left Jeroboam speechless.

When Solomon died, his son, Rehoboam, went north to Shechem, where all the Israelites crowned him king. When Jeroboam heard this, he went to speak with the new king.

"Please, Rehoboam, your father made the people work hard and taxed them harshly. Lighten the load, and we will be your servants," he offered. Because Jeroboam had served as an officer in charge of King Solomon's workers, he was able to represent the voice of the people.

King Rehoboam thought about Jeroboam's request for three days and rejected it. As a result, the ten tribes of Israel rebelled against the new king and followed Jeroboam instead. Only the tribes of Judah and Benjamin remained loyal to Rehoboam— just as God had said. From that day on, Rehoboam ruled in Jerusalem over those in Judah who remained loyal to the house of David, and Jeroboam ruled in Israel, with Shechem as his capital. The nation of Israel had been torn apart.

The thought of his people traveling to the temple three times a year to offer sacrifices made Jeroboam nervous, but all Jewish men were commanded by Law to do so. *By traveling into Rehoboam's kingdom, they might be influenced to join back up with him, then turn around and kill me! I must do something to keep them from going and offering their sacrifices in Jerusalem!* Jeroboam schemed.

It didn't take long to come up with a plan.

There, that'll do it! Jeroboam thought smugly, looking at the high places and shrines he had set up. He had made two golden calves for the people to worship as their gods, placing one in the northern city of Dan and one in the southern city of Bethel. The high place (altar) in Bethel was strategically located on the main road, just thirty miles before a traveler would reach Jerusalem. Jeroboam knew that this would distract worshippers from continuing their journey. "Why go all the way to Jerusalem, when we can offer our sacrifices *here?*" they would say to themselves. The high place in Dan would be more convenient for those living in the north.

Jeroboam called the northern tribes together and made his proclamation. "The journey to Jerusalem is too long and not needed," he announced. "For right here are the gods who brought you out of your Egyptian slavery and into this land!"

Jeroboam introduced the golden calves and led the hearts of the people away from their obedience to God. He then appointed priests from among the people (even though none were from the tribe of Levi!) and came up with his own version of the sacred festival held once a year in Jerusalem. Picking a time of his own choosing, Jeroboam cleverly instituted a new festival to be held exactly one month later than Judah's. He knew this would keep the Israelites from longing for their former ways of worship. *That'll do it!* he said in his heart, pleased with himself.

"That'll do it!" God would respond—in judgment.

Footwork

Turn to 1 Kings 14:8. What did God say to Jeroboam? Drop down and read verses 9–10. What was going to happen to him? Now, look at the consequences of Jeroboam's sin in verse 16.

Fruit

Jeroboam set up "convenient" places of worship as a distraction for the Israelites. There, they worshipped idols in high places instead of worshipping the one true God at the altar. What "high places" or distractions might you (or others in your life) have set up that keeps you from worshipping God?

King David dies; Solomon, his son,

For Better or For Worse
Taken from 1 Kings 13

Foundation

Stop for a moment and pray. Ask God to give you listening ears and a teachable heart so that you will be able to receive what He wants to share with you from His Word today. Tell Him what's on your mind so you can better learn what's on His.

Focus

Do you ever struggle with being influenced by the behavior of those around you?

The prophet stepped out from the crowd and leveled his message from God at King Jeroboam—not just against the king's wickedness but against the altar he was making a sacrifice on. The altar and a gold calf had been built as a substitute to keep the Israelites from journeying to Jerusalem and worshipping there.

"As a sign that my message of judgment is true," the prophet declared, "this very altar will split in two, and the ashes on it will fall to the ground."

"Enough!" Jeroboam snapped. Then pointing at the prophet, he shouted, "Grab him!"

But as soon as Jeroboam stretched out his hand, it withered and became paralyzed! God's power and authority had overruled Jeroboam's. The king watched helplessly as the altar split apart, just as the prophet had said.

ecomes third king over Israel,

"Please," Jeroboam begged the prophet in a panicked voice, "ask your God to restore my hand."

The prophet did as Jeroboam requested, and the king regained the use of his hand. Then the king extended a generous offer to the prophet to come back to the palace to feast. His intention was to influence the prophet, but the young man refused.

"Even though you give me half of everything you own, I wouldn't go with you to eat bread or drink water, for I was commanded by the Lord that I must not eat bread or drink water in Bethel, nor return by the way I came." With that, the prophet obeyed the Lord and took a different road out of town.

Meanwhile, when word of the prophet reached the ears of an older prophet in Bethel, he raised his eyebrows. "So," he said under his breath, "this young man believes that he has a ministry from God? Hah! We'll just see about that!"

In his years of living in Bethel—the very center of Jeroboam's system of false worship—the old prophet had gotten lazy and complacent. The influence of his surroundings had hardened his heart, and he no longer valued obedience to God. *Talking with this young man of God will be of great interest!* he thought to himself.

So the old prophet mounted a donkey and rode after the young prophet. When he found a man sitting under an oak tree, he asked, "Are you the prophet from Judah?"

"Yes," came the reply.

"Then come with me to Bethel and join me for a meal," the old prophet invited.

> **Kings commonly kept palace prophets to tell them only the prophecies they wanted to hear. Perhaps this was what Jeroboam wanted to offer the young man of God.**

When the young man declined, explaining that God had forbidden him to eat or drink in the city of Bethel, the old prophet tried to influence him. "I'm a prophet of God as well," he reassured, "and an angel speaking for God told me to bring you back to my house to eat and drink with me." The old prophet made this up, for he wanted to persuade the man of God to return home with him. It didn't matter to him that God had forbidden it.

I know that God told me not to partake of any food or drink in Bethel—the city of idolatry, the young prophet thought. *Yet this older man is a prophet himself and claims that God has given him other directions for me to follow.*

After briefly weighing this in his mind, the man of God agreed to return to Bethel to eat and drink with the older prophet—directly against God's command.

Midway through the meal, God delivered a message through the lips of the older, disobedient prophet. It was a message of judgment for the man of God. "You have disobeyed the command God gave you, and defied God's authority by coming back to the place where He told you not to eat or drink. Because of your actions, you will die and be buried in a tomb not belonging to your fathers.

When the young prophet left the older prophet's house and began his journey home, he was attacked on the road by a lion and killed. The older prophet heard of this and felt guilty. So he brought the young prophet's body back to Bethel, buried it in his own tomb, and mourned for him. Because he had allowed himself to fall under Jeroboam's sinful influence and brazen disobedience, the older prophet had influenced another prophet to do the same. And the results were deadly!

Footwork

Open your Bible to 1 Kings 15 and come along on a quick tour of the power of Jeroboam's influence. The first stop is 1 Kings 15:25–26. What does it say? (Go on, look this up in your Bible—it's something you won't want to skip over.) Now look ahead to verses 33–34 and read them. Then turn to 1 Kings 16:25–26 and read what these verses say. Finally, read verse 31. What do you learn from these verses about the power of influence?

Fruit

Influence is a powerful thing—it can be used for either good or evil. It can make others either spiritually stronger or spiritually weaker. What kind of influence does your life have on others? Take a moment to think about the people you influence. Now think about the lives of those you allow to influence you. Ask God to forgive you for choices or actions that lead you (or others) away from Him. Then remember to practice three simple steps to help keep you on the right path:

1. *Evaluate* everything according to God's standards. (To do this, you need to be in His Word so you know what His standards are!)
2. *Pray* before you act (or react).
3. *Renew* your commitment to serve God—daily!

Promise?
Taken from 1 Kings 17—18

Foundation

Begin your time today with prayer. Start by thanking the Lord for the lessons you've been learning as you get to know Him better through His Word. Thank Him for His faithfulness and for being a God who cares deeply for your needs.

Focus

Do you sometimes worry about how your needs will be met?

It had been forty years since King Jeroboam died. From that time until now, Israel (the ten northern tribes) had endured five different kings— each following in the wickedness Jeroboam had established, each leading Israel further away from the Lord. Now a man named Ahab was ruling the northern kingdom. King Ahab had little concern for God and considered the sins and idolatry of Jeroboam to be trivial. So God sent the prophet Elijah as His spokesman to challenge Ahab.

"Just as surely as God lives," Elijah proclaimed to King Ahab, "no dew or rain will come in the next few years until I say otherwise!"

Elijah obediently delivered God's message of warning to the king of Israel, then he followed the Lord's next command for him: "You are to leave here and go to the Kerith Ravine, just east of the Jordan River, to hide. I will send ravens to feed you and you will have water to drink from the brook."

Elijah did as God said, and God did as He promised. The ravens brought Elijah bread and meat both morning and evening, and Elijah drank water from the brook. When the brook finally dried up because of the lack of rain, God directed Elijah to go and stay in the village of Zarephath. "I've commanded a widow there to provide food for you to eat."

Arriving at the town gate, Elijah saw a widow collecting sticks. It was obvious the woman was poor and had very little. Her face looked hollow and drawn from hunger. "Would you please bring me a little drink of water in a jar?" Elijah politely requested.

Zarephath was a town on the Mediterranean Coast in Phoenicia and was the homeland of Ahab's wife, Queen Jezebel.

The Obadiah mentioned here was in charge of King Ahab's palace. He also secretly hid one hundred of the Lord's prophets so Queen Jezebel wouldn't kill them (1 Kings 18:4). This is not the same Obadiah for whom the Old Testament book is named.

As the widow turned to go fetch the water, Elijah added, "And would you also bring me a little bread?"

The widow turned back toward Elijah and looked into his eyes. She knew it was the custom to take care of visiting prophets, but she also knew that she had no bread to offer him. Her sad, tired eyes communicated the situation without spoken words.

"Just as surely as the Lord lives," she sighed, "all I have is just a handful of flour left and a small amount of oil in the bottom of my jug. I have no bread to offer and was just gathering a few sticks in order to cook this last meal—then my son and I will die."

Elijah looked at the woman, who seemed to have so little. He thought about how God had been faithful to provide for his own needs, feeding him from the mouths of ravens. Then he replied kindly, "Do not fear, but return home to cook your meal—only before you cook it, first make a small piece of bread out of what you do have and bring it to me. Afterwards, make something for you and your son to eat," he instructed. "For the God of Israel says: 'Your jar of flour will not go empty, and the oil in the jug will not run out until the Lord sends rain again.' "

The widow acted in faith and did as Elijah told her. She put her trust in the Lord to meet her needs and wasn't disappointed. The jar of flour wasn't used up, and the jug of oil didn't run dry, just as God had promised! Elijah stayed with her, and the Lord continued to provide for the needs of the widow—as well as Elijah.

When the third year of the famine had come, the word of the Lord came to Elijah telling him to pay King Ahab a visit. Meanwhile, the king had gone in search of grass to keep his horses and mules alive.

"Obadiah, you go in one direction, searching all the springs and valleys," the king commanded his servant, "and I'll go in the other."

Obadiah obeyed and set out immediately, but instead of coming across grass, he came across something more remarkable. *That's Elijah the prophet,* he thought, recognizing Elijah from a distance. Obadiah knew that Elijah was a wanted man and that the king blamed him for the terrible drought. (Even though Obadiah served under King Ahab, he was a believer in the Lord.)

"Go and tell King Ahab that I want to meet with him," Elijah instructed Obadiah.

Obadiah hesitated. "I have worshipped the Lord since my youth," he said. "Why are you sending me to tell Ahab I've seen you? Have I done something wrong? Ahab has sent servants into every nation and kingdom to look for you! Now you're asking me to go and say, 'I've seen Elijah'? If I tell Ahab this and you aren't there, he'll kill me!"

Elijah reassured Obadiah, "Rest assured, as the Lord Almighty lives, I promise you I will show up and meet with Ahab today."

Elijah was confident in God's ability to handle the situation and meet his needs. It was a lesson he learned firsthand from his experiences during the drought.

Footwork

Look up 1 Kings 17:17–24 in your Bible. Through the hands of Elijah, the widow experienced another miracle. Notice her response. What does she say?

Fruit

Trusting God to meet our needs frees us up to act boldly, confidently, and in obedience to Him. As a result, God is able to use us in powerful ways. On a small piece of paper, write down one or two needs in your life that you're concerned about. These could be needs for physical or even emotional things. Commit your list to God, then take the next step: Trust Him and step out in faith. God promises to be there for you. He won't let you down.

Solomon dies; kingdom of Israel divide

Attention, Please!
Taken from 1 Kings 17—18

Foundation

Take a moment to pray and really talk to God. Don't just list things you want Him to do for you; spend time praising Him. Thank Him for His power and that He alone is the one true God. Nothing and no one else can compare to Him.

Focus

Have you ever been afraid to stand up for the Lord when others attack the honor of His name?

"More water."

"More?"

"Yes—until it overflows into the trenches."

Silence fell upon the crowd. Some stood curiously wondering; others stood mocking a crazy man. King Ahab stood impatiently tapping his foot and remembering when Elijah first came to him …

"As the Lord, the God of Israel lives," Elijah had said, reminding the king of the one true God of Israel that he should have been worshipping, "the One whom I serve …"

King Ahab had flinched at those words and grown restless. And with anger mounting in his heart, he had muttered to himself, "Doesn't he know who he's speaking to?"

Everyone knew that Ahab's wife, Queen Jezebel, had plans to make Baal worship the national religion of the Israelites. She had already killed off many of God's priests and replaced them with 450 prophets of Baal and 400 prophets of Asherah. Jezebel had also destroyed the altars dedicated to the worship of the Lord.

Mount Carmel *means "God's vineyard" and is aptly named. Standing one thousand feet high, it's the most heavily forested area in all of Israel. Today its slopes are covered with olive groves and vineyards.*

Elijah *means "Yahweh is God." Just saying Elijah's name must have been detestable to King Ahab!*

Baal is the god of this land and will soon be the god of these people as well, King Ahab had reminded himself. But he wasn't prepared for the challenge that came from the lips of Elijah.

"There will be no rain on the land during the next few years unless I speak the word," Elijah had stated boldly.

Foolish man, Ahab had laughed softly to himself, *doesn't he know that the god in control of rain and the richness of the soil isn't the God of the Israelites? It's Baal—the god of the land! It's Baal who brings forth crops and green grass. Yahweh is a god of the desert—this is the land of Canaan, and the richness of this land is due to the Canaanite gods.*

Ahab had scoffed at Elijah's words and found them quite amusing—but he didn't laugh for long. Now, three years later, the smile had all but disappeared from King Ahab's lips. The once fertile soil lay dry and cracked due to drought.

"Call the people together and come to Mount Caramel," Elijah had told King Ahab. "Have all your prophets of Baal and Asherah join you as well."

When the people had joined Elijah on the mountain, Elijah confronted them. "You must choose this day whom you will follow—Baal or the God of Israel. Both of them can't be the one true God! So make up your minds! Follow Baal if he is god, or the Lord if He is God!"

That troublemaker Elijah has challenged the power of Baal! Ahab had raged in his heart. *Now he will see the power of our gods!*

Gathering the 450 prophets of Baal, the 400 prophets of Asherah, and the people of Israel, King Ahab had journeyed up the mountain to meet Elijah.

"Take your bull and arrange it on your altar, but don't light the wood," Elijah had commanded. "I will do the same. Then call on the name of your god, and I will call upon the name of mine. The god who answers by fire— He is God."

The Baal worshippers had smiled to themselves. They knew that Baal was the god of weather and was often portrayed carrying a thunderbolt. *Hah!* King Ahab had reasoned, *this time Elijah will be proven wrong!*

All morning the prophets had cried out to Baal, begging him to answer. But there had been no response. They had shouted louder and danced around the altar—but still no answer.

Around noon Elijah had begun to taunt them. "It seems as if your god Baal is preoccupied in his thoughts, or busy with other things. Perhaps he is off traveling or taking a nap and needs to be awakened!" Elijah of course knew the reason they weren't having success: Baal wasn't God.

The prophets of Baal had shouted all the louder, slashing themselves with swords and spears, continually calling out to their god—but still there had been no response. Nothing! No one had answered. No one had paid attention. The prophets of Baal and the prophets of Asherah had had their turn. Now it was Elijah's turn!

After having called the people to gather around, Elijah repaired the altar of the Lord, which had been torn down. He had then cut up his bull and arranged the pieces on the altar over the wood. Next, Elijah had done something that had surprised everyone—he had called for water to be poured over the sacrifice, making it all the more difficult to light....

The king's attention returned to the events taking place before him. The last of twelve large jars of water were being poured over the altar and the sacrifice, filling the trench below to overflowing. Elijah stepped forward and prayed a simple prayer to the Lord. Then suddenly, just as Elijah finished praying, a lightning bolt ripped down from heaven and consumed the sacrifice, burning up the bull, the wood, the stones, the soil, and all the water in the trench!

The people instantly fell down, crying out, "The Lord, He is God; the Lord, He is God!" Their attention and allegiance were now back with the Lord.

Moving swiftly, Elijah had all the false prophets of Baal seized and put to death in the Kishon Valley. God had gotten the people's attention!

Footwork

Open your Bible and turn to Elijah's prayer in 1 Kings 18:36–37. What two requests did Elijah first make in verse 36? According to verse 37, what was the driving purpose behind his requests?

Fruit

Elijah had a lot of guts! He wasn't afraid to stand up against the culture and protect the honor of God's name. Because of his courage to do that, the hearts of many were turned back to the Lord.

Take a moment to evaluate your life. Do you turn a deaf ear and remain silent when God's honor is challenged, or do you allow yourself to be used by God to make a difference? What steps could you take to be more like Elijah? (Example: not remaining silent when a friend takes God's name in vain.) Think of a few things you can do, and make a point of doing one of them this week. Write them down here in the margin so you won't forget.

2 Kings

Second Kings begins where 1 Kings leaves off—with twists, turns, great adventure, and terrible mishaps. Powerful nations had surrounded Israel and Judah—nations God would use to accomplish His purposes and carry out His judgment.

Reading through this part of Scripture can get confusing because it often switches between the kings of Judah and the kings of Israel. When you read about the kings in your own Bible, you might want to take two different colored pencils and highlight the different kings. For example, you could use red for the kings of Israel, since God would put a stop to their kingdom first. Then use green for the kings of Judah, since God would preserve their nation and eventually bring about the birth of the promised Messiah through their descendants.

As you explore 2 Kings, you'll notice examples of obedience and disobedience to God—sometimes coming from the same person! You'll see faith in action and faith in need of repair, good actions and chain reactions, brief moments of victory and years of defeat. But most of all, you'll see God's hand always there, preventing total disaster. As you read through these passages, keep your head up so you don't lose your way—or your perspective—and keep your eyes on the Lord. That's something Israel and Judah didn't do. Enjoy the journey!

Check out four bonus lessons online at www.cookministries.com/FaithFactor: "Oh" (taken from 2 Kings 6—7), which talks about believing and claiming God's victory; "Charrrge!" (taken from 2 Kings 9—10), which talks about not getting carried away with our emotions; "No Offense?" (taken from 2 Kings 16), which talks about tolerance; and "Never!" (taken from 2 Kings 18-19), which deals with trials that teach!

ingdom of Israel; one year

Says Who?

Taken from 2 Kings 1

Foundation

Before you begin today's lesson, make sure your heart is prepared. You can do this by simply taking the time to talk with God before you dig into His Word. Ask Him to quiet your heart and your thoughts so you can learn what He wants to show you.

Focus

Does it irritate you to be around people who think they can simply order others around?

"What are you doing back so soon?" King Ahaziah asked, groaning in pain as he tried to reposition his body. "Surely you couldn't have gone to Ekron and back in such a short time!"

The messengers hesitated before giving their report to the king. Ever since he had fallen through the lattice of his upper room, he had suffered from both the pain of his injuries and a fear of dying.

"Go to Ekron in the land of the Philistines and inquire of their god, Baal-Zebub, to see if I will recover from my injuries," the king had commanded his messengers.

But on the way they received an answer from an unexpected source who met them on the road.

"Are you going to consult the god of Ekron because there is no God in Israel?" Elijah challenged.

The messengers looked at one another, unsure how to respond. All they knew was that they needed to return home with an answer for the king.

"Since Ahaziah has done this, go back and give him this message from the Lord: 'You will not recover from this, but will die in your bed!'"

With these words Elijah left the men standing in the middle of the road looking at one another and wondering what to do next. After a slight hesitation, they decided to return to the king and deliver Elijah's message.

"We met a man on the road who stopped us," the messengers finally said in response to the king's surprise at their quick return.

"What kind of man was he—what did he look like?" the king asked.

When the messengers described the man's clothes made of hair and the leather belt he wore, the king immediately recognized who it was. "Elijah!" he spat. "That man was Elijah the prophet!"

Dismissing his messengers, King Ahaziah summoned one of his captains. "Take your company of fifty men and bring Elijah here at once!" he demanded.

So the captain left to arrest Elijah and found him sitting on a hill. "Elijah, man of God! Come on down from there! You have been ordered by the king to come along with us."

Elijah knew that the king hated him and the God he represented. The fact that Ahaziah had sent a band of soldiers to arrest him and drag him

Baal-Zebub, "lord of the flies," was a pagan idol worshipped chiefly in Ekron. Thought to have healing powers, Baal-Zebub was not the same as Baal (the main god of the Canaanites).

There were two King Ahaziahs who ruled twelve years apart from each other. The Ahaziah mentioned here is the son of King Ahab. He ruled in Israel (the northern tribes) for two years, beginning in 853 BC. The other Ahaziah ruled over the southern tribes of Judah nearly twelve years later. Both Ahaziahs were evil and didn't seek after God.

to the palace like an outlaw only reaffirmed it. God's honor was being challenged, and Elijah would have no part of it!

"If I truly am what you say I am—a man of God—then may God defend me, and strike you and your fifty men down with fire from heaven!" Elijah responded.

As soon as those words came from Elijah's lips, fire blazed down from heaven and destroyed them all. But instead of learning from this, King Ahaziah grew impatient and sent another captain with fifty men to find Elijah.

"You man of God," the captain called out with great authority, "the king commands you to come down and return with us to the city right now!" He believed that his message would convince Elijah to come down immediately. *What King Ahaziah wants, he always gets,* the captain thought. But he wasn't ready for Elijah's response.

"If I am what you say I am—a man of God—and I do only as the Lord God instructs me to do, then may He send down fire from heaven and destroy you and all fifty of your men with you!" Elijah once again stated.

In that instant, fire once again came down from heaven and destroyed the captain and his band of soldiers.

King Ahaziah, still refusing to accept the fact that he couldn't control God, sent yet another captain and his soldiers to Elijah. This time, however, the captain had respect for both the Lord and His servant. He called Elijah a "man of God" not with contempt but with sincerity. He then made his request of Elijah humbly and didn't command Elijah as if he were giving orders to a dog. The Lord saw this and encouraged Elijah to go with the captain—and Elijah did, obediently.

Footwork

Open your Bible to 2 Kings 1:16–17 and read what it says. According to these verses, what happened when Elijah met with King Ahaziah?

Fruit

King Ahaziah knew that it was wrong to seek counsel from the gods of other nations, yet he chose to do so anyway. Doing evil in God's eyes was of little concern to him, for King Ahaziah had set himself up as his own authority. This proved that he was an arrogant person who had nothing but contempt for God and those who followed Him.

Life today is no different. It's almost guaranteed that you'll meet up with arrogant people who think they own the world and can command anything or anyone. Follow Elijah's example and don't blindly and fearfully march at their command. Such people feed on the sense of power they get from ordering timid people around. Instead, stand your ground and ask yourself, "Says *who?*" Then let power fall where it rightly belongs—into God's hands.

May I Have That . . . and More?

Taken from 2 Kings 2

Foundation

Before beginning today's lesson, stop and pray. Ask God to give you a renewed passion to live for Him in such a way that others would desire to know Him all the more because of your life.

Focus

Have you ever wanted what someone else has—for nonselfish reasons?

"No," Elisha replied respectfully, "I choose not to stay behind but to go with you." *This is now the third time Elijah has tried to keep me from coming with him. Doesn't he know I'm committed to staying with him—even to the very end?* Elisha wondered.

Apparently satisfied with Elisha's response, the prophet Elijah invited Elisha to continue on with him as a school of prophets from Jericho followed at a distance. They knew Elijah would soon be taken from them, and watched as the older and younger prophets walked together toward the Jordan River.

The younger prophet recalled the first time he and Elijah met. He had been busy plowing with twelve pair of oxen when Elijah approached him in the field and threw his cloak over him.

"Allow me to say good-bye to my father and mother," Elisha had responded, "and then I'll come with you."

Elijah nodded in agreement, and Elisha slaughtered his oxen and burned his plowing equipment to cook the meat. After offering the meat to the people, he then set out to follow Elijah (1 Kings 19:19–21).

The two had now reached the Jordan River and could go no farther. Removing his cloak, Elijah folded it up and hit the water with it. The water parted, and both men crossed to the other side. Elisha couldn't help but think of how God had parted the Red Sea for Moses and the Jordan River for Joshua—and now He had done it for Elijah. The same God who had performed those miracles long ago was still showing His power in and through His servants.

"Before I am taken, what would you like me to do for you?" Elijah asked the younger prophet, who would soon fill his shoes.

"Please, let me become your successor and inherit twice your spirit!" Elisha responded.

Even though Elijah understood what the young prophet desired, he knew it wasn't his to give. "This is a difficult request," he answered, "but, if you see me when God takes me, it will be a sign that He has given you what you've asked."

As the two continued walking and talking together, a chariot of fire suddenly appeared out of the heavens and swooped down between them. Then a whirlwind came and swept Elijah off the face of the earth and into God's presence.

As Elijah was caught up into the whirlwind, his cloak fell to the ground near Elisha's feet. The

> Elisha *means "my God is salvation."* Through Elisha's life, God would work miracles that would point others to Him. You can read about these in 2 Kings 2—6.
>
> ---
>
> *A prophet throwing his cloak around someone represented passing on his authority to that person.*
>
> ---
>
> *Elisha asked for "a double portion" of Elijah's spirit. Interestingly, the Bible records that he did almost twice as many miracles!*

young prophet tore his clothes in mourning, as he looked heavenward after Elijah. He then bent over, picked up the cloak, and carried it with him to the river's edge. There, Elisha stopped.

I know I asked that I might be able to carry on the ministry of Elijah and do even greater things for Your glory, Lord. I also saw Elijah being taken up—a sign that You would grant me my desires, he prayed softly. Looking at the cloak in his hands, Elisha knew what it meant. God would use him as His next prophet to bring others to Himself. Elisha slowly rolled up the cloak, and full of faith, he called out, "Now where is Elijah's God—the Lord God Almighty?" and struck the waters of the Jordan River. And just as God had done for Elijah, He parted the Jordan so Elisha could cross back over.

Seeing what Elisha had done, the school of prophets, who had been watching from a distance, knew Elisha was operating under God's power. He was picking up where Elijah had left off and would be the next great prophet to do mighty works in the name of the Lord. Little did Elisha know how God would use him and how greatly the prayer of his heart would be answered.

Footwork

Not long after this event, Elisha encountered a difficulty. Open your Bible to 2 Kings 2:23–25 and read about it. What happened? How did Elisha respond? Do you think he overreacted?

It's important to know that the youths were really a gang of young men—possibly false prophets of Baal. When they shouted "Go on up!" they were implying that if Elisha were as great as Elijah, he should just follow Elijah's example and disappear into heaven himself! Elisha saw the contempt for God in their eyes. His curse wasn't to protect his own pride but to address their disrespect for the Lord.

Fruit

Although you and I will probably never do any miraculous things for God, we're still called to be the Lord's servants, just like Elijah and Elisha were. God wants to work in and through our lives in such a way that the world might know that He is God. Elisha's heart was in the right place; he wanted what God had to offer so that he could use it for God's glory.

Lord, there are so many times I fail You. Please forgive me. I want to live my life in Your power so that You can do great things in and through me. However You choose to use me, I give my time, abilities, desires, and all that I am to You. Help me to seek Your best and not settle for anything less than what will bring glory to You. Amen.

By the Way . . .
Taken from 2 Kings 5

Foundation

Before you begin today's lesson, spend time thanking God for who He is. Ask Him to help you better reflect faithfulness, truthfulness, and integrity in your thoughts, motives, and actions.

Focus

Do you secretly try to manipulate others for your own personal benefit?

"My master Naaman would be healed of his leprosy if only he would go and see the prophet who lives in Israel," the Israelite girl said to her mistress, Naaman's wife.

Naaman was a commander of the Aramean army and was very valuable to the king. Unfortunately, he had leprosy, a disease that would eventually take his life. The king of Aram was afraid of losing his best commander, so when he heard about the possibility of Naaman being healed, he wrote a letter of introduction for Naaman to carry with him and hand to the king of Israel. The letter simply stated, "With this message I present my servant Naaman to you to be healed."

"What?" the king of Israel said to his attendants in disbelief. "This king sends me a leper to heal! Am I God that I can destroy and bring back to life? Is the king of Aram using this leper to pick a fight with me?" he shouted. *I can't heal him any more than I could heal myself! Why is this king insisting on stirring up trouble and putting me in such a position?* he thought to himself. Then the king of Israel tore his robes, expressing both grief and deep concern over the situation at hand. The thought of calling on the Lord, or even God's prophet, Elisha, never once crossed his mind.

When Elisha heard about the king's distress over Naaman, he sent the king a message asking why he had torn his robes. "Send the man to me," Elisha directed, "so he might know there is a true prophet of God in Israel."

Not long after this, Naaman came to Elisha's home with all his horses and chariots. But instead of speaking directly to Naaman, Elisha sent his servant to the door with instructions. "Go to the Jordan River and wash yourself seven times, and your leprosy will go away." Naaman stood there stunned. He was a proud man and didn't like being treated like an ordinary person.

"No healing ceremony? And this prophet won't even speak to me himself?" he muttered under his breath. "What kind of joke is this? Wash myself seven times in the Jordan River?" he repeated to himself. "Never! Aren't the rivers in Damascus better than this filthy river?" Then he left, furious over how he had been treated.

Naaman's servants could see their master's pride had been wounded, but they believed that he had nothing to lose and encouraged him to obey Elisha's instructions.

"If he had told you to do something difficult, wouldn't you have done it?" they gently coaxed. "Surely then, if he tells you to do something simple, why not do it and be cured?"

Aram was a pagan nation that frequently waged war with Israel. The Arameans often swooped down in raids and took captives back with them. The Israelite servant girl in Naaman's household was one such captive.

In Elisha's day, there were many false prophets who made a habit of lining their pockets by accepting gifts for their services. Elisha wanted to show Naaman that God's gift of healing couldn't be bought.

Naaman looked at his servants and saw their concern. His anger began to fade, and he went to the Jordan River to do as Elisha had instructed. When Naaman came out of the water, everyone was amazed—his leprosy was gone! Not only that, but Naaman's skin had been restored to what it had looked like during his childhood! Quickly, Naaman returned to Elisha to thank him and offer gifts as payment for this great deed.

"Now I know that the God of Israel is the one true God!" Naaman exclaimed. With that, he offered Elisha the gifts he had brought with him—750 pounds of silver, 150 pounds of gold, and ten sets of clothing.

Elisha looked at the generous gifts but refused them. But Gehazi, Elisha's servant, looked at them with desire and began scheming how he could manipulate Naaman in order to get the "goods" Elisha turned down. *If Elisha won't take them from Naaman, then I will!* he thought, trying to catch up to Naaman's caravan. *After all, he was more than willing to give those gifts*, Gehazi reasoned.

"Is something wrong?" Naaman asked, concerned.

"No," Gehazi replied, "everything is fine … except that my master, Elisha, sent me with word that two prophets came to visit him unexpectedly, and … well … he was wondering … could you please give him seventy-five pounds of silver and two sets of clothing?"

"It would be my pleasure!" Naaman responded generously, believing Gehazi's lie.

Gehazi's eyes gleamed, and he secretly delighted at his gain. When he saw Naaman didn't give just one bag of silver but two, Gehazi delighted all the more! *I've got it all!* he breathed to himself, pleased that he had been able to manipulate the situation to his advantage.

When Gehazi arrived home, he quickly stashed the silver and clothes in his house and returned to Elisha …

Footwork

Quickly turn in your Bible to 2 Kings 5:25–27 and read it. (Go on, look it up!) What did Elisha ask Gehazi? What was Gehazi's response in verse 25? Gehazi's motive was to gain something for himself. According to verse 27, what did God allow Gehazi to gain?

Fruit

Gehazi fell into the temptation of looking out for his own personal interests instead of serving the Lord. He readily manipulated Naaman to get what he wanted and ended up getting more than he bargained for!

When opportunity comes knocking on your door, will you try to get all you can for yourself, or will you be satisfied with letting God get the glory?

Every Little Bit Helps
Taken from 2 Kings 21—23

Foundation

Spend a moment to pray and clear your mind of distractions. Ask God to show you the importance of living your life for Him. Just one life can make a difference!

FOCUS

Do you ever feel like giving up because it's too hard to resist all the evil around you?

"You found what?" King Josiah demanded, jumping to his feet.

"The book of the law of Moses!" Shaphan the temple secretary eagerly repeated. "While cleaning out the temple as you commanded, we came across this scroll! Shall I read it?"

The king of Judah sank back into his chair in wonder. His mind clouded with thoughts of all the wicked things his father, King Manasseh, had done.

Lord, You know how my father worshipped the sun, the moon, and the stars; built altars for Baal; and set up an Asherah pole in the temple—Your temple! You saw when he rebuilt the pagan shrines my grandfather had torn down, practiced sorcery, and consulted with mediums and psychics, Josiah prayed. He stopped for a moment, overwhelmed at all the evil his father had done. *Lord, I want to make a difference!* Josiah thought with deep passion.

"King Josiah ... sir?" Shaphan asked once more, "Shall I read from the scroll?"

King Josiah's attention returned to Shaphan. He nodded and then listened with delight and dread to God's words in the law of Moses. Tears streamed down the king's face, and he tore his robes in distress. Although Josiah strove to bring the kingdom of Judah back to following the Lord, he knew much damage had already been done.

O Lord, our ancestors haven't obeyed the words in this scroll, he prayed in great desperation. *As a result, Your anger is burning against this place, for I know in Your righteousness and holy judgment, You will do as You promised according to Your Law.*

Needing direction from God, King Josiah sent Hilkiah the priest along with Shaphan and three others to visit the prophetess Huldah.

"God has seen King Josiah's sorrow and how he humbled himself before the Lord when he heard what God said about Jerusalem and its people," she said. "Because he tore his clothes in despair and repentance, God will not bring the disaster He promised on this place until after King Josiah has died and is buried in peace," the prophetess concluded.

The men returned to King Josiah with the message that God intended to destroy Jerusalem, but not until after he was gone. Not content to give up on resisting the evil around him, Josiah summoned all the leaders of Judah and Jerusalem. He then went to the temple of the Lord and stood before the priests, prophets, and people—from the least to the greatest.

King Josiah tore down the altar at Bethel, and to defile that place forever, he burned on the altar the bones of the false prophets who had been buried nearby. This was a direct fulfillment of the prophecy in 1 Kings 13:2–3!

The Mount of Olives, a favorite place to build shrines and high places for idol worship, was often called the "Hill of Corruption" (2 Kings 23:13). Interestingly, in New Testament times, Jesus often chose the Mount of Olives as a place to sit and teach His disciples about serving God alone.

Opening the scroll, King Josiah began to read aloud and didn't stop until he had read the entire book of the covenant. Silence filled the air. Some of the people looked down at their feet, ashamed. Others shifted their weight uncomfortably, knowing they had strayed far from the very God who called them by name.

When King Josiah finished reading, he looked out at the sea of faces before him. He then took the lead and pledged himself to obey the Lord heart and soul by keeping all God's commands, regulations, and laws. The people then followed his example and dedicated themselves as well, renewing the terms of the covenant that were written in the scroll. After that, Josiah commanded the people to celebrate the Passover, making sure to follow all of God's laws very carefully. No Passover like this had been celebrated in the land since the days of the judges.

Although King Josiah knew that God was going to carry out His judgment against His people, he also knew that God wanted him to make a difference and resist the evil in the land while he lived. So King Josiah finished having the temple of the Lord cleansed. He removed all the tools and utensils used to worship Baal, Asherah, and the stars and burned them in a nearby valley. He also removed the Asherah pole from the temple and burned it; put to death the pagan priests appointed by previous kings of Judah; and destroyed all the pagan altars, shrines, and idols. Not one remnant of idolatry was left in the land of Judah because of the difference Josiah made.

Footwork

Open your Bible to 2 Kings 22:19–20. What does it say? Now turn to 2 Kings 23:24. What was King Josiah's response? Do you think you would have done the same?

Fruit

King Josiah didn't just think about himself. He strove to make a difference and change what he could—even when God told him he wouldn't be around to see His judgment on the nation. King Josiah cleansed the land in spite of the coming judgment. He didn't give up, and he didn't give in.

Take a moment to evaluate your own life. What difference are you making? What can you do to make more of a difference in the lives of those around you? Think of one thing you can start to do, and begin doing it today.

Great. What Next?
Taken from 2 Kings 23—25

Foundation

Take a moment to pray before you begin this last lesson in 2 Kings. In the quietness of your heart, think about your life and everything that affects you—both
good and bad. Ask God to help you understand and accept the fact that everything
happening in your life happens for a reason.

FOCUS

*Have you ever felt like your whole world was beginning to fall
apart before your very eyes?*

"King Josiah, turn and go back to Jerusalem," Neco, the king of Egypt, warned.
"The quarrel I have isn't with you but with Babylon."

But King Josiah refused to listen. He feared that Egypt and Assyria might join
together to come against Judah in the future, so he engaged the Egyptian pharaoh
in battle. It was a deadly mistake, costing King Josiah his life, and the kingdom of
Judah to fall under Egypt's control. All of Judah mourned King Josiah's death as
they buried him in Jerusalem, and then chose his middle son, Jehoahaz, to be
their next king.

When Pharaoh saw this, he thought to himself, *Jehoahaz has far too much
leadership strength, and this could be a problem. I will appoint his older brother as
ruler instead. He is weak and will make a good puppet king.*

So the king of Egypt took Jehoahaz away in chains and made his brother Eliakim

movement; Homer writes Iliad and

king over Judah, changing his name to Jehoiakim. Then Neco imposed a heavy tax on the people—a tax Jehoiakim readily paid.

During Jehoiakim's reign, an unexpected turn of events took place. Nebuchadnezzar, king of Babylon, defeated Pharaoh Neco in battle. Now Babylon would be the new world power, gaining control over Egypt and all the kingdoms Egypt controlled—including the kingdom of Judah! Things were not looking good ...

To make sure Judah is securely under my control, King Nebuchadnezzar thought, *I'll raid Jerusalem and take the captives back to Babylon with me.*

The attack sent a strong message of Babylon's power to King Jehoiakim, and as a result, he submitted to the Babylonian king— but only for three years. Hoping to revolt, he sought help from Egypt but was unsuccessful. No one could stand against the Babylonian Empire.

As Judah became weaker, the nation fell victim to raiding bands from Babylonia, Aramea, Moab, and Ammon. God was removing Judah from the Promised Land and using other nations to accomplish His purposes.

When King Jehoiakim died, his son, Jehoiachin, came to the throne at the age of eighteen. He had been in power only three months when Nebuchadnezzar came back through on a second raid, eight years after his first one. Jehoiachin readily surrendered and was taken prisoner to Babylon along with ten thousand others—all the officers

When the Babylonians conquered a land, they took the cream of the crop as captives—often providing them with food and limited freedom in order to win their allegiance. The poor were left behind to tend the land because they were no threat. In Nebuchadnezzar's first raid against Judah in 605 BC, Daniel was taken as one of the captives (see Dan. 1:1–3).

In 597 BC, Nebuchadnezzar raided Jerusalem a second time and looted Solomon's temple, fulfilling the prophecy in 1 Kings 9:6–9. The third and final raid was carried out in 586 BC, when Jerusalem's walls were destroyed and the city was burned.

and fighting men, craftsmen and artisans. Only the poorest in the land were left in Jerusalem.

All the treasures from the temple of the Lord and the royal palace were taken away as well. Even the gold articles that Solomon had made for the temple of the Lord were carted off and used in Nebuchadnezzar's temple. Women were also taken captive along with the officials and leading men of the kingdom. Nebuchadnezzar appointed Jehoiachin's uncle, Zedekiah, to be king and rule over the people who remained in Judah.

Zedekiah did evil in the eyes of the Lord as the other Israelite kings had. In the ninth year of his reign, he revolted against Babylon by seeking help from Egypt. Once again, Babylon was too powerful. And those who had remained in Jerusalem only suffered all the more.

"Ram the city walls!" Nebuchadnezzar ordered his soldiers—and they did. With the walls of Jerusalem destroyed, the people of Judah would be unable to stand against their attackers. Zedekiah tried to escape, but the Babylonians caught him and blinded him so he couldn't lead any more revolts. They also killed his sons so there would be no heirs to the throne. Things looked hopeless for the remnant in Jerusalem.

Nebuchadnezzar finished tearing down the city walls, broke the large bronze pillars of the temple in order to carry them off (as well as other temple furniture), and then ordered the city to be burned. He carried off the majority of poor people, leaving only a few farmers to keep the land from growing completely wild. Jerusalem was left in ruins, and the people of Judah had been taken as captives to Babylon. Yet through the smoldering ashes, God would raise a spark of hope.

Footwork

Open your Bible to 2 Kings 25:27–30 and read it. The Babylonian king who replaced Nebuchadnezzar gave former King Jehoiachin of Judah special favor and loosened the prison restrictions. Although the people of Judah were in another land, they were together—and being preserved. God was still faithful to them even while they were experiencing God's judgment as a nation.

sport in northern Europe. ● 785-77

Fruit

When our world falls apart and nothing seems to be going right, often our first response is to become angry or even rebellious. Instead of seeking what God might want to show us in our circumstances, we only look for a way to escape our difficulties—and miss the whole point of our trials. This week, as you experience difficulties, watch your attitude and reaction. Turn your disappointments and difficulties over to God. Trust Him to make something great out of them—even the ashes.

1 Chronicles

Just a glance at the first nine chapters of 1 Chronicles seems like enough to put anyone to sleep! It appears to be nothing more than a list of names and genealogies—all-important historical records, but not necessarily something on your list of hot items to read. But don't be discouraged—or fooled! After the genealogies, 1 Chronicles gives vital information on the kings of Judah and offers more detail than the books of 1 and 2 Kings. Although Kings and Chronicles are similar, 1 and 2 Chronicles were written after the books of Kings.

Jewish tradition says that Ezra wrote this book about 150 years after the events happened. The Babylonians had conquered the southern kingdom of Judah and taken the people into captivity to Babylon, where they lived in exile for seventy years. Then in 538 BC, the survivors began to return from exile to Jerusalem. Ezra returned from exile around eighty years later, and the Israelites needed to regroup. They needed to be reminded of who they were, where they had been, and where they were going. That is the point of the Chronicles.

Perhaps the best way to view this particular book is to think of it as a flashback in history, remembering the details of some of the nation's highlights and low times. Since we already covered some of the background history in the books of 1 and 2 Kings, we'll only take a short time to explore 1 Chronicles. But don't zone out! There's more here than you think. So keep your eyes open, and enjoy the journey!

Watch Your Step!
Taken from 1 Chronicles 13—15

Foundation

As you begin your journey through 1 Chronicles, ask the Lord to guide your heart and thoughts. Ask Him to point out areas in your life that seem more like the world's approach to God rather than God's guidelines for approaching Him.

Focus

Have you ever tried to do something good but only got in trouble for it?

What a great celebration it was! After one hundred years of not having the ark of God in their midst, the Israelites were witnessing its return. Their new king—King David—planned to bring the ark into Jerusalem so it would have a permanent resting place among the people. Excitement mounted as the Israelites went down to Kiriath Jearim to retrieve it from the house of Abinadab, where it had been kept after the Philistines returned it.

The Israelites remembered only too well how the ark of the Lord had been brought down to the battlefield during King Saul's time and used as a good-luck charm against the Philistines in battle. They remembered with horror how the ark of God—the very symbol of His presence with them—had been captured and carted off by the enemy. Later, they had seen the ark returned on a cart pulled by cattle. They remembered and regretted. But today was not a day for regrets! It was a day of celebration!

The priests, Levites, and even King David wore their linen garments as they went to Abinadab's house to retrieve the ark. They loaded it onto a new cart and began the journey back to Jerusalem with Abinadab's sons, Uzzah and Ahio, carefully guiding the cart. King David and all the Israelites rejoiced. Music from songs, harps, lyres, tambourines, cymbals, and trumpets filled the air. It seemed like nothing could go wrong—well, almost.

> *To this day, on the road to Jerusalem (about one or two miles from Kiriath Jearim) is a small village named* **Khirbet el-Uz,** *which means "the ruins of Uzzah"!*

"Easy! Easy does it!" someone warned, seeing the uneven ground on the threshing floor.

"Watch it!" a shout went out as the cart lurched to one side and the ark of God began to slide. Looking up in time to see the disaster, Uzzah quickly reached out his hand to steady the ark. Although he meant well, his actions brought only trouble. Uzzah died as punishment for touching the holy ark of God.

David felt both angry and afraid at this display of God's wrath. "How can I ever bring the ark of God back into my care?" he asked no one in particular. So he decided not to move the ark into Jerusalem, but instead took it to the nearby home of Obed-Edom, where it remained for three months.

David came back after that time to move the ark and complete its journey to Jerusalem. But this time he would do it differently. In preparation, David gathered all the Levites. He then summoned Zadok and Abiathar the priests.

"As heads of the Levitical families," he said, "you are to purify yourselves so you may bring the ark of the Lord back."

David looked at the faces of the men who were gathered before him. All of them remembered what happened to Uzzah and didn't want to see a repeat performance—especially if it meant their own deaths!

"No one but the Levites may carry the ark, and this must be done according to God's commands!" David announced. "It was because you Levites didn't carry the ark that God became angry with us. We didn't ask God how to move the ark—the way He commanded of Moses!"

Silence filled the air as the importance of the lesson sank in. Then, with a new determination and much celebration, the Israelites went down to Obed-Edom's house and returned in triumph with the ark. This time the ark wasn't placed on a cart and hauled like merchandise. Instead, it was carried on long poles and shouldered by Levites, just as it had been carried years ago when Moses led the Israelites through the wilderness.

Footwork

Turn in your Bible back to Numbers 4, and read verses 4–5 and 15. According to these verses, how was the ark of God to be treated? The Kohathites were descendants of Kohath, the second oldest son of Levi (from whom the Levites got their name).

Fruit

David's first mistake was to move the ark of God on a cart much like the pagan Philistines had done earlier. This showed little respect for the holiness of God. The ark represented God's presence among His people. It was to be treated with respect, not casually and without regard. We can't approach the things of God the way the world does. God deserves—and demands—better treatment than that. Watch your step!

It's Mine
Taken from 1 Chronicles 28—29

Foundation

As you begin your time today, be still before the Lord and evaluate how you feel about your possessions. Think of all you have (not what you don't have or wish you did). Spend a moment to thank the Lord for the good things He's given you. Ask Him to challenge you to realize who really owns them.

Focus

Do you have a hard time letting go of what you own?

David paused a moment, scanning the crowd of leaders who were listening attentively to his words. *These, Lord, are the leaders who will help my son Solomon when he becomes king. These are the men who will continue to lead Your people long after I'm gone,* he prayed silently. *Help them do what is right and good in Your eyes.*

Clearing his throat, David continued with his message. "As you know, I brought the ark of the Lord here to Jerusalem that it might be among us in a permanent place. I also made plans to build a temple to house it. Yet the Lord, the God of Israel, told me that because I'm a warrior and have killed people, I'm not the one to build Him a temple," David informed them. "Instead, God has chosen my son Solomon to sit on the throne over all Israel and to be the one to build the Lord's house."

All eyes shifted quickly over to Solomon, then back to King David. He explained how Solomon's throne would be established, and he challenged the Israelite leaders to be careful to follow all the Lord's commands. Then David turned his gaze to his son.

BC — Rome is founded and named after

222

"And you, Solomon," David said with a tender voice, "serve God with a whole heart and a teachable mind, because God searches the heart and understands the motives behind every thought. Seek Him, and He will make sure you find Him; but if you turn your back on Him, He will reject you forever."

Solomon looked up into his father's eyes and nodded. He both heard and understood. King David then handed Solomon the complete plans for the temple—plans that God had given him for a temple that he was not to build. "You are the one the Lord has chosen to build the temple. Be strong, and do the work He has given you."

Solomon carefully opened the plans and looked at them. The task seemed enormous! There, written down, was everything he would need—from the plans for each room and its furnishings to job assignments for the priests and Levites once the task was completed. Everything was described in detail—right down to the exact weight of gold to be used for decorating the temple! Solomon looked up at King David who now addressed the rest of the group. He heard his father's words urging the people to support Solomon's efforts and encouraging them to join in the work.

> *It's not what we have to give that counts with God, but rather our willingness to give what we have. It's interesting to note that both the tabernacle and the temple were built with voluntary gifts!*

"With all I have available to me as king," David said, "I have given for the temple of my God—gold, silver, bronze, iron, wood, onyx, turquoise, and all kinds of fine stone and marble. All of these have been given in large amounts."

The leaders looked on approvingly. As king, David had used his resources wisely.

The king continued, "Over and above what I have provided, I now also give my personal treasures of gold and silver—all for the temple of my God."

The leaders looked at King David in silence. His example of giving went above and beyond the call of duty and showed his wholehearted devotion toward the things of the Lord.

"Now then, who will follow my example?" he asked. "Who is willing to give offerings to the Lord today?"

It didn't take long for the leaders to step forward.

"I will!" each of them said.

Encouraged by David's personal example of integrity, all the leaders gave willingly and wholeheartedly to the Lord. The Israelites rejoiced when they observed their leaders' actions, and King David looked on with great joy, for through their generosity, God's name would be honored.

Footwork

Wait! Don't skip this part. Open your Bible to 1 Chronicles 29:16–18 and read what it says. According to these verses, what is David's perspective on ownership? Now look at verse 18. Does David's prayer describe you and your own attitude?

Fruit

Whether or not you recognize it, what you have to offer God is only what He Himself has first given you. Take a look at the things you own. Just whose are they—really? Think about this for a moment. Do you hold on to your possessions with a tight fist, or are you willing to open your hand? Talk to God about it right now.

2 Chronicles

The purpose of 2 Chronicles is to deliver a pep talk to the Israelites who had just been released from captivity. By the close of the book of 2 Kings, the Assyrians had already conquered the northern kingdom of Israel and taken the people into exile. Assyria's king had resettled Samaria with his own people, thus putting an end to the northern tribes. Their identity was lost and they were no more.

The southern tribes of Judah, however, were carried off into exile by the Babylonians, but would later be allowed to return to their homeland in Jerusalem. The book of Chronicles was written to these refugees. Since seventy years of captivity had passed, they would need to be instructed and encouraged in the things of the Lord. God had lived among them in the past—would He do it again?

Second Chronicles focuses mainly on the kings of Judah, since the northern tribes of Israel were no more. Israel only had bad kings, who brought the nation down 136 years before Judah! Although Judah also had some bad kings, a few good ones helped preserve the nation and turn it back around, if only temporarily.

As you explore this book, you'll get a close-up look at the lives of Jehoshaphat and Joash, two kings of Judah. What did they do right—and what did they do wrong? Exciting adventures and great lessons await you in 2 Chronicles. Read on!

Friend ... or Foe?
Taken from 2 Chronicles 18—22

Foundation

Start your time today by committing your day into God's hands. Ask Him to go before you and help you make wise decisions, and thank Him in advance for His guidance.

FOCUS

Have you known of a situation when a person's choice of friends soon became a source of trouble for him or her?

"That sounds acceptable to me," King Jehoshaphat said to King Ahab, "but first, let's inquire of the Lord."

"Who? Oh ... right," Ahab responded as he called his four hundred prophets to come before them.

"O king!" the false prophets agreed in unison, "today you will have victory over Ben-Hadad, the king of Aram, and his enemies!" The report satisfied Ahab, but Jehoshaphat was uncomfortable.

"Don't you have a prophet of the Lord you can inquire of?" Jehoshaphat asked.

King Ahab reluctantly summoned one of the Lord's prophets, Micaiah, but his report wasn't favorable. He spoke of defeat, not victory.

Instead of listening to the counsel of the Lord, King Ahab became so angry with Micaiah that he threw the prophet into prison. Then Ahab turned to Jehoshaphat and declared, "Together we will go and fight against Ben-Hadad."

King Jehoshaphat readily accepted King Ahab's offer, ignoring the past sins of his new ally. "Agreed!" Jehoshaphat said foolishly.

It didn't take long for Jehoshaphat to realize that his friendship with King Ahab wasn't the wisest choice he could have made. Just before going to battle, King Ahab selfishly instructed Jehoshaphat to wear his royal cloak while Ahab himself would be disguised as a regular soldier. This put Jehoshaphat's life in serious danger.

"You are only to go after Ahab, the king of Israel!" King Ben-Hadad instructed his warriors.

So when the warriors saw Jehoshaphat in his royal cloak, they assumed it was King Ahab and pursued him. But in the nick of time, Jehoshaphat cried out, and the warriors realized he wasn't the one they were after. Not long after, an arrow shot randomly into the air found its mark between the sections of King Ahab's armor and killed him.

Learning of Ahab's death, Jehoshaphat asked God's forgiveness for seeking to ally himself with those who despised God. He then turned his attention to strengthening the spiritual condition of those in his kingdom, just as his father, King Asa, had done. Jehoshaphat appointed judges to carry out the laws of the land and Levites and priests to administer God's laws and settle controversies.

When the countries of Moab and Ammon threatened war against Judah, King Jehoshaphat sought God and led his people in prayer and fasting. Because of this, the Lord fought their battle for them, and they won. Yet in spite of King Jehoshaphat's efforts to do what was right in the eyes of the Lord, his unwise choices in friendships would affect his family long after he was gone.

When Jehoshaphat died, his oldest son, Jehoram, inherited the throne.

> *Jehoshaphat made an alliance with King Ahab in hopes of bringing peace between Judah and Israel, but this unwise choice only brought turmoil in the future.*
>
> *King Jehoshaphat also made an alliance to build a fleet of trading ships with Ahab's wicked son, Ahaziah. Before the ships could sail, Jehoshaphat's plans were sunk—literally (see 2 Chron. 20:35–37)!*

Unfortunately, Jehoram was evil and didn't follow in the steps of his father. Instead, he was influenced toward wickedness by his wife, Athaliah (daughter of King Ahab and Queen Jezebel). Jehoram immediately killed all his brothers and then rebuilt the high places to Baal that his father had torn down. Jehoram led the nation of Judah into both idolatry and destruction. Because of his wickedness, God sent a message through the prophet Elijah stating Jehoram would suffer a severe bowel disease that would lead to his death.

When Jehoram died, his son Ahaziah ruled Judah for one year—under Queen Athaliah's influence—before Jehu murdered him. Jehu was a military warrior who vowed to purge Ahab's evil influence out of Judah and Israel. In his murdering rampage he had Athaliah's mother, Jezebel, thrown from a window, slew seventy princes, and killed all the priests and prophets of Baal.

Seeing her opportunity for power, Queen Athaliah began to destroy the whole royal family of the house of Judah. She succeeded in killing all—but one. Being as wicked as her parents, Athaliah had little regard for the things of God and didn't care that she had turned against her husband and her descendants.

"I will rule!" she vowed—and did since there were no longer any capable heirs left.

Queen Athaliah reigned for six years, not realizing that her infant grandson, Joash, had survived the massacre. He had been hidden by Jehosheba, King Jehoram's daughter, and secretly lived in the temple, growing up under Jehoiada the priest's godly instruction.

Footwork

Turn to 2 Chronicles chapter 22 and read verse 3. This verse talks about Ahaziah, who was Judean King Jehoram and Queen Ahaziah's son. What does it say? Now, skip down and look at verse 10 in this same chapter. Athaliah not only introduced Baal worship into Judah, she also nearly destroyed the entire royal line of David!

Fruit

Friendships really do matter, and they can have a dynamic, long-lasting impact on your life. Decisions you make in relationships today will affect your future in one way or another. Jehoshaphat learned this the hard way. How wisely do you choose when making friends?

Excuse Me—Is This Yours?

Taken from 2 Chronicles 23—24

Foundation

Spend a few minutes preparing your heart and quieting your thoughts before the Lord. How well do you know Him? If all your supports were kicked out from underneath you, would your relationship with God still stand strong? Tell God about it, and honestly admit to Him any weaknesses. God wants you to know Him personally—He calls you by name.

Focus

Have you known anyone whose faith in God relied heavily on another person?

"Now is the time," Jehoiada whispered to himself after enduring six years of Queen Athaliah's rule over Judah. The queen had single-handedly undone everything her godly father-in-law, King Jehoshaphat, had accomplished during his lifetime. As daughter of King Ahab and Queen Jezebel, Athaliah followed in her parents' wickedness and reintroduced Baal worship to Judah. She even corrupted her son Ahaziah to follow in her wickedness.

When Ahaziah died, Athaliah was furious and attempted to kill off the entire royal line of David! But unknown to the queen, Princess Jehosheba had secretly saved one infant heir and hidden him in the temple, where Joash grew in safety under Jehoiada the priest's instruction.

Now that Joash is seven, he's old enough to take back the throne of his grandfather Jehoshaphat and rule as king over Judah, Jehoiada thought with great pleasure. Because Joash was so young, Jehoiada would be there for him as a trusted friend and adviser. *He'll need help to turn Judah around,* the priest said to himself.

Jehoiada assembled the Levites and all the people at the temple. He armed the Levites with weapons and gave them orders to guard the temple, the palace, and the Foundation Gate. With an additional group of Levites assigned to protect Joash at all times, Jehoiada and his sons brought out the young boy and placed the crown on his head. Then they presented Joash with a copy of the covenant—as God required—and pronounced him king. At that moment a great celebration broke out among the Israelites. Trumpeters blew their trumpets, and singers with instruments led praises.

What's that noise? Athaliah wondered, making her way to the temple to investigate. When she arrived, she stopped cold in her tracks. Before her very eyes, people were shouting, "Long live the king!"

At the sight of the young king standing at the entrance to the temple, Queen Athaliah flew into a rage. "This is treason! Treason!" she shouted.

When she realized that Jehoiada had sent soldiers to arrest her, Athaliah ran back to the palace. But the soldiers caught her at the entrance and put her to death.

Because Joash was only a boy when he became king over Judah, Jehoiada stepped in to help. His first act was to make a covenant with the Lord that he, the people, and the king would live for the Lord. Then all the people went to the temple of Baal and destroyed it, along with the altars and idols. They also put the priest of Baal to death, ridding the land of

> *Living to an old age was believed to be a sign of God's favor. Jehoiada lived to be 130, putting him up there with Moses, who lived to be 120, and Aaron, who lived to be 123.*

rade copper, lead, iron, zinc,

idolatry. After this, Jehoiada placed the care of the Lord's temple in the hands of the Levites, who would carry out sacrifices and burnt offerings according to God's commands. It was a great time of revival for God's people.

Years went by and Joash was now a young man. Seeing the temple of the Lord in need of repair, he decided to restore it to its former glory, along with the articles and dishes Queen Athaliah had ruined. Joash had craftsmen build a chest and he placed it outside the gate of the temple where the people came and generously gave their contributions. The king also made sure that burnt offerings were continuously offered in the temple of the Lord according to the law of Moses.

This was trues long as Jehoiada the priest lived. However, Jehoiada was reaching old age and finally died, leaving King Joash on his own. King Joash was unprepared to stand alone without another to give him strength spiritually.

"King Joash, listen to us! We know what you should do!" some of his officials said.

Unfortunately, Joash listened to their poor advice and followed it. As a result, he and his people stopped worshipping God in the temple, and it wasn't long before they abandoned God altogether. Since Jehoiada the priest was no longer around, the people returned to their old ways. Asherah poles and idols once again replaced the worship of God. Sadly, Joash went right along with the changes, for now that Jehoiada was gone, Joash's source of spiritual strength was gone as well!

Footwork

Look up 2 Chronicles 24:2 in your Bible and read the entire verse. Now read just the first half of the verse. What does it say? Unfortunately that first half of the verse hinges directly on the second half. Much like Joash, the first half of the verse can't stand alone. Take a close look at it!

Fruit

One mistake King Joash made was to rely on others to be spiritually strong for him. He did what was right in God's eyes as long as Jehoiada was priest. The problem King Joash had was that he didn't "own" his faith—it wasn't his. Nor did he seem to have a personal relationship with the Lord. Do you own your faith, or do you depend on others for spiritual support? It's easy to pretend we're something that we're not. God wants us to depend upon Him. He wants to be the source and foundation of our faith. Do a quick spiritual inventory by asking yourself these simple questions:

1. What is my spiritual foundation like? Do I even have a relationship with the Lord to build on? (If you can't answer this one, turn to the back of this book. There's a special message there just for you!)

2. How have I been building on my foundation?
   - Am I mostly dependent on others for spiritual support (parents, friends, pastor)?
   - Do I read the Bible daily for myself?
   - Do I pray (talk to God) and take my concerns to Him first?

3. Have I determined in my heart to follow God and learn more about what that means—in spite of what others around me do (or don't do)?

Close your time in prayer, asking God to help you in your areas of weakness.

Ezra

As you explore the book of Ezra, you will come to know the person for whom this book is named. You will also be set for an adventure! Before you begin your journey, let's review where the nation of Israel has been and where it's headed. As we learned in the books of Kings and Chronicles, the Israelites split into two different kingdoms after the death of King Solomon. The northern kingdom called itself *Israel,* and the southern kingdom called itself *Judah.* But the people who lived in *both* these kingdoms were called *Israelites*. But don't let that confuse you! (If you haven't read 1 and 2 Kings or 1 and 2 Chronicles yet, now would be a good time to do so.)

Israel had nothing but wicked kings, while *Judah* had a few kings who sought after God even though most of its kings were also wicked. Because the kings in both kingdoms were wicked and led their people astray, God judged the Israelites and removed them from the land as He promised He would do. At the end of 2 Chronicles, we see most of the Israelites from the kingdom of *Judah* being carted off to Babylonia as captives. (The kingdom of *Israel* had been destroyed much earlier.)

The book of Ezra tells us what happened next and picks up where 2 Kings leaves off. It's a record of a fresh start and second chances. Will the Israelites finally begin to live wholeheartedly for the Lord, or will they fall back into their same old idolatrous ways? You'll just have to read to find out!

As you explore this book, keep in mind that a few other books in the Bible fit in this same time frame. For instance, the events in the book of Esther take place around the same time as the events in chapters 6 and 7 of Ezra. And the books of Haggai and Zechariah were written to encourage and challenge these Israelite refugees as they rebuilt the temple—an event described in the book of Ezra.

Enjoy your journey through this fascinating book!

Be sure to check out www.cookministries.com/FaithFactor for a bonus lesson titled "Aha!" (taken from Ezra 4—6) that talks about how God raises up encouragement to meet our needs. ⎯⎯⎯⎯⎯⎯⎯⎯

First Things First!
Taken from Ezra 1—3

Foundation

As you begin your journey through the book of Ezra, start your time with prayer. Commit your life to God and ask Him to help you be more consistent in following Him with your whole heart.

 Focus

Do you struggle with putting God first in your life?

Many years had passed since King Nebuchadnezzar had destroyed Jerusalem and taken the Israelites into captivity to Babylon. The walls protecting the city had been knocked down and left as rubble, and the city had been burned to the ground. The temple of the Lord had also been burned down after being stripped of its gold and silver. The once glorious city had been left in ruins, charred beyond recognition. In spite of all that, nearly fifty thousand exiled Israelites were willing to make the nine-hundred-mile trip back to their homeland—a dangerous journey that would take almost four months!

"This is what Cyrus, King of Persia, decrees ..." came the announcement to the Jews living in Babylon.

No longer was King Nebuchadnezzar king over Babylon, and no longer was Babylon a powerful kingdom. Nebuchadnezzar's death brought a weakening in power under the rule of his descendants. As a result, King Cyrus of Persia conquered Babylon. A kind ruler, Cyrus gave the captives great freedom. In an effort to set up buffer zones around his kingdom for protection and to create loyalty, he even allowed all the captives to return to their homelands to live and worship their own gods. The Persian king knew that if his empire were ever attacked, the released captives would fight loyally to protect the freedoms they enjoyed.

"Israelites from Judah may go up to Jerusalem to build a temple for the Lord, and may your God be with you!" King Cyrus declared. "Furthermore, those who live in any place where Jewish survivors are found are to give them silver and gold, livestock and supplies, as well as a freewill offering to help with the work on God's temple."

After nearly seventy years of captivity, the Israelites welcomed this good news. Many of them had been yearning to return to the land God had given them—and to worshipping the Lord. Others, however, had never seen Jerusalem. Babylon was the only home they had ever known. These Israelites chose to remain in Babylon for the time being. But all those whose hearts God had moved began to make preparations for the long and dangerous journey to Jerusalem. They loaded up all the supplies they would need to rebuild the temple, as well as

> *The prophet Isaiah mentioned King Cyrus by name and foretold the decree he would make 150 years before it happened! (See Isa. 44:28; 45:1–13.)*

> Zerubbabel, *which means* "begotten in Babel," *was the grandson of King Jehoiachin, who reigned only three months before surrendering to Nebuchadnezzar (see 2 Kings 24:10–12).*

the articles their neighbors had given them—just as King Cyrus had commanded. Then the king himself brought out the articles that had once belonged to the temple of the Lord. Although King Nebuchadnezzar had carried them off and placed them in the temple of his own god, they had been preserved for this very moment. They would be returned to their rightful place to be used once again in the service of the one true God— the God of the Israelites.

The first group of Israelites eagerly set out for Jerusalem under the leadership of Zerubbabel. Many were priests and Levites who were uncertain what lay ahead in the rubble of Jerusalem. *What will we return to?* they wondered. *After almost seventy years, what will we find?* No one really knew.

When they arrived in Jerusalem and made their way to the ruins of the temple, silence hung over them like a heavy cloud. They were relieved they had made it safely, yet stunned by the destruction that stretched out before them.

If only we had obeyed the Lord, none of this would have happened! many thought, picking their way through the debris. Considering the task ahead, some of the family leaders unloaded their valuables and gave generously toward the rebuilding of the Lord's temple on its original site. Each of the leaders did the same. After they had done this, some of the refugees settled in the villages around Jerusalem, while others returned to their hometowns in Judah. Once the people were settled, they assembled back at Jerusalem to begin the work of rebuilding.

Under Zerubbabel's direction, repairing the altar of the Lord would be the first and most important priority. As soon as the altar was rebuilt, the Israelites could once again come to God in worship, approaching Him as He instructed and being obedient to His commands. *Yes,* Zerubbabel said to himself, *the altar will be built before anything else, so that we might put God first ... and keep Him there.*

Footwork

Turn to Ezra 3:3 in your Bible. According to this verse, what did the Israelites fear? Notice what the Israelites did *not* build—walls for protection. They decided to put first things first! God would have a prominent place in their lives, and He would be the center of all their activities, interests, and concerns.

bury swords with their dead; Etrusca

Fruit

How does God rate in your priorities? Can others tell that He is truly first in your life? Perhaps the best way for you to answer this question is to ask yourself how much time you spend with Him. People refer to this different ways, such as having a "quiet time" (QT for short), "personal devotions," or even doing their "spiritual disciplines." What you call your time with God isn't important. The important thing is that you do it—daily. Take a moment now to think about the condition of the "altar" in your life. Do you regularly meet with God? Follow these simple steps of rebuilding what needs repair in your life:

Step 1: Designate a time and place to be alone for five to ten minutes each day. (This could be first thing in the morning when you wake up or last thing at night before you go to sleep.)

Step 2: Begin your time with a simple prayer and really talk things over with God.

Step 3: Open His Word and read it for yourself. A good place to start is reading in the book of Proverbs. Since there are thirty-one chapters, that allows you to read one chapter a day for a month. (Example: On day seven of the month, you'll read chapter 7.)

Step 4: Think about what you've read, and try to focus on one thing you can put into practice. Ask God to use what you've read to change your life. Then close in prayer, thanking Him in advance for what He will do.

Haven't We Been Here Before?

Taken from Ezra 6—10

Foundation

Pause for a moment and give your time to the Lord today. Ask God to help you learn to rely on His power so that you might not be trapped in the cycle of sin.

Do you find yourself repeating the same sins over and over?

"Surely, Lord, this is Your hand of blessing upon us!" Ezra whispered under his breath. With great excitement he continued reading the letter in his hand.

"Greetings from Artaxerxes, the king of kings, to Ezra the priest, an instructor of the law of God who lives in heaven," the letter began. "I hereby proclaim that any of the Israelites in my kingdom who wish to go with you to Jerusalem are free to go—including priests and Levites."

In the letter, King Artaxerxes explained he would give them gold and silver to return with, as well as permission to get more in Babylon. They would be free to offer sacrifices to the Lord on the altar at the temple and make their own decisions on how to use the gifts they had received.

Ezra read on, eagerly devouring each word on the page.

"And you, Ezra, are to use the wisdom God has given you to appoint judges familiar with God's laws to govern all the people. You are also to teach those who are unfamiliar with these laws," the king added.

Ezra looked up from the letter and out across the horizon. It had been eighty years since Zerubbabel left Babylon under a decree by King Cyrus to rebuild the temple. *Eighty years!* Ezra sighed. The temple had now been up for fifty-seven years. He couldn't help but wonder how it would feel to celebrate the feasts and sacrifices once again in obedience to what God had commanded. He yearned to travel to Jerusalem and join the others in worship, teaching them to love God's law, for Ezra had a deep understanding and appreciation of God's Word.

With King Artaxerxes' decree in hand, Ezra gathered together those Israelites who wanted to return to Jerusalem. His group totaled nearly four thousand people, including women and children, and although this group was much smaller than the first group that returned under Zerubbabel, it didn't bother Ezra. With determination and a love for the Lord, he would bring these people to Jerusalem. It would be a victorious time—or so he thought. Ezra wasn't prepared for the problems he would face when he arrived.

"How could the people *do* that?" Ezra cried out when he heard the reports from concerned leaders in Jerusalem. "Don't they know it was because of this very thing that God judged our nation and sent us into exile?"

The leaders stood by silently, uncertain how to respond. Although the Israelites had been offering sacrifices and celebrating the feasts and ceremonies according to the law of Moses, they had not been not living in obedience to God. Old habits had found their way back into the people's hearts. Several of the Israelites married foreigners who lived in the land—something God specifically forbade them to do.

> **Take action*!*
> **A**—Anchor yourself in God's Word.
> **C**—Confess your shortcomings daily.
> **T**—Take responsibility for your actions.
> **I**—Include God in your day.
> **O**—Organize and set your course under God's control.
> **N**—Never underestimate the power of a habit.
>
> ---
>
> *Artaxerxes was Xerxes' son. Xerxes was the king who married Esther.*

Ezra was speechless. Falling on his face before the Lord, he asked for God's mercy and forgiveness on behalf of the people. "O Lord, our sins are so many— they nearly reach the heavens! I am ashamed at our guilty condition before You— too ashamed to even lift up my face to You," he agonized. Even though he hadn't taken part in these sins, Ezra identified with the people, for their sin would affect the well-being of the entire nation.

"From the days of our forefathers until now, our guilt has been great. Once again, we have disobeyed the commands You gave through Your servants, telling us not to marry the pagans in the land you gave us or to make treaties with them," Ezra continued.

As Ezra prayed on behalf of the Israelites, they were deeply grieved at what they had done. Realizing the same mistakes were being repeated, they desired to correct the matter with God's help.

Ezra then gathered all the people together in Jerusalem to tell them what the Law commanded them to do: They were to get rid of their foreign wives and separate themselves from the surrounding nations. Ezra knew this would be a difficult thing for them to do, but he also knew it was necessary. The pattern of sin that had taken hold in the Israelites' lives had to be broken. Having once experienced the consequences of their sins, the Israelites knew the sin cycle was one cycle they did not want to repeat again. They had traveled down that road before!

Footwork

Open your Bible to Ezra 7:10 and read the description about Ezra. What does it say? Notice the word "devoted." What did Ezra devote himself to do? (See if you can find three things listed in this verse that Ezra did. The first two actions lay the foundation for the third.) How do Ezra's actions compare to yours?

Fruit

Ezra was a man of prayer and action! He not only prayed for forgiveness and guidance, but he acted as well. This is the only way to break the cycle of repeating the same sins over and over. Ezra made it a habit to set his course, ground himself in God's Word, and then actt on what it said. Have you made this your habit as well?

Nehemiah

The book of Nehemiah is an extension of the book of Ezra, continuing the story of the Israelites' return to Jerusalem and what they faced. If you've been reading the devotions in order, you'll have a great background and history of the Israelites as well as a good understanding of what they were doing in Babylon in the first place! If you haven't been reading the lessons in order and you're curious—good! Put a bookmark in this spot, flip back to the devotions on 2 Kings, and read them. There's great stuff back there waiting for you to explore!

By this time, two groups of Israelite refugees had left Babylon and returned to Jerusalem and Judea. The first group returned in 538 BC, led by Zerubbabel, who supervised the rebuilding of the temple. The next group returned eighty years later (458 BC), led by Ezra, who helped turn the Israelites back to the Lord.

Now the stage is set for the book of Nehemiah. It's appropriately named for the man who led the third group of Israelites back to Judea. Nehemiah sought to rebuild the walls of Jerusalem, and this is his account of what happened.

As you explore this book, you'll see the results of prayer and the importance of teamwork. You'll also crawl up difficult inclines and look for light at the end of the tunnel—just like Nehemiah did. Watch closely how he handled the challenges he faced, then take your cues from him. You can learn a lot from Nehemiah's life!

Be sure to check out www.cookministries.com/FaithFactor for two bonus lessons titled "Join the Team" (taken from Nehemiah 2—4) and "You Win the Prize!" (taken from Nehemiah 5). These lessons deal with needing and serving one another.

. . . Amen
Taken from Nehemiah 1—2

Foundation

As you begin exploring Nehemiah today, commit your time to the Lord and ask Him to challenge you to desire a greater and more meaningful prayer life. Don't read on until you've done that!

Focus

Do you ever struggle with not wanting to pray, or not knowing how?

Nehemiah was speechless, stunned at what he had just heard.

"Those who live in Jerusalem in the province of Judah are in terrible shape and disgrace," the men had reported.

They had just traveled through Judea on their way back to Susa, where Nehemiah lived and served as cupbearer to King Artaxerxes. Nehemiah had eagerly questioned the men, excited for any news about how his fellow Israelites were faring. But the report wasn't good, for the men had concerns over the state of matters in Jerusalem.

"The walls in Jerusalem are a wreck, and the only thing left of the once strong gates are charred remains," they reported in dismay.

Nehemiah felt heartsick. He could only wonder about the recent decree King Artaxerxes had issued concerning Jerusalem in response to a false report by Samaritan officials.

"You should know, O king, that the Jews who came to Jerusalem are

Serving as the king's cupbearer was a position of importance and trust. The cupbearer would taste the wine before serving it to the king to make sure it wasn't poisoned.

When the Israelites in Judah were carted off to Babylon as captives, foreigners were brought in to marry those who remained, preventing them from uniting as a strong nation and rebelling. The offspring of these mixed marriages became known as the Samaritans.

restoring that defiant and evil city by repairing the walls and rebuilding the foundations!" the spiteful officials said. "Furthermore, you should know that if they are successful at their task, they will rebel against you and refuse to pay their obligation of taxes, tributes, and duties. If this happens, your royal treasury will suffer! Now then," the Samaritans wrote deceitfully, "we are sending you this message since we remain loyal to you and don't want to see you dishonored in any way. Search the records, and you will see that this city is a place of rebellion against kings from ancient times. That is why it was destroyed. If it is rebuilt, you, O king, will be left with nothing."

Taking the advice of the wicked Samaritans, King Artaxerxes had the historical records searched and found that indeed powerful kings had once ruled Jerusalem. So the king issued a decree ordering an immediate halt to all of the rebuilding efforts in the city. When the regional governors received the decree, they immediately enforced it, and all rebuilding stopped dead in its tracks.

So nothing has been done since then, Nehemiah sadly realized. His heart grew heavy with concern, for once a Persian king made a decree, no one could change it except the king himself. As he thought about this, Nehemiah fasted and prayed for several days, acknowledging God's character, power, and attributes. He also asked God to grant him favor in the eyes of the king. Then Nehemiah waited.

"Why are you looking so sad?" King Artaxerxes asked Nehemiah one day.

Serving as the king's cupbearer, Nehemiah knew that showing any negative emotion was dangerous, for it could easily be interpreted as dissatisfaction with the king. Speaking humbly, Nehemiah told the king he was sad because the city where his ancestors were buried lay in ruins.

"What would you like me to do?" the king asked.

Nehemiah knew that God had opened a door of opportunity for him to lay his request before the king. He also knew it was a dangerous request.

Shooting a quick prayer to the Lord, Nehemiah answered. "If it pleases you, O king, I would like to go to Jerusalem, the city of my fathers, so that I can rebuild it," he said.

"How long will you be gone?" the king asked, hinting at his approval.

Nehemiah gave the king a time, and the king agreed. Then Nehemiah asked, "Would the king be willing to write letters to the governors in the provinces, asking them to ensure my safety until I reach Judah? Would the king also write a letter to Asaph, the keeper of the king's forest, asking him to give me timber to use as beams for the city wall and the gates, as well as for a house for myself?"

> *Ezra 4:7–23 is the companion passage that tells about King Artaxerxes' decree to stop construction in Jerusalem. Because of Nehemiah's request (and prayers), the king issued a new decree to allow construction to resume.*

King Artaxerxes agreed to all of Nehemiah's requests and issued a royal decree giving Nehemiah permission to rebuild the walls of Jerusalem. God had answered his prayers.

Footwork

Turn in your Bible to Nehemiah 1:1–2 and read it. The month of Kislev is around November or December, depending on how the Jewish calendar fell that year. Now read the last verse of chapter 1 and the first verse of chapter 2. The month of Nisan is in the March–April time frame. How long had Nehemiah been praying and patiently waiting? (*Note:* The cupbearer could not go before the king unless the king summoned or requested him.)

of Assyria, destroyed. ✦ 605 BC

Fruit

Nehemiah spent time in extended prayer, pouring out his heart to God (Neh. 1:5–11). He also shot up a quick "arrow prayer" while in the middle of a conversation with the king (see Neh. 2:4–5). Prayer was something Nehemiah did both purposefully and spontaneously.

Ironically, we try to make prayer more than it is, and it becomes so cumbersome that we often end up skipping it altogether. We lose sight of the fact that prayer is simply talking to God, much like we would talk to a person standing in front of us. Next time you pray, use this simple tool to help you remember some important guidelines:

P—Pour out your heart to God.

R—Remember that God is concerned about you and is listening.

A—Avoid the temptation to put off praying until another time.

Y—Yearn to develop a close relationship with God through prayer.

E—Enjoy your time with God.

R—React to your situations by first talking to God about them.

Good Riddance!
Taken from Nehemiah 6

Foundation

Pause a moment to pray and commit this time into God's hands. Instead of rushing on, really talk to God and tell Him about a difficulty you've been experiencing lately. Don't worry! God can't be surprised, but *you* can when you experience the freedom that comes from placing your troubles into His care.

Focus

Have you ever wanted to run from your problems?

"That Nehemiah is really getting on my nerves!" Sanballat hissed under his breath.

Tobiah and Geshem nodded in agreement. In spite of their threats, the building of the walls of Jerusalem had continued under Nehemiah's leadership. When Sanballat threatened to attack, Nehemiah had simply reorganized the builders so that some worked while others stood guard. Instead of fear dividing the Israelites and discouraging them from their mission, it only brought them together as a team. This annoyed Sanballat and his companions all the more. After failing at their earlier attempts of attacking the builders, they changed their strategy and attacked Nehemiah directly.

"Please come and meet with us in one of the villages on the plain of Ono," Sanballat's message stated.

abylon; Daniel taken captive.

Nehemiah looked out toward the horizon and considered the intent behind the message. *Why would Sanballat have such a desire to meet with me at this time, and at the place he selected?* he wondered. Ono was about twenty-five miles northwest of Jerusalem, a whole day's journey away. It also bordered Samaria, Sanballat's hometown. Nehemiah read the letter over again, carefully reading between the lines. *This message makes it sound as if Sanballat wants to make peace with me,* Nehemiah thought, feeling hope stir in his spirit. And yet …

> **Sanballat was a Samaritan official who targeted Nehemiah as an enemy. Sending Nehemiah an unsealed letter easily enabled its contents (all rumors!) to be made public.**
>
> ---
>
> **According to Numbers 3:10, only God's priests (the Levites) were allowed to enter the temple. All others would be put to death.**

Nehemiah knew that Sanballat's actions in the past had been nothing more than attempts to keep the Israelites from rebuilding the walls of Jerusalem and reclaiming their city. *Perhaps this is just another one of his attempts,* Nehemiah thought, not even considering the possibility that Sanballat was trying to ambush and kill him.

"Tell Sanballat that the project I'm working on demands my full attention and I can't leave it," he replied to the messenger. "There would be no reason to have the work stop so I might go and meet with you."

Nehemiah's response was a test for Sanballat to prove his sincerity. *If Sanballat is really interested in seeking peace,* Nehemiah reasoned, *then he can come to Jerusalem and meet with me here.* As Nehemiah soon found out, this wasn't the case. Four different times Sanballat sent his message to Nehemiah, urging him to leave Jerusalem. And four different times Nehemiah refused. By this time Nehemiah knew that Sanballat only intended to harm him.

Soon another message came to Nehemiah—this time in an unsealed letter. It contained lies and unfounded rumors aimed at Nehemiah.

"All the nations report—and Geshem says the rumors are true!—that you Jews are repairing the wall because you're plotting a revolt against me!" Sanballat accused. "It's also been reported that you intend to become king and have already hired prophets to spread the word. You can be very sure that I will hear about this, so I suggest we meet to talk about it."

Nehemiah was shocked. *Nothing could have been further from the truth!* his heart screamed within him. Collecting himself, Nehemiah sent his response back with the messenger.

"These are all lies! None of what you've described is happening." The messenger left, and Nehemiah sank to his knees. *Strengthen me, Lord,* he prayed.

One day, the prophet Shemaiah asked to meet with Nehemiah. "Let's go inside the temple and meet behind closed doors where you'll be safe, for a group of men are coming to the city to kill you!" the prophet whispered, pretending to be concerned for Nehemiah's safety.

Nehemiah listened carefully to Shemaiah's words, not knowing the prophet had been hired by Sanballat in order to lure Nehemiah into the temple—a place where only priests could go. But when Nehemiah looked into the cold, steely eyes of the false prophet, he realized that no true prophet would ask him to sin against the Lord by disobeying His laws. This was just another attempt to discredit him and give him a bad name! "Should someone like me run away from danger?" Nehemiah challenged. "Should I run into the temple and sin just to save my life? I won't do it!" he said firmly. Nehemiah had better things to do with his time and his problems ...

Footwork

Read Nehemiah 6:8–9 in your Bible. What was Nehemiah's first course of action? (*Hint:* Look at the end of verse 9.)

Fruit

Nehemiah faced many difficulties at the hands of his enemies who tried to oppose him. Yet God gave him the strength and wisdom to handle his conflicts. Instead of running from problems, Nehemiah ran to God—and then stood his ground.

The next time conflict comes your way, which way will you run?

What's the Expiration Date?

Taken from Nehemiah 8—13

Foundation

As your journey through the book of Nehemiah comes to an end, reflect
on what you've learned. What lessons have hit close to your heart? Tell
God about them and invite Him to use them in your life. Then thank Him
for His Word (Scripture), which gives you strength and direction.

Focus

*Have you ever tried to change, only to find yourself quickly
falling back into the same old habits?*

All eyes were fixed on Ezra as he stood on a wooden platform high
above the crowd. After spending the past two months rebuilding the
walls of Jerusalem, the Israelites would now rebuild their spiritual lives.
Men, women, and children gathered in the square, listening expectantly
as Ezra cleared his throat and read from the law of Moses. His voice
projected across the square, and God's Word penetrated their hearts.
Once again, all were reminded that they had fallen short of God's ways.
Many wept. Others resolved to begin seeking God more faithfully. It was
a solemn time for everyone.

Seeing the people weeping, Nehemiah encouraged them not to grieve.

uilt   in   Ephesus.   ✦   597   BC   —

"This day is sacred to God! Go and celebrate with a feast, sharing with others who didn't bring anything. The joy of the Lord is your strength!"

The Israelites looked up at Nehemiah, considered his words, and then left encouraged. They would celebrate with great joy, for that day they had heard and understood the Scriptures.

The next day everyone gathered again to hear Ezra read from the Law. Every day during the Feast of Tabernacles, Ezra read from the book of the law—all in keeping with the Scriptures. At the end of the month, the Israelites gathered for a special assembly to worship God and confess their shortcomings.

"You alone are the Lord, who made the heavens and the earth and all that is in them," they acknowledged in worship. "You are the one who gives life to everything, and all the heavenly beings worship You."

For three hours the people took turns asking God's forgiveness for their sins and recognizing His power and faithfulness toward them. They remembered how God made a covenant with Abraham, delivered their ancestors out of slavery in Egypt, provided for them in the desert, and brought them into the Promised Land. Because of His loyal love and faithfulness, God kept His covenant and did not abandon His people—even when they turned away from Him.

"In all that has happened to our people, Lord, You have been just, acting faithfully while we did wrong," the Israelites confessed. "Because our ancestors disobeyed Your laws and refused to pay attention to Your warnings, they were taken from this land just as You said would happen. Now, we are like slaves because another kingdom rules over us and enjoys the goodness of the land. Hear our cry, O Lord, for we are in distress!"

> *The law of Moses includes the first five books of the Old Testament—Genesis through Deuteronomy. We often refer to it as the* Pentateuch—penta *means "five." According to Deuteronomy 31:10–13, the Law was to be read aloud publicly every seven years.*

> *God is never impressed by what we do for Him in our own efforts. He's only pleased with what we do through Him—and with what He does through us.*

Wanting to show their sincere change of heart, the people recorded their commitment on parchment, which would stand for all time. "We promise not to let our sons or daughters marry the pagan people of the land. And when foreigners enter our city to sell their goods on the Sabbath—or any other holy day, we will refuse to buy anything from them. We promise to obey the command to pay the temple tax and to bring the first part of every harvest to You. We promise to supply the storerooms of the temple with food so the priests may be provided for as they go about their jobs—just as You commanded. We will not neglect God's house, and we will not neglect You, Lord."

Once the Israelites' promises had been recorded, the leaders, Levites, and priests put their seal to them. In the eyes of the people, they had decided to make a change, and they would live by it … or so they thought.

His job done, Nehemiah returned to Babylon to serve under King Artaxerxes as he had promised. Later, when an opportunity came for Nehemiah to return to Jerusalem, he was shocked at what he saw. Eliashib, the priest in charge of the temple storerooms (which lay empty), had allowed a foreigner to move in and live there. The foreigner was Tobiah, the same man who had tried to stop the rebuilding of the city walls! Nehemiah also discovered that the priests had gone back to work the fields and were neglecting their duties in the temple because the people hadn't kept the storerooms supplied.

Furious with the people for neglecting God's house, Nehemiah kicked Tobiah out of the temple storerooms and rebuked the officials who had let them go empty. When Nehemiah noticed foreigners coming into the city on the Sabbath and selling merchandise to the Israelites, he rebuked the people and ordered the city gates to be locked until the Sabbath was over.

It seemed the promises the Israelites had made to change had only been good for a short time.

Footwork

Open your Bible to Nehemiah 9:38 and read what it says. Do you think the Israelites were sincere about what they were doing? Now turn to Nehemiah 8:10 and read the last sentence in that verse. What do you think this means? Do you find it a little odd? According to Nehemiah, where should the people's focus have been?

Fruit

The Israelites had a great revival, and everyone was emotionally charged to live wholeheartedly for God. Unfortunately, the people didn't realize that true revival is more than enthusiasm and keeping to a new set of standards or rules. It's a plan of action carried out by dependence upon God for help. Turning over a new leaf is never effective when it's our own power that is doing the turning. Yes, we need to be determined, but more importantly, we need to be dependent. If we depend on our own efforts, revival will be fruitless. Be careful of "self-effort"; it's a trap that will keep you from experiencing true and lasting strength in a relationship with the living God.

Esther

The story of Esther takes place in 483 BC after the first group of exiles, led by Zerubbabel, had returned to Jerusalem and before Ezra returned with the second group. Historically speaking, if we were to plug the book of Esther into its proper time sequence, it would fall between chapters 6 and 7 of the book of Ezra.

Apparently, Esther's family chose not to return to Jerusalem, even though King Cyrus's decree had granted them permission to do so. Many Jews enjoyed great freedom in the Persian Empire, and they had become accustomed to their way of life. Others simply feared the long and dangerous journey back to their homeland. For whatever reasons, Esther's family remained in Persia, and God had a plan for it.

As you explore the book of Esther, you'll see the glory of God's timing and the twists and turns of man's pride. Although a short book, Esther is packed with great life lessons! There's more to Esther than meets the eye.

It's No Coincidence
Taken from Esther 1—4

Foundation

Start your time today with prayer. Invite God to help you apply what you learn and to understand that He has a specific plan and purpose for your life right here and now. Ask Him to show you that purpose.

Focus

Have you ever secretly wished you could do something great—something that really made a difference?

For my guests, I shall have the best of everything! King Xerxes of Persia decided.

Important leaders and dignitaries would share his table during a six-month celebration. Not only would this help solidify a battle strategy for invading Greece, it would also provide an opportunity for King Xerxes to show off his vast wealth, thus proving his ability to carry out his plan. But in a moment of thoughtless merriment, King Xerxes decided to show off more than his riches.

"Summon Queen Vashti to come and show off her beauty for my guests!" he commanded.

The edges of his lips curled into a satisfied smile as he waited in anticipation for Vashti to arrive. But his smile soon faded, for Queen Vashti refused to come. Knowing that the king and his cohorts had become drunk, she refused to be a part of it. This angered the king greatly, and as a result, he dethroned the queen, sending her away from his presence. Vashti would easily be replaced by another queen.

"The search has begun to find King Xerxes a new queen!" The announcement

two years during Babylonian captivity.

soon spread across the land. Officials were appointed to bring young women from every province to Susa, the capital of Persia, to be placed in the king's harem. After undergoing beauty treatments for twelve months, they would be presented to King Xerxes. Until that time, or unless the king specifically called for them by name, the young women would remain in the king's harem. Among them was a young Jewish woman named Hadassah (Esther in the Persian language).

Mordecai paced, wondering how his cousin was faring. She had been taken to the king's palace for the selection process. Every day Mordecai walked back and forth near the courtyard of the harem to find out what was happening to her. Ever since the death of Esther's parents, Mordecai had taken his cousin in and raised her like his own daughter.

"Don't tell anyone your nationality," he advised her before she was taken away. Esther had obeyed, not realizing how important that simple act of obedience would be.

When Esther was finally presented to King Xerxes, she quickly found favor in his eyes. The king was more attracted to Esther than he was to any of the other women, so he selected her as his new queen and placed a royal crown on her head. An announcement was made and sent throughout all the provinces declaring a national holiday, and a huge banquet was held in Esther's honor. King Xerxes was greatly pleased.

One day while Mordecai was at the king's gate, waiting to find out how Esther was getting along, he overheard a conversation. Two of the king's officers were talking between themselves in hushed tones. They were angry with King Xerxes and planned to kill him.

I must inform Esther so she can warn the king! Mordecai thought. So he contacted Esther and revealed the plot against the king. Esther then reported the plot to King Xerxes and gave credit to Mordecai for finding it out. After an

> *The beauty treatments the women had to undergo required six months of skin treatments with oil from myrrh and six months with perfumes and cosmetics (Est. 2:12).*

investigation found the report to be true, the guilty officers were hung on the gallows, and the whole event was recorded in the king's royal records—along with Mordecai's name.

Not long after these events, King Xerxes honored a man named Haman and elevated him to a position higher than all the other nobles. According to the king's command, all the royal officials had to kneel down and pay honor to Haman. Mordecai, however, refused to bow to Haman.

God had commanded the Israelites not to bow to anyone but Him. But there was another reason Mordecai refused to bow to Haman. Haman was an Amalekite. In Deuteronomy 25:17–19, God commanded the Israelites to destroy the Amalekites and wipe their memory from the face of the earth. Bowing to an Amalekite was something Mordecai could not and would not do as a Jew.

"Why won't you bow to him?" the royal officials asked Mordecai. "Why are you refusing to obey the king's commands?"

Every day they asked Mordecai the same question, and each day he refused to bow or to give a reason for his actions. When word of this reached Haman, his anger boiled. When he discovered that Mordecai was a Jew, a plot began to take shape in his mind.

One day Haman came before the king with a request. "There is a certain people in the provinces of your kingdom whose customs differ from ours. They don't obey your laws and should not be tolerated," he said. "If you announce a decree stating they should be destroyed, I will gladly donate 375 tons of silver into the treasury as payment for the men needed to carry out such a decree."

King Xerxes thought Haman's request was reasonable and handed Haman his ring to officially seal the decree. He didn't realize the people Haman spoke of were Jews—and that Queen Esther was one of them!

When the decree was announced, Mordecai grieved and sent word to Esther. He knew it was no coincidence that she had been chosen to be queen. "Perhaps you can present yourself before the king and plead for your people," Mordecai urged.

Footwork

Turn to Esther 4:14 in your Bible. Especially look at the last part of the verse. What does it say? Now look at verses 15–17. What was Esther's response? Want to know what happens next? You'll have to read the next lesson or take a sneak peek at chapters 5—8 in your Bible!

Fruit

God places you in different situations so He can use you. Sometimes you'll find yourself in positions of great honor and prestige like Esther, and sometimes you'll be in behind-the-scenes positions—outside the palace gate like Mordecai. Whether you find yourself on center stage or behind the scenes, God has you there for a reason. It's no coincidence, and both positions are equally important. Do you value the place where God has you right now?

I Deserve It!
Taken from Esther 5—6

Foundation

Spend a moment or two preparing your heart before you begin today. Quiet your heart before God and ask Him to help you learn to put pride in its proper place.

Focus

Does it ever bother you when others receive special honor and you don't?

Queen Esther's heart was pounding wildly within her as she stood before the doors to the throne room. *I know I risk death by coming before the king without being summoned, but the risk of not doing so is even greater!* Esther thought. The matter at hand was urgent and involved more than just her own life. She had already spent three days praying and fasting as she sought God's direction—and protection.

The doors opened, and the king looked up. Esther froze, unsure whether the king would receive her. Her bold actions could easily cost her life. She fixed her gaze upon the scepter King Xerxes held in his hand. If he raised it, she would be pardoned for such an interruption, and her life would be spared. If he didn't …

King Xerxes tightened his grip on the scepter and pointed it in her direction. He then raised it. Esther sighed in relief knowing that her life had been spared, but the burden of her mission still weighed heavily on her heart. Approaching the throne, she touched the end of the scepter and bowed before the king.

"What is your request, Queen Esther?" the king asked her kindly. "All you have to do is ask and it's yours—even if it means half of my kingdom!"

Queen Esther knew that God had opened a door for her request, but she also knew such matters had to be handled delicately. Instead of making her charge against Haman's wicked decree to kill all her people, Esther decided to approach things differently and wait for God's timing to make her request.

"If I have found favor in your sight," Queen Esther responded, "please grant my request to come today to a banquet I've prepared for you and Haman." The king agreed, and he and Haman went to the banquet.

The king was very pleased with the banquet Esther had given him and said, "What do you want me to do for you, Esther? I will give you whatever you ask, even up to half of my kingdom."

Esther replied, "O king, if I have again found favor in your sight, please grant my petition by coming to a banquet I prepare for you and Haman tomorrow. Then I will answer your question."

Again, the king agreed.

When Haman arrived at home, he boasted to his wife and friends about all the ways the king had honored him above other nobles and officials. "Not only *that*," Haman eagerly added, "but I'm the only person Queen Esther invited to join the king at the banquet!"

Everyone was impressed with the honor Haman had received. But Haman got little satisfaction from it. "Even though these are all wonderful things, I am unable to find pleasure in them as long as I see that ... that ... *Jew* Mordecai who sits at the king's gate!" he stated bitterly.

"Why not have a huge gallows built and tomorrow morning ask the king

Because Persian kings were protective of their wives, it was very unusual to be invited to a private banquet with the queen.

Although the king's records contained twelve years of events, the official "happened" to read from the portion concerning Mordecai, an event that had occurred five years earlier in which Mordecai's life-saving act had gone unrewarded!

to have Mordecai hung on it!" his wife and friends suggested. "Then simply go to the dinner party and enjoy yourself!"

A fiendish smirk broke out across Haman's face, and he gave immediate orders to have the gallows built.

That night King Xerxes had difficulty sleeping and ordered his book of records to be read to him. The king listened intently as his attendants read about the plot to assassinate him. "A man named Mordecai discovered the plot, and through his quick action the king's life was spared," the record stated.

King Xerxes looked up and asked his official, "What reward was given to this Mordecai?"

"None," came the response.

Realizing that Mordecai hadn't been properly rewarded, the king resolved in his heart to attend to the matter in the morning.

Just then he heard a noise in the outer court. The official noticed that it was Haman and summoned him in to see the king.

"You're just the person I want to talk to!" Xerxes said. "Tell me, what should I do to honor a man who truly pleases me?"

Haman's heart pounded with delight. He knew the king had to be speaking about him! "Instruct one of the most noble princes to dress that man in the king's robe, place him on the king's own horse, and lead him through the city square proclaiming: 'This is a man whom the king finds worthy of honor!' " Haman eagerly replied.

King Xerxes nodded in agreement, pleased with the suggestion. "Go without delay and do everything exactly as you said for Mordecai the Jew, who sits at the gate!"

Footwork

Quickly open your Bible and read Esther 7:1–6. Then read verses 9–10. After Haman honored Mordecai as the king commanded (against his will, no doubt!), he was summoned to Esther's banquet. What happened there?

Greek mathematician and philosopher,

Fruit

Haman had a real problem with wanting others to show him honor, and he got what he deserved. In striving to be appreciated, Haman only ended up humiliated. Don't let yourself fall into the same trap of being ruled by your pride and thinking you deserve to be honored, for only God deserves to be honored and worshipped. Often, honor comes to those who don't seek it. That's God's blessing. Those who proudly set themselves above others only come to ruin. Don't be one of them!

Job

As you've already seen, the books of the Old Testament aren't necessarily presented in chronological order in our Bible. Job is no exception. Although scholars have debated the exact date this book was written, many facts support the idea that Job lived around the time of the patriarchs (Abraham, Isaac, and Jacob). If this is true, then the correct placement of this book would be somewhere in the middle of the book of Genesis.

The book of Job is full of surprises—and disappointments. It allows us to witness an insider's view of suffering as well as the outward reactions of observers. Many have regarded this book as a great piece of literature. But a word of caution is needed before we begin. Because Job centers on the sufferings of one man and the bad counsel of his friends, it's important not to pull the Scripture verses out of context. To do so would be to treat examples of bad advice as truth!

As you explore this book, you'll gain an inside view into Job's life and wrestle with an age-old question: If God is good, then why do the godly suffer? Enjoy the journey—and watch out for hidden surprises.

Ready ... Aim ... Fire!
Taken from Job 1—3

Foundation

Before you begin exploring Job, pause a moment to prepare your heart. Ask the Lord to show you what He wants you to learn—then allow Him to use it to change your life.

Focus

Have you ever felt like a target, with everyone and everything firing at you?

"The Sabeans did *what?*" Job asked with disbelief, turning his full gaze on the man bringing him the bad news.

The messenger repeated his words, trying to calm himself as he spoke. "Your field hands were plowing with the oxen and donkeys were grazing peacefully nearby," he explained once again, "when the Sabeans attacked, killed all your servants, and carried off all the animals. I'm the only one who escaped to tell you!"

Job was stunned. *All my servants—gone?*

The Sabeans' attack had been totally unprovoked, unexplained, and unexpected. Job knew there was a great loss of life, for he had many servants who helped care for his one thousand oxen and five hundred donkeys.

While the messenger was still giving Job his report, another servant came up with equally bad news. "Sir," he said, out of breath, "fire fell from heaven and burned up all seven thousand of your sheep as well as your servants! I'm the only one who escaped to report it to you!"

As this messenger was still speaking, yet another messenger appeared. "The Chaldeans came and took all three thousand of your camels and killed your servants," he announced.

Job looked from one messenger to another, hardly able to believe that such events had taken place. Then, just as the third messenger finished telling Job of the tragedy, another servant approached. Job looked up, wondering if he could take any more bad news. This messenger's news was the worst yet.

"Sir, a strong wind like none I've seen before came through and ripped apart the house where your sons and daughters were celebrating a feast together. The house collapsed in a pile of rubble and killed them all. I'm the only survivor," he said quietly, observing the effects of his solemn news on Job.

Job stood in shocked silence as great anguish welled up inside him. He tore his robe in deep grief, shaved his head, and fell to the ground in worship before the Lord.

"I came into this world with nothing, and one day I'll leave it with nothing. God gave me everything, and He has taken it all away. Praise His name!" he said. Even though he was in deep sorrow, Job could not and would not raise his fist against God.

Unknown to Job, Satan had come before God to accuse God's people. "They only love You for what they can get from You!" Satan accused, his words full of spite and hatred. "If You removed Your blessings," Satan added, "people would curse You and not worship You!" Satan's words were an attack not only on humanity but also on God's character.

God gave Satan permission to test his theory on Job. He knew that Satan's accusations would be quickly silenced and Job's faith greatly strengthened. In a fury of destruction, Satan acted quickly, firing one disaster on top of another at Job and stripping away everything that gave Job a sense of security. Satan's first attack was on Job's wealth and his beloved children. The final attack would be on Job's own health.

> **The Sabeans were people from southwest Arabia. The Queen of Sheba, who visited King Solomon in 950 BC, was a Sabean.**

"You're still holding on to your precious uprightness?" Job's wife spat with disgust. "Just curse God and be done with it all!"

But Job refused. Instead, he reached for a piece of broken pottery while sitting among the ashes and scraped his inflamed sores, which seeped with infection and itched. Job had lost his appetite and his strength. Pain wracked his body, and his flesh seemed to rot on his bones as it turned black and fell off. Dark circles gave Job's eyes a sunken look, and depression curved his lips downward as he sat stooped over in misery. Feverish and restless, he gasped for breath. Each effort only intensified his physical pain and added to his emotional agony. Yet even though he was in a state of hopeless misery, never once did he curse God. He did, however, curse the day he was born.

"Oh, that my mother had never given me birth!" he moaned in great pain and sorrow. "Why did God give life to me if I was destined to live in distress with no future?"

Footwork

Turn in your Bible to Job 3:25–26 and read it. What does Job say? Have you ever felt like saying this?

Fruit

Unfortunately, many people seek God and worship Him only to gain something for themselves. They worship God as long as they experience a successful, happy life—or at least one without pain and difficulty. But when success and happiness are gone, their faith in Him disappears as well! Job was different. His love for God was real—and God knew it. Job knew that no matter what, God was in control of the circumstances of his life, and God deserved his allegiance.

Today, if you were to experience extreme testing like Job did, how would your faith hold up? Talk to God about it.

If You Ask Me . . .
Taken from Job 4—14

Foundation

Take a moment to pray, asking God to check your thoughts, motives, and actions. Ask Him to help you avoid making false assumptions about others—or yourself.

Has anyone ever given you bad advice?

Suffering hung over Job like a heavy blanket that threatened to suffocate him. Words couldn't describe the mental, emotional, and physical pain he was feeling as he sat on the ash heap. For a week now, Job had sat in silence and mourning. Only the sound of a piece of broken pottery scraping against his infected skin broke the silence. As a customary sign of respect for his grief and suffering, Job's friends Eliphaz, Bildad, and Zophar sat with him, saying nothing. Even though they had said nothing for the past seven days, they hadn't been able to quiet their thoughts. And their thoughts about Job's unusual suffering all boiled down to an obvious explanation: Job's suffering was the result of sin.

Job groaned, and his three friends looked at him expectantly. Coughing and clearing his throat, Job finally broke the long days of silence. "If only my mother had never given me birth!" he whispered. "Cursed is the day I was born! The very thing I feared most has happened! I am tormented inside and have no peace. There is no rest for my broken heart," Job moaned.

He looked at his friends briefly, then dropped his head to stare at the ground in agony. Eliphaz took this as his cue to speak. As the oldest of Job's friends, he would give his thoughts on the matter first. Clearing his throat, he began to offer his explanation for the suffering he saw Job experiencing.

"Will you listen to something I have to say?" Eliphaz asked Job, not waiting for his reply. "Under such circumstances, who couldn't speak? In the past, you've supported the weak. Your words strengthened and encouraged others who had fallen or wavered. But now that trouble strikes you, you are faint and downcast," Eliphaz observed. He paused for a moment before challenging Job. "Has an innocent person ever perished? When has an upright person ever been destroyed?" Eliphaz reasoned. "My own experience tells me that those who plant evil and cultivate trouble only experience the same! God stands beside the upright and punishes those who do evil; therefore, do not challenge the Lord's punishment on your life."

Job heard Eliphaz's words and felt the sting of what they implied. *Eliphaz thinks that if I just confess my sins to You, Lord, my suffering will end! Yet I have lived uprightly before You. I've done nothing wrong and haven't committed any sin that I need to confess!* Job prayed. He knew deep down that Eliphaz was wrong in assuming that the godly never suffer. Eliphaz relied on his own experiences and gave advice from that point of view. His advice was not helpful.

Bildad was the next to speak. After hearing Job's response to Eliphaz, Bildad became more forceful and spoke not from his own experience

In three rounds of different speeches, Job's friends offered their bad advice. First they questioned whether Job had sinned, then they assumed he must have. In their last round of advice, they openly accused Job of sinning! But in chapters 38—42, God had the final word and set the record straight.

It was the custom of the day to remain silent until a grieving person spoke first. Placing ashes on one's head or sitting in an ash heap was a cultural way of showing grief and mourning.

but used examples of past generations and tradition to give his words more authority. "Even former generations all know that if a man is guilty God will reject him; if he is blameless, God will grant him success and strengthen him," he erroneously counseled. "When your children sinned against God, He gave them what they deserved. But if you are upright, God will remove your suffering. If not, then ..."

Job understood the intent of Bildad's words. Like Eliphaz, Bildad believed that only the wicked suffered, while the godly experienced nothing but success. He wrongly assumed that Job's children had been killed because they were unrighteous.

It didn't take long for Job's third friend, Zophar, to chime in with his own observations. Zophar pressed his point even more forcefully than the others. "God is wiser than you, Job! He knows deceitful men and brings them to account!"

Although Zophar's words were true, Job hadn't been deceitful, nor had he tried to hide his sin from other people—let alone God. Once again, the advice of his friend didn't apply.

As much as Job's friends tried to argue, persuade, dominate, and reason with Job, they did so in vain, for they assumed they knew God's mind in the matter. Their advice was based on personal experience, the experience of others in the past, and the logical religious thinking of their day. Job knew that the advice he received from them was shallow and that his friends had quickly jumped to false conclusions. Although Job didn't fully understand the reason for his suffering, he knew what it was *not* caused by. Job allowed God to be big enough to have other reasons for allowing him to suffer.

Footwork

In your Bible, look up Job 5:27. What does it say? What does the person saying this assume?

(If you are reading from the NIV, notice the words "we," "examined," "true," "so ... apply it.")

Fruit

Much goes on behind the scenes in a person's life that we know nothing about. Unlike God, we can't judge people's thoughts or the motives of their hearts. Often when we try to help someone, we draw wrong conclusions. Sometimes we even tell ourselves lies. Suffering is *not* always because of sin. Be wary of people who tell you otherwise.

Interestingly, in New Testament times, Jesus was confronted with this very question of why people suffer. In John 9:1–3, Jesus and His disciples came upon a man who had been born blind and was forced to beg on the streets. Immediately, the disciples asked Jesus whether the blind man or his parents had sinned to cause such suffering. Jesus responded, "Neither this man nor his parents sinned … but this happened so that the work of God might be displayed in his life" (vs. 3). Jesus later healed the blind man. You can read all about it in your Bible and in *Faith Factor NT*!

Psalms

The book of Psalms is the longest book in the Old Testament—but don't let that scare you! It's also one of the most moving, for it speaks directly to the heart. Although David wrote many of the psalms, he wasn't the only writer. Korah's sons (Korah led a revolt against Moses in the desert) and a man named Asaph wrote some as well. God used each of these men to pull together the message He wanted to communicate to us in His Word.

Although the ancient Hebrews called this book "songs of praise," the word *psalm* comes from a Greek term designating "music on stringed instruments." Psalms took the form of personal testimonies, songs of praise and thanksgiving, prayers, and even prophecies of the future and the coming Messiah. It's interesting to note that New Testament writers quoted the book of Psalms more than any other book, and they recognized that the "Messianic" psalms had been fulfilled in Jesus' life.

For our purposes (and available space!) we'll only cover one Psalm. However, online there are seven more available for you and your friends to read—and even more than that for you to read in your own Bible!

Be sure to check out www.cookministries.com/FaithFactor for seven more lessons on the book of Psalms. In these devotionals you'll explore Psalms 40, 51, 73, 101, 103, 119, and 139.

King Cyrus overthrows Babylon, one yea

Get Real!

Taken from Psalm 13

Foundation

As you explore the book of Psalms, don't just read it for head knowledge. Instead, allow God to use today's lesson to transform you from the inside out. Commit your time to Him and come expectantly and openly.

Focus

Have you ever been afraid to let God know what's really on your heart—thinking He might be disappointed with you?

David agonized. Hurt, pain, frustration, and a feeling that God had abandoned him were mounting in his heart. It was a terrible situation to be in. David valued his relationship with God and knew that he couldn't sweep his emotions under a rug and pretend they didn't exist. He also realized that God knew his heart and secret thoughts anyway. Being honest with God wasn't an option; it was a necessity. David's honest prayer came from the deepest, darkest corners of his heart.

"How long will You forget me, Lord? Will it be forever? How long will You turn Your face away from me and look the other way?" he cried out in anguish. David's pounding heart felt as though it would break through his chest as he admitted his true emotions. But there was no holding back. David knew that God despised liars. It would be far better to

ater · makes · decree · permitting

express his honest feelings than it would be to try to cover them up for fear he might somehow offend God. David refused to play games with the Lord.

"Must I keep struggling with my thoughts and the sorrow in my heart forever?" he asked impatiently. For David, it was a bitter disappointment that God was allowing his enemy to get the upper hand. It was not only a personal embarrassment but a threat to David's kingship. Would it also threaten his trust in God?

> *Real prayer can be words off the top of your head or a well-thought-out poem. It doesn't matter how you pray, as long as you're communicating with God and sharing with Him what's in your heart.*
>
> *Although we aren't told in the Scriptures what situation David was referring to in this psalm, we do know it was something that was intensely painful and disappointing.*

"How long will You let my enemy be victorious?" David cried out with his complaint. "Turn and answer my prayer, O Lord! Don't let my enemy gloat, saying, 'Aha! I've conquered Him!' Don't let my foes rejoice at my downfall!" he added, expressing both the fear and frustration in his heart.

David sat a moment in silence. Then relief began to wash over his soul. The pounding in his heart and the frustration on his lips melted away as his words spilled forth. Even though God hadn't delivered David from his situation and seemed to delay in coming to his rescue, David knew He was trustworthy. Nothing David could say or do would shock God, for God already knew it all. This comforted David, for he knew he could come to God just the way he was and be accepted. His relationship with God was based on honesty, not on the fear of saying or doing the wrong thing. David knew he could be real with God and not be rejected, and that encouraged his trust.

"I confidently rest in Your unfailing love, and the salvation You provide causes my heart to be filled with joy," David was able to admit. "I will sing to You, for You have been good to me," he whispered quietly.

Footwork

Turn in your Bible to Psalm 34:4. What did David say in this psalm? Take a close look at the first half of the verse. What does David say he did here? Now look at the second half of the verse. What two things did God do as a result of David's seeking Him?

Fruit

God wants us to come to Him with our deepest feelings—whether good or bad, complaints or praise. That's the whole purpose and point of prayer: communicating with God. He knows us intimately and longs for us to be in relationship with Him. But that can't happen if we hide behind a lie or kid ourselves that everything is okay when it's not. We can come to God honestly with our deepest feelings and without fear. Give it a try! Let God into the dark corners of your heart and get real with Him.

In the quietness of your heart, open up those doors and closets where you've conveniently stored your hang-ups, fears, and "unacceptable" emotions. Let them air out in God's presence. Here are some sentences you can complete to help you get started:

Lord, it hurts when _____.

I feel frustrated because _____.

I don't think it's fair when _____.

Now, just as David did, trust God to help you with those emotions. If they keep coming back, keep handing them over to the Lord. He will be there for you, just as He was for David.

Proverbs

Faith facts

The book of Proverbs is fun, fast-paced, and full of golden nuggets just waiting to be mined. While the other Old Testament books tell stories about historical events that offer us examples of how to live (or not to live!), Proverbs is a collection of short statements that offer wise and practical advice for everyday living. Compiled by King Solomon (who wrote more than three thousand proverbs), this book gives instruction on how to live, how to be successful, and how to relate to others. If you have a problem or question in life, you will most likely find it addressed here!

Proverbs is written in poetic form so you'll remember it—but don't let that scare you off. Poetry is simply a "compactor" of spoken language. It squashes large thoughts into the smallest amount of space possible, often comparing or contrasting two statements to make a point. As you read through Proverbs, look for the words *but* (showing the *difference* between two things), *like* or *as* (showing how two things are *similar*), and the word *and* (which gives more information to *expand* the original thought). These words give us hints for how to think about the big idea being made.

In this devotional we'll take a quick look at only one of the many topics in Proverbs: wisdom. You'll definitely want to explore the other topics in this interesting book on your own. Enjoy the journey!

You Talkin' to *Me?*
Selections from Proverbs

Foundation

Take a moment to be still before God. Ask Him to search your heart and pinpoint areas in your life where you need to walk more wisely—relying on His wisdom and not your own.

Have you ever met people who think they're pretty smart?

"My child, accept my words and value what I have to say. Tune your ear to wisdom and focus on understanding—even to the point of crying out for insight and understanding. Seek them as you would look for a secret treasure. Then you'll know what it's like to fear the Lord and gain knowledge about God. For the Lord is the one who gives wisdom …" (see Prov. 2:1–6).

How well Solomon knew what he was writing about! God had given him wisdom beyond his years and enabled him to rule a vast empire (1 Kings 3—4). He had found wisdom not because he was intelligent but because he desired and sought after God. With all that in the back of his mind, Solomon wrote, "The fear of the Lord is the beginning of wisdom, and knowledge of the Holy One is understanding" (Prov. 9:10). He also recorded, "The wise in heart accept commands" and "A man of understanding delights in wisdom" (10:8, 23).

Solomon couldn't help but think of those who rejected God's wisdom and chose to live by their own understanding. Having seen plenty of those types of people around him, Solomon readily grouped them into three categories:

[Ezra 1). ● 516 BC — Completion

(1) Those who are *simple*, (2) those who are *fools*, and (3) those who are *mockers*.

"A simple man believes anything," Solomon wrote, "but a prudent [wise] man gives thought to his steps" (14:15). He knew that the simple didn't give much thought to their lives and were too lazy to change. They stumble through life, going from one thing to the next without ever looking beyond the surface for deeper understanding and meaning. "Leave your simple ways and you will live; walk in the way of understanding" (9:6), he urged.

Thinking of fools, Solomon documented, "He who trusts in himself is a fool, but he who walks in wisdom is kept safe" (28:26). He knew that this group of people thought they were smart and didn't need any wisdom from God. As a result, their lives were often wrecked on the highway of their own poor choices. Believing themselves to be professionals in the driver's seat of life, they don't even realize they don't know how to drive! "Do you see a man wise in his own eyes?" he challenged. "There is more hope for a fool than for him" (26:12).

Solomon further described fools as being "hotheaded and reckless" (14:16), despising "wisdom and discipline" (1:7), delighting "in airing [their] own opinions" (18:2), and focusing only on the things of this earth (17:24). Knowing mankind's natural tendency toward reckless, prideful foolishness, Solomon added a warning: "He who walks with the wise grows wise, but a companion of fools suffers harm" (13:20).

Finally, Solomon addressed mockers. These people reject God's wisdom and are the most dangerous. They are hopeless fools who have taken a fatal next step: They deliberately rebel against God and make their prideful position known to everyone around them. Of them, Solomon wrote, "The proud and arrogant man—'Mocker' is his name; he behaves with overweening [excessive] pride" (21:24). Not only does the mocker operate with the pride of a fool, but he campaigns for arrogant rebellion, trying to enlist others to follow his lead. "A mocker resents correction; he will not consult the wise" (15:12), Solomon recorded, describing the unteachable heart attitude of those in this group. He then added, "The Lord detests all the proud of heart. Be sure of this: They will not go unpunished" (16:5).

Solomon knew that all three types of people were on the wrong path in life and needed to turn from their sinful ways. "How long will you *simple* ones love your simple ways?" he challenged. "How long will *mockers* delight in mockery and *fools* hate knowledge?" (1:22).

He also knew that the only way they could turn their lives around was to seek the Lord with a humble and trusting heart. "Trust in the Lord with all your heart," Solomon urged, "and lean not on your own understanding; in all your ways acknowledge [Him], and [He] will make your paths straight" (3:5–6). For "when pride comes, then comes disgrace, but with humility comes wisdom" (11:2).

Footwork

Turn in your Bible to Proverbs 2:6. What three things come from God? Now turn ahead a few chapters and read Proverbs 9:10. According to this verse, what is the beginning of wisdom, and what is the basis of true understanding? (Don't just guess! Look this up.)

Fruit

If you want to know how wise you are, here's an easy test: What is your "awe factor" toward God? "The fear of the Lord is the beginning [the very source and life-spring] of [true] wisdom" (Prov. 9:10). When we fear God (deeply respect and honor Him for who He truly is), we are teachable (able to learn from Him).

Take a moment and examine your life. Of the people described in Solomon's proverbs, which one are you most like? The wise? The simple? The fool? The mocker? Tell God about it right now. If you need to, ask Him to forgive you and help you grow in understanding and knowledge. It's never too late! Proverbs 20:12 says, "Ears that hear and eyes that see—the Lord has made them both." God provides you with all the equipment you'll ever need to become truly wise. He's talking to you—are you listening?

Ecclesiastes

King Solomon wrote Ecclesiastes, or the book of "the preacher," which is what the name *Ecclesiastes* means. Unlike the book of Proverbs, which contains Solomon's advice for wise living, Ecclesiastes is a record of mankind's attempt to find meaning and fulfillment on earth apart from God. Solomon wrote this book from personal experience during a dark time in his life when he wandered from the Lord. How did that happen? What did Solomon discover? That is what Ecclesiastes is all about!

As you read through this interesting and challenging book, you'll notice that Solomon repeatedly uses the phrase "under the sun"—twenty-nine times to be exact! It's a poetic way of saying "down here on earth." The phrase "Everything is meaningless" or "All is vanity" simply means that life was empty and unable to fulfill or satisfy Solomon. Why was his life empty and unsatisfying? You'll just have to read on to find out!

Is This All There Is?
Taken from Ecclesiastes 1—2

Foundation

Praying before you begin exploring God's Word isn't just an empty routine; it's a way to make sure you're on track with God. Spend a moment now and thank Him that He cares about you, that He wants to be involved in your life, and that He alone can meet the deepest longings of your heart.

Focus

Have you ever looked forward to something, and when the time for it finally came, it wasn't as exciting as you thought it would be?

"Everything is meaningless! Total emptiness! Everything is empty!" Solomon penned. Then he stopped a moment to think about how high he had risen in life. Not only was he the son of David, but he was also a king himself! Wiser than anyone who ruled over Jerusalem above him, he built great projects, owned many slaves, and had huge herds of sheep and cattle. He had it all! Great wealth, a large harem, and many wives—everything the world could offer that promised pleasure and a sense of accomplishment. And yet ...

"Emptiness," Solomon admitted. *This shouldn't be! What's wrong?* he wondered. *What's life really about? What am I missing?*

Although he had been blessed with God's wisdom, Solomon had

Some people doubt that Solomon wrote the book of Ecclesiastes. Although the author didn't name himself directly, he did give us clues. The wisdom (1:16), pleasures (2:3), building projects (2:4–6), numerous servants (2:7), and wealth (2:8) the author enjoyed all point to none other than Solomon himself.

Slaves? The many slaves Solomon acquired were most likely Canaanites who labored in his stone quarries and built his palaces and cities.

failed to heed his own advice. As his kingdom grew larger, his power and fame spread so that he was known in foreign nations. Many foreign kings offered their daughters to Solomon in marriage, hoping for political favors. As the number of Solomon's wives grew (he had seven hundred in all!), Solomon's heart began to shrink from loving the Lord. His wives brought their foreign gods with them to Jerusalem and began to influence Solomon. In spite of the wisdom God had given him, it wasn't long before he began to seek happiness and fulfillment in everything under the sun.

Even though I control all major trade routes on the land and have fleets of trading ships that bring me gold, silver, ivory, apes, and baboons, I find no satisfaction in it! Solomon sighed. Picking up his pen, he recorded more of his thoughts: "I thought to myself, since I have become so wise, I will put my mind toward pursuing even more knowledge and the understanding of all that knowledge. But I found that there is no end to books, and much study only wearies the body. I have also observed that even the smartest of men will in the end suffer the same fate as the fool. Both will die and soon be forgotten. This is an empty, dead-end road!

"I then set my heart to pursue pleasure. I didn't deny myself anything my eyes saw and desired, nor did I hold back on what my heart found enjoyable. But this only left me feeling all the more empty. I tried music, acquiring men and women singers. Empty. I then surrounded myself with beautiful women. Still empty. I even tried going the other way and sought meaning in living a morally upright life. Nothing. Seeking happiness is like chasing after the wind! It cannot be caught and grasped with the hand."

Then Solomon thought about all his striving and planning. "I have observed that a man toils under the sun, but in the end he takes nothing with him when he dies. Just as man comes naked from his mother's womb, so he departs in the end. Everything under the sun is vanity and meaningless; it cannot be held on to, nor does it satisfy!"

Solomon put his pen down in frustration. He would write more later.

Footwork

In your Bible, turn to Ecclesiastes 2:10–11 and read what Solomon says here. What two things did he *not* do in verse 10? What was the reward for all his labor? Now look at verse 11. What did Solomon discover in the end?

Fruit

Many things in the world today falsely promise to bring you happiness and satisfaction. They include things you own, good health, friendships, fun activities, a great job, honor and fame, food, and riches. Although you may enjoy many of these as a blessing from God, keep in mind that they come with God's "thumbprint" of frustration on them. Seeking to find fulfillment in them instead of God will only leave you empty, frustrated, and longing for something more—like Solomon. God has put a longing for Him deep inside us, and this longing is His built-in way of bringing us back to Him, for He has made us for better things than feeling frustrated. At the end of Ecclesiastes, Solomon made this statement about what he came to realize: "So what is every person's duty? Don't lose sight of God. Fear Him and keep His commandments. This applies to everyohe."

How is your relationship with God doing? (If you aren't sure if you even have a relationship with Him, turn to the back of this book. You'll find a special message there just for you!) Do you know anyone who is caught in the trap Solomon was in? Pray for that person today. Then make a point of sharing with your friend what you learned in Ecclesiastes this week. Solomon had been there and done it all, only to find that the emptiness of everything "under the sun" (what this world has to offer) isn't all there is to life. We only need to read Ecclesiastes to be reminded of that!

Song of Songs

This book has also been called "The Song of Solomon" and was written by—you guessed it—Solomon. Of all the 1,005 songs King Solomon wrote, God specifically included this one in the Bible. Why? Because it celebrates the love of a newly married man and woman as they delight in each other. God, not people, invented the idea of love and physical intimacy, and He is not ashamed of it. Nor should we be.

Although the majority of this book looks at marriage, we'll be looking only at the first few chapters, which deal with the couple's courtship (before they were married). While reading in Song of Songs, you'll notice language that seems confusing and hard for our modern ears to understand. For instance, telling a young lady today that her "nose is like the tower of Lebanon looking toward Damascus" (Song 7:4) would *not* be considered a compliment! In Solomon's day and language, however, it was. For just as the tower reflected a sense of strength as it protected Damascus, so Solomon was saying that his beloved's features reflected her strong and beautiful character. So when you come across comparisons that seem like insults, don't get stuck on what that object looks like. Instead, stop to ponder how the people of that day may have felt emotionally about the object being compared. Then you'll be on track to better understand what the author of this book was trying to say to his beloved.

Ewwwww!
Taken from Song of Songs 1—4

Foundation

Take a moment to pray and prepare your heart before reading today's lesson. Ask God to help you understand His perspective on love and how it is expressed.

FOCUS

Does "mushy stuff" turn you off (or perhaps tempt you)?

"Your love is more enjoyable than a fine wine," the Beloved (Solomon's bride-to-be) said, describing how his affections refreshed her and brought her joy. "The aroma of your perfumes is like your character, pleasing and attractive. No wonder many are drawn to you! If only you could whisk me away right now—that I might be able to be with you!" she added, looking forward to the day they would celebrate their wedding.

But as the Beloved reflected on her appeal to her Lover (Solomon) and compared herself with the other women in Jerusalem, she suddenly felt insecure. They lived in the city, but she worked in the vineyards.

"Dark am I like the tents of Kedar," she expressed, comparing her sun-darkened skin to tents made from black goat's hair. "Don't look at my darkness, for my brothers forced me to work outdoors in the vineyards," she said, apologizing for not keeping up her own "vineyard," her appearance.

"My darling," the Lover responded, "I compare you to a mare harnessed to one of Pharaoh's chariots." He knew that his Beloved would understand the meaning of his words, for stallions (male horses), not mares (females), were used to pull chariots. A female horse among all the males would create quite a stir! Solomon was telling his bride-to-be that she was beautiful and sought after—just like the only female in a world full of males would be.

Solomon's kind response to his Beloved's insecurity allowed her to bloom in confidence and feel valued. As a result, she longed for him even more, as did he for her.

"You are like a sachet of myrrh I wear around my neck," she exclaimed, thinking of the sachet's constant fragrance and how often she thought of him. "And like a bouquet of white henna flowers from the fields of En Gedi," she added. Compared to him, all other men were like a desert, but he stood out like the beautiful white henna flower on the oasis of En Gedi near the Dead Sea.

Her words expressed how much she valued him, and that brought his appreciation. As Solomon thought of her character, he couldn't help but see it reflected in her face. "You are so beautiful, my darling! So very beautiful! Your eyes are like doves," he stated. (A person's eyes were thought to be an indication of his or her character, and doves were known for their cleanliness and peacefulness.)

"No, but I am just a rose of Sharon, a lily of the valleys," she corrected, comparing herself to a common wildflower.

"Not so!" her beloved replied, "Among all other women, you are like a lily among thorns!"

Solomon deeply loved his bride-to-be and made a point not only to tell her but also to show his love in tender ways. He wasn't ashamed of her, nor would he do anything to compromise her character.

> *The Kedar people were nomads and descendants of Ishmael who lived in northern Arabia. They were known for their flocks and their archery skills.*
>
> *Myrrh, a pleasant and fragrant-smelling resin (gum), came from small trees in Arabia and was one of the gifts brought to Jesus when He was born.*

> *Sharon was a fertile coastal region of Israel running from Caesarea to Joppa. The "rose of Sharon" is mentioned in the Song of Songs numerous times and is only mentioned one other place in the Old Testament (Isa. 35:1), where it is translated "crocus."*
>
> *The rose of Sharon was a common meadow flower.*

This made the Beloved feel secure and protected. It also made her feel honored. She rejoiced in his tender protection and stated to all the women around her, "He is an unexpected surprise, like finding an apple tree in a forest! I am delighted to sit in the protection of his shade, and taste his sweet fruit [the enjoyment of their close relationship]. His banner flying over me is love." Just as a banner, a type of military flag, was held high so it could be easily seen by the troops as they marched, Solomon's love for her could be easily seen by anyone who observed their relationship.

"Oh, he is absolutely lovely!" she exclaimed. "This is my beloved—and this is my friend."

Footwork

In your Bible, turn to Song of Songs 3:5. (It may be called Song of Solomon in your transla-tion.) What does it say? The "Daughters of Jerusalem" were those who lived in the city. Gazelles and does were graceful and agile mountain animals and good examples to follow. Here, the Beloved is telling others not to rush into a relationship with someone just to enjoy what she and Solomon had, but to wait patiently for God to bring this kind of relationship into their lives. "Do not arouse or awaken love until it so desires." Let God handle things, and let Him be at the center of the relationship.

Fruit

What God has designed, people often abuse. This includes what we see around us as well as our relationships. Our culture isn't the standard for how we're to relate to people of the opposite sex—or how we're to relate to anyone of the same sex! God has set the pattern, and He has given us a beautiful picture of that in Song of Songs. There is no shame; there are no regrets. God's design is for love to be fully explored and enjoyed in the setting of a husband-and-wife relationship. This kind of relationship may seem far off in the distance to you and may be the last thing on your mind. Or it may be your deepest longing. Wherever you are in that process today, guard your heart! This week, protect what you allow your ears to hear (on the radio or your iPod) and what you allow your eyes to see (on TV or your computer). God—not society—is the Author of love, and He knows how it is best enjoyed.

Isaiah

The book of Isaiah begins the section in our Old Testament called the "Prophetic Books." Whereas Psalms, Proverbs, Ecclesiastes, and Song of Songs were considered "Wisdom Literature" that contained reflections on life, the books from Isaiah onward were written to warn the Israelites about what was to come and encourage them to follow the Lord. Some of the prophecies were long range (foretelling the coming of Jesus), and some were short range (warning the Israelites of coming danger if they didn't turn from their sinful ways).

Often you'll hear people dividing this section of the Bible into Major Prophets and Minor Prophets. Don't let that confuse you. The message of the Minor Prophets (Hosea through Malachi) is just as important as the message of the Major Prophets (Isaiah, Jeremiah, Ezekiel, and Daniel). The Major Prophets are major only because we have more of their messages contained in our Scriptures.

As you may well have guessed, Isaiah wrote this book that bears his name. Although he was a prophet, Isaiah came from a princely line and was brought up in the royal courts. Having received the best training, he rose to serve as a statesman and prophet under the reigns of Uzziah, Jotham, Ahaz, and Hezekiah—all kings of Judah. Isaiah himself lived in Judah and began to see much that not only grieved his own heart but God's heart as well. His book was God's special message of warning and encouragement to the struggling kingdom of Judah. And it's God's message of warning and encouragement to us as well. ————————

In _____ We Trust
Taken from Isaiah 1 and 36

Foundation

Stop and pray. Take time to thank God for what He has allowed in your life (blessings and trials) and thank Him that He is there for you in the good times as well as the bad.

Focus

Do you find it easier to trust in your circumstances (or things you think you can control) than to trust in God?

The people of Judah felt anxious. To the north of them lived the strong Assyrian conquerors, and to the south of them lived the powerful, threatening Egyptians. Both were racing to become world empires, and Judah lay smack-dab between the two. Already they had seen Shalmaneser, king of Assyria, attack and conquer the northern tribe of Israel—after a three-year-long siege of Samaria, Israel had been completely destroyed and the kingdom had ceased to exist. Now it seemed only a matter of time until Assyria—or even Egypt—would swallow the southern tribe of Judah into its power-hungry empire. What were the people of Judah to do? To whom should they turn? Should they team up with one enemy nation to seek protection from the other? Although Judah was consumed with this situation, the prophet Isaiah knew it was the least of Judah's problems—and the least of God's concerns.

The tunnel King Hezekiah built was hewn out of solid rock and measured 1,777 feet long! It redirected water from the spring of Gihon (which was vulnerable to enemy attack) into a large twenty-by-thirty-foot collecting pool that was located safely inside the city walls. This pool was known as the Pool of Siloam, a place where Jesus healed a man born blind (see John 9:6–11).

Be sure to check out www.cookministries.com /FaithFactor for a free bonus lesson titled Never! (2 Kings 18—19), which tells the exciting story of how King Hezekiah was delivered from the Assyrians. Or you can read it for yourself in the Bible!

"Listen to what I have to say to you! For this is what the Lord says," Isaiah exclaimed as he relayed God's case against the people. "The children I have reared and raised up have rebelled and turned from Me. Even an ox knows its master, but Israel (the tribe of Judah) does not know hers. Ah, sinful nation, you are loaded with guilt for you have forsaken the Lord and turned your backs on Him."

Isaiah couldn't help but think about the covenant God had made with His people long ago—a covenant they had readily forgotten. They were commanded not to worship, bow down, serve, or sacrifice to any foreign gods, but worship God alone who had delivered them from Egypt with His mighty power. They were to carefully obey all the Lord's decrees and commands, and in so doing, God would deliver them from the hand of all their enemies.

Those thoughts burned in Isaiah's mind as he listened to King Hezekiah's question: "What shall I do, Isaiah?"

It was the fourteenth year of Hezekiah's rule and the king had already come to Isaiah once before for counsel concerning how to handle the threat from Assyria. Like many kings before him, Hezekiah was tempted to seek help from other countries in defending Judah against her enemies. Against Isaiah's earlier counsel, King Hezekiah had formed an alliance of small kingdoms. He had then reinforced Jerusalem's defenses by building an underground tunnel to ensure a constant water supply and led an outright rebellion against Assyria. But to the king's horror, the Assyrians had swooped down in a counterattack, leveling forty-six walled cities and carrying away more than two hundred thousand captives.

"I have done wrong," King Hezekiah had cried out to King Sennacherib of Assyria. "Please withdraw from me, and I will pay whatever you demand." So Sennacherib exacted three hundred talents of silver and thirty talents of gold from Hezekiah. This required all the silver found in the temple of the Lord and in the treasuries of the royal palace as well as the gold stripped from the temple doors and doorposts.

Now, King Sennacherib was back, threatening to attack Jerusalem. Supported by a large army, the king's field commander arrived to deliver a message to King Hezekiah.

"Tell Hezekiah," the field commander called out, "that the true great king—the king of Assyria—asks upon what are you basing your confidence when you boldly say you have a plan and military might? If you are depending on Egypt for help, you will be defeated. And if you say, 'We are depending on the Lord our God,' understand that no god of any nation has ever been able to defend his land against the mighty king of Assyria!"

When Hezekiah heard those words, he sought Isaiah's counsel. "Turn to the Lord, and trust Him, for the Lord will deliver you from the hand of your enemies," Isaiah once again reminded the king. This time Hezekiah listened and obeyed the prophet. And God did exactly as promised.

Footwork

In your Bible, turn to Isaiah 2:22. What does it say? Now read verses 17 and 18. According to these verses (as stated in the NIV), what will be "brought low" and what will "totally disappear"?

Fruit

The nation of Judah had experienced loss because they neglected their covenant with God and relied on something that gave them a false sense of security. Although they returned to God and trusted Him this time, they would eventually fall back into old habits and suffer for it.

What makes you feel secure? Is it family? Being surrounded by good friends? Experiencing success at a task? All of these blessings pass first through God's hands. Have you stopped to thank Him? On a piece of paper, trace your hand and wrist. Where you traced your wrist, write the word *God,* and then in the palm, list everything that brings you a sense of security and well-being. Post the paper on a bathroom mirror this week as a reminder to trust and thank God for what He provides for you.

Now Can You Hear Me?
Taken from Isaiah 36—53

Foundation

Before you begin today, ask God to give you a teachable heart so you might hear what He wants to tell you about Himself.

Focus

Have you ever wished that God would speak directly to you and tell you what His will for your life is?

As Isaiah pondered what God had revealed to him concerning the future of the Israelites, he couldn't help but think of their recent past. They had lived in confidence, luxury, and prosperity under King Hezekiah. Although they performed religious rituals, their hearts were not seeking after God. Even the king, who had been one of the more godly rulers of Judah, had slipped into bad judgment.

How well Isaiah remembered King Hezekiah's bitter tears when Isaiah informed the ill king that he would soon die! The king had called out to God after that. Isaiah also remembered the look on Hezekiah's face when he later received a new message from God, saying that God had seen his tears and heard his prayer. He would be given fifteen more years to live, and God would defend Jerusalem from Assyrian attacks. *What exciting news that had been,* Isaiah thought. But what a disappointing turn of events occurred because of a poor decision the king had made.

Isaiah recalled it all too well. When King Merodach-Baladan of Babylon

In 605 BC, the beginning of Isaiah's prophecy was being fulfilled. Some of King Hezekiah's descendants—including Daniel—were taken into captivity to Babylon.

Isaiah 45:13 foretells that King Cyrus would issue a decree allowing the Israelite captives to return to rebuild the temple and the walls of Jerusalem. This prophecy was given years before Judah was taken into captivity and one hundred years before Cyrus was born! The many fulfilled prophecies in God's Word truly are proof of His power!

heard that King Hezekiah had recovered, he sent messengers bearing a gift to celebrate Hezekiah's recovery, as well as an invitation for him to join a growing rebel alliance against Assyria. In a moment of pride and with a desire to impress, Hezekiah showed the foreigners everything of value in his palace, his storehouses, and his kingdom. When Isaiah heard about King Hezekiah's foolish act, he informed the king that not only would his wealth be carried off to Babylon, but some of his descendants would be forced to serve in the Babylonian royal court as well.

Isaiah looked out on the horizon. The Lord would allow the remaining people of the tribe of Judah to be taken captive and carted off to Babylon. The temple would be destroyed, and it would seem to God's people that all hope was lost. But Isaiah knew that all hope was not lost. God had given him a vision of things to come and a special message for the struggling Israelites: "Fear not, for I have redeemed you; I have called you by your name; you are Mine." God wasn't going to squash the nation or give up on His covenant with the people. Instead, He would remove them from the land in order to draw their hearts back to Him.

Isaiah reassured the people of God's plan for them and that although they had not acknowledged Him, He would strengthen them so that all nations would know there is no other God but Him. He also told them how a man named Cyrus would one day set them free from exile to go back to Jerusalem and rebuild it. He then recounted God's words to the people that summarized their sorry current condition: "I have taught you by My commands and have directed you in how you should live, but you refused to listen. If you would have heeded what I told you, you would have experienced peace beyond measure. Your righteousness would have been constant, like the rolling waves of the sea."

Isaiah sighed. He knew things could have been different, but the Israelites had chosen not to hear God. Now, God would need to get their attention in a more dramatic way …

Footwork

Turn in your Bible to Isaiah 45:22. Who is this verse talking to? What does God say about Himself? What is the first thing God tells us to do in this verse—and for what reason?

Fruit

God's will for us is to be in a right relationship with Him, and He has gone through great lengths to make that possible. In Genesis 22:18 we read how God set apart the Israelites to be a people through whom salvation would come to all the nations of the earth. Although they failed in their task, God remained true to His covenant with them. Through the preserved line of David (the tribe of Judah), God would send a Savior for the world. Isaiah 53 foretold this, and it was fulfilled in the life of Jesus Christ. Jesus Himself, while reading from the scroll of Isaiah in the synagogue, said, "Today this scripture is fulfilled in your hearing" (Luke 4:16–21).

Where is your relationship with God today? He is calling your name and is longing for a close relationship with you. Are you listening?

jeremiah

Jeremiah, the author of this book, was a descendant of the priestly line of Aaron. His hometown, Anathoth, was a little over two miles northeast of Jerusalem and was one of the cities designated by Joshua for the priests. Although he was born into the Levitical priesthood, Jeremiah began serving as God's prophet in 627 BC (during the thirteenth year of King Josiah's reign), when he received the word of the Lord. Sometimes known as "the weeping prophet," Jeremiah's heart was heavy with the warnings God gave him to deliver to the people of Judah. For many years Jeremiah preached God's message to them. It was a message that told of coming judgment—a message they cared little to hear. Overall, Jeremiah's ministry lasted more than forty-one years.

As you read through Jeremiah, you'll quickly see that it isn't arranged in chronological order. Jeremiah had a secretary, Baruch, to whom he dictated his messages. When King Jehoiakim destroyed Jeremiah's scroll, Jeremiah then dictated a more complete version—the one we have today—as God brought things to his mind. Because of the prophet's careful documentation, however, we can easily organize his messages if we know the order of the kings who reigned during his time. Here's the kingly lineup: Josiah (the last righteous king of Judah), Jehoahaz, Jehoiakim, Jehoiachin, and Zedekiah (who was the last of Judah's kings).

As you'll see, God's mission for this prophet was to preach a powerful and unpopular message. What were the results? You'll have to read on to find out. ——

You're Kidding, Right?
Taken from Jeremiah 1 & 16—20

Foundation

Take this time to prepare your heart for today's lesson. Tell God about the difficulties you're facing right now. Ask Him to give you the strength to do what He asks you to do and to learn what He wants you to learn from today's lesson.

Focus

Have you ever had something important to say, but no one took you seriously?

"Before I formed you in your mother's womb, I knew you, Jeremiah. And before your mother gave birth to you, I selected you to be a prophet to deliver My message to the nations."

How God's words seared Jeremiah's heart! What a daunting task God had called him to! Fear motivated Jeremiah to look for excuses.

"But, Lord, I'm just a child; I can't speak!" he protested, hoping that would be a satisfactory enough answer for God.

It wasn't. "Don't tell me you're 'just a child,'" God declared. "You must go and give My message to everyone I send you to. Don't be fearful of who they are or the power they may hold, for I will be with you and will keep you from harm," He promised, adding, "My words have now been placed in your mouth."

a 400—year span of "silence" begins.

Even if Jeremiah wanted to run from the task, he couldn't. God immediately gave him two visions that would be the basis of his messages. One was the branch of an almond tree, representing how God would be closely watching to make sure that His word was fulfilled (the Hebrew words for "watching" and "almond tree" were similar). Jeremiah's messages would be backed up by God's actions.

The second vision was that of a boiling pot tilting from the north to the south, as if its scalding hot contents were about to be poured out. Because God's people had forsaken Him, burned incense to other gods, and worshipped what their hands had made, God would allow invading armies to come from the north and conquer them.

Jeremiah's heart grew sad. He knew God had allowed the Assyrians to swoop down and destroy the northern kingdom of Israel one hundred years earlier for the very same reasons. And now Judah would possibly suffer the same fate at the hands of another enemy.

Because of the seriousness of the message Jeremiah was to proclaim, and the difficulties he would face in delivering it, God instructed him not to marry or even to attend social events. Jeremiah was to focus entirely on the task at hand.

One day the Lord instructed Jeremiah to purchase a clay jar from a potter, gather up the priests and elders, and go to Topheth near the Valley of Ben Hinnom just southwest of the city. Jeremiah cringed, for he knew that Topheth was a high place for child sacrifice and Baal worship. The Valley of Ben Hinnom was Jerusalem's garbage dump where trash was burned.

"Listen to the words of the Lord, all you kings of Judah and people living in Jerusalem," Jeremiah shouted, "Because you have forsaken God and built this high

> *Although Babylon lay to the east of Judah, its invading armies followed the trade routes along the Euphrates River, which brought them down from the north. This happened exactly as God said it would in Jeremiah's vision.*

> *Ben Hinnom, or the Valley of Hinnom, was called Gehenna in the Greek. In the New Testament, it represented the fiery, smoldering decay that characterizes hell.*

place to Baal where you offer sacrifices that are detestable to God, this place will no longer be known as Topheth or the Valley of Hinnom, but rather the Valley of Slaughter!"

Then Jeremiah lifted the clay pot he was holding in his hands and smashed it on the ground as the leaders looked on. "God says that just as this clay pot is smashed, so will Jerusalem be destroyed because its people are stiff-necked and will not listen to Him."

When Jeremiah returned from Topheth, he repeated the same message in the court of the Lord's temple. When one of the priests heard Jeremiah's prophecy, he had Jeremiah beaten with forty lashes and put in stocks for public ridicule. When Jeremiah was released the next day, he refused to change his message. Instead, he told Pashhur the priest that God had changed his name from Pashhur to Magor-Missabib, meaning "terror on every side." Because he refused to listen to Jeremiah's message, the priest would witness the terrible destruction Jeremiah had foretold.

Jeremiah had faced much opposition. While he was proclaiming God's true message of coming doom if Judah didn't repent, other prophets and priests were falsely proclaiming that God wouldn't allow His people to suffer harm. As a result, Jeremiah's unpopular message was rejected. And so was he. But even though Jeremiah suffered ridicule, scorn, and beatings, God held true to His word and protected Jeremiah when Jerusalem fell to the Babylonians.

Footwork

How did God protect Jeremiah? If you're curious, you can read about it in Jeremiah 38—40. But for right now, turn to Jeremiah 1:19. According to this verse, what was God's promise? God would not abandon His prophet, nor would He abandon His people. Now flip ahead to Jeremiah 29:10–14 and read what it says. Look especially at verse 11. What does God say in this verse? Does this encourage you?

Fruit

Jeremiah knew the cost of bringing God's message to his culture. His own people rejected him and ridiculed his message. Yet whenever he felt loneliness, fear, sadness, or insecurity, Jeremiah stayed the course because he loved and trusted God, and as a result, God used him powerfully and effectively. What about you? The world will mock you for taking a stand for God. "You've got to be kidding!" people will say. But God can use you in spite of this, and He isn't kidding. Are you willing?

Lamentations

Some have said that Lamentations is the saddest book ever written. In fact, the name Lamentations comes from the first word in the book: "Alas!" or "How." It was a common word used to express deep, heartfelt emotion, such as grief. Although the author of the book isn't mentioned, many believe that the prophet Jeremiah wrote these laments while grieving over the horrible destruction of Jerusalem in 586 BC. So, for the purposes of *Faith Factor, OT,* we'll assume that Jeremiah is the author.

As Jeremiah looked around at the destruction of the city he loved and the suffering of the people, he didn't have an "I told you so!" attitude; rather, he mourned with compassion and wrote five funeral poems of lament, each beginning with a letter of the Hebrew alphabet. Even though all seemed lost to Jeremiah, out of the dust and rubble of the city rose a ray of hope …

This Is Unbelievable
Taken from Lamentations 1—3

Foundation

Take time to pray right now. Don't rush through this part, but really talk to God. Tell Him what's on your mind, and let Him tell you what's on His.

FOCUS

Have you ever wondered how God, who is supposed to be loving, could allow evil things to happen?

"How empty is this city that used to be overflowing with people!" Jeremiah began, using the first letter of the alphabet to begin his sad funeral poem. It was true. All the roads and gates leading into the city were deserted. People who used to come for the appointed feasts and celebrations at the temple had either been killed or taken into captivity. "The splendor of Judah is now gone, and there is no comfort. When Jerusalem fell into enemy hands, there was no one there to help her. The enemy has triumphed!"

Jeremiah then went on to lament how the invading army of Babylonians had stormed the holy temple—a place God had prohibited foreigners from entering. Not only had foreigners entered the temple, they had also looted and burned it. It felt like the final straw, as if God had finally given up on His people.

"The Lord has acted like an enemy by swallowing Israel up," Jeremiah agonized. "He has destroyed His place of dwelling like a farmer who tears down his temporary shelter when he's finished harvesting his field."

As Jeremiah looked around him, his heart cried out in despair. Because there had been a long siege before the Babylonians finally overtook Jerusalem, the food supply was almost nonexistent. Young and old were both affected. The bodies of weak and dying people littered the ground, and children cried out in the streets from starvation. "The old and the young lie like rubble in the dusty streets. Both the young men and maidens have been slain by You, Lord. In anger You killed them without pity."

Jeremiah felt broken in body and spirit. In anguish, he wrote, "I have no peace. I have forgotten what Your favor is like! Everything I had counted on You for is gone. I am full of despair."

Jeremiah could write no more. Tears filled his eyes and finally spilled onto the parchment.

> *The Hebrew word for God's lovingkindness used in Lamentations 3:22 is hesed (pronounced heh-said), which means "covenant love, or loyal love." No matter how things may look, God never abandons those who are His!*

Footwork

It would be truly sad if Lamentations left off here, but it doesn't. Open your Bible and turn to Lamentations 3:19–23. It's a wonderful turning point. What do these verses say? Many people all through the ages have been comforted by Jeremiah's words. Now skip ahead and read verses 31-33; then look at verses 39-40. These verses are the key to what Jeremiah finally came to see as he poured out his heart before God. And they help us understand why he could go from weeping over God's judgment to a confident trust in Him.

Fruit

Jeremiah was able to be real with God about everything he was experiencing. He didn't sugarcoat the situation he wrote about, nor did he deny or try hiding his feelings from God. Because of that, God answered the deep questions of his heart with the calm assurance of His loyal love.

When is the last time you were real with God? Do you have such an open and honest relationship with Him that you can take your arguments to Him and express your disappointments without fear of offending Him? Just as Jeremiah didn't try to pull himself up by his own bootstraps and fix his emotions, you don't need to either. God will take you just as you are. And He's able to handle what you're feeling.

On a small piece of paper or index card write "The Lord is my portion; therefore I will wait for [Him]. The Lord is good to those whose hope is in [Him], to the one who seeks [Him]; it is good to wait quietly for the salvation of the Lord" (Lam. 3:24–26). Carry these verses around with you this week, and memorize them if you can. The next time you're faced with something "unbelievable" that has you feeling discouraged or in despair, tell God about it and wait quietly for Him.

Ezekiel

Faith facts

Ezekiel's name means "strengthened by God" or "God strengthens," and that's exactly the message Ezekiel gives in this book. The words "They will know that I am the Lord," and "This is what the Sovereign Lord says," appear frequently throughout the book as Ezekiel tries to center the thoughts of the Israelite captives who had been carted off to Babylon. Instead of focusing on being delivered and returning to the land of Judah, they needed to focus their hearts on returning to God. But it isn't until they hear that Jerusalem has finally fallen that they begin listening to what Ezekiel has to say.

To better understand the setting of this book, you'll need to know a little background information. When Nebuchadnezzar, king of Babylon, invaded the southern kingdom of Judah (the Israelites), he didn't attack Jerusalem in one fell swoop. Rather, Jerusalem's destruction came in three different stages. The first stage was in 605 BC when Jehoiakim was king of Judah. This defeat resulted in the exile of such key figures as Daniel and his friends to Babylon. Then, nearly eight years later, when King Jehoiakim and then King Jehoiachin rebelled against Babylon's rule, King Nebuchadnezzar forced the Israelites to submit a second time. This time he took ten thousand Israelites as captives to Babylon, including King Jehoiachin and the prophet Ezekiel. Then in 586 BC, King Nebuchadnezzar invaded a third time, totally destroying Jerusalem after a long siege.

While in exile in Babylon, Ezekiel writes this book to encourage and challenge those exiled with him. Let's see what he has to say. ———

I Do

Taken from Ezekiel 16 and 36

Foundation

Take time to pray before you dig into today's lesson. Ask God to give you a teachable heart, and thank Him for His faithful love.

Have you ever loved someone who didn't return your love?

"This is what the Sovereign Lord says to Jerusalem …" (Ezekiel 16:3) Ezekiel began, delivering yet another message to the stiff-necked people of Judah. Judgment was coming, for they had chosen to turn their backs on the living God, acting as if they had no need of Him. Instead, they had given their love, trust, and worship to foreign gods and pagan idols that had no power or ability to love them back. Not only that, they had gone as far as trying to appease these angry gods by offering their own children as human sacrifices. Perhaps then the false gods would know of their sincerity and not be angry with them anymore. Perhaps the gods would grant them a good growing season for their crops and would protect them from their enemies, they mistakenly thought.

All of this grieved God's heart. The very people He had adopted as His own—a nation He had created with a special purpose in mind—had no clue how far off track they had gotten. So to turn their hearts back to Him, God judged the nation of Judah, sending them into captivity in Babylon. God also gave Ezekiel a powerful word picture for the people—the picture of a husband and an unfaithful wife. Although it talked about Jerusalem's beginnings, it would soon be clear that God was really speaking about them.

"You, O Jerusalem, were born in the land of the Canaanites," Ezekiel began. It was true. Before King David conquered Jerusalem, their beloved city had been a Canaanite town belonging to the descendants of Noah's son Ham. Just as Ham had chosen to act foolishly and disobey God's laws, so did the Canaanites. They were steeped in the worship of false gods and wicked living.

"But this is what God has to say to you: 'When you were born, no one cared enough to wash you, rub salt over your skin to dry and toughen it, or wrap you in warm blankets. Because you were despised at birth, you were thrown into the field and left to die, but seeing you there, helplessly kicking about and near death, I rescued you, and gave you new life. You grew like a wildflower and became a beautiful jewel. When you became old enough for love, I spread the corner of My garment over you and entered into a solemn covenant with you, taking you as My own. I clothed you in the finest of linens and most expensive garments. I adorned you in gold and silver jewelry—bracelets, earrings, and necklaces—and placed a royal crown upon your head. You rose to be queen and the beauty of your splendor, splendor I had given you, became known among all the nations.'"

Exekiel stopped to consider God's choosing of them and all that had taken place in the history of the Israelites. He then continued on with God's direct message to them.

Canaan, one of Ham's sons and the son Noah cursed in Genesis 9:25, became the father of the Hittites, the Jebusites, and the Amorites, among others. The Jebusites lived in Jerusalem at the time King David conquered it.

Spreading the lower part of your garment over another person was a symbolic act of showing protection and entering into a covenant agreement for marriage. A good example of this is in the book of Ruth.

"'But although I lavished all this splendor on you, you turned and trusted in your own beauty, using your fame to seek out other lovers, and inviting them to the marriage bed,' God says. 'You then took the gold jewelry I had adorned you with and melted it down to make idols to please these false lovers, and you clothed those idols in the costly garments I provided for you. You took the fine flour, honey, and olive oil I provided for you to eat and offered it to them as incense. If that wasn't enough, you even went so far as to sacrifice the sons and daughters you bore to Me as food to those idols! While you engaged in all these detestable acts, you ignored all I had done for you and rejected your marriage covenant with Me. Because of your unfaithfulness, I will turn you over to your lovers, and they will become your undoing. But even though you have forgotten your binding covenant with Me, I will remain loyal to you, and one day your beauty and our relationship will be restored.'"

> **God used Ezekiel to tell the Israelites, "If you love Me ..."**
> **L—Listen to My words.**
> **O—Obey what I tell you.**
> **V—Verify your love for Me by the way you live your lives.**
> **E—Enjoy My love.**

Ezekiel once again pondered God's vivid word picture and looked forward to the day God would restore His relationship with His people.

Footwork

In Ezekiel 36:22-25, God said that He would restore the Israelites for the sake of His holy name, which they had "profaned among the nations." As a result, God declared that "the nations will know that I am the Lord" (v. 23). How would God bring about this change? Turn to verses 26-28. What do they say? In verses 26-27 God promised to give His people a new heart and His spirit to live in them. Through faith in Jesus Christ, that promise is true for us today.

Alexander the Great conquers Greece; an

Fruit

People, who are prone to breaking promises, will frequently disappoint you, but God won't. He doesn't love us out of convenience or to benefit Himself. He loves us, period! Through Him, we gain the capacity to truly love others, even if they don't love us back.

Remember this about the difference between God and us: When we say, "I won't!" God still says, "I do!"

Daniel

Faith facts

The book of Daniel is unique. Not only did Daniel write in the customary Hebrew language, but he also wrote in Aramaic, which was the language of the Gentile (non-Jewish) people living in his day. Daniel had a message for God's people—a message that described God's prophetic plan not only for His people Israel but for the Gentile world powers as well. His book is filled with detailed prophecies about future world events and is a key to understanding the book of Revelation in the New Testament. But that's not all Daniel is about. Daniel and his friends serve as powerful examples of following God in less-than-favorable circumstances.

As we explore the book of Daniel, we'll focus on the lives of Daniel and his friends. Through their stories we'll learn how to trust God in difficult situations and take a stand for Him, even if it means risking our lives. We'll also see God's awesome power and His ability to control world events and empires.

So keep reading! You won't want to miss any of the action!

Looks Crystal Clear To Me!

Taken from Daniel 1—3

Foundation

Take a moment and prepare your heart before reading today's lesson. Ask God to show you areas in your life that need changing. Thank Him that He is a God who is deeply interested in your life, not a God who is cold and distant.

Does the way you live your life cause others to want to know God?

Daniel had a good life. He was from a royal family, he was good-looking, and at the age of sixteen, not only was he well educated, but also a promising future leader.

"Find among our captives those of nobility who are handsome, able to learn, and who would be qualified to serve in my palace," King Nebuchadnezzar ordered a chief court official.

When invading a country, the Babylonians often took the educated higher-class people as captives, leaving the poor and uneducated behind to work the land for the king. This kept the king supplied with a fresh crop of promising leaders whom he could retrain and prevented the nations he conquered from organizing and rebelling. Daniel and his friends Hananiah, Mishael, and

Azariah were among the first crop of Israelite captives carted off on the five-hundred-mile journey to Babylon. They would also be among the first young men King Nebuchadnezzar would retrain—or so he thought.

"Here," the chief court official offered, sliding plates heaped with wonderful food and glasses of wine in front of Daniel and his friends.

Already the four young men had been plunged into Nebuchadnezzar's three-year training program in which they were taught mathematics, astronomy, history, science, and magic in an effort to retrain their thinking. The Babylonians had also given them new names in an effort to change the young men's loyalties: Daniel was named Belteshazzar, Hananiah was Shadrach, Mishael was Meshach, and Azariah was Abednego—all Babylonian names honoring the Babylonian gods. Now they were being offered food from the king's own table in an attempt to change their lifestyles. Daniel and his friends knew they couldn't eat what the king provided, for doing so would go against their beliefs about eating food prepared by Gentiles. More important, since the meat had most likely been offered up to idols, Daniel and his friends would defile themselves in God's eyes by eating it.

"Please don't make us eat this food," Daniel urged respectfully, "for we cannot defile ourselves in this manner."

The official considered Daniel's request, and because God had caused him to look at the young men favorably, he agreed to Daniel's alternate plan. For ten days the four men would eat only vegetables and drink only water. Then at the end of that time, if they were as strong as the others who had been eating the king's food, they could continue following their special diet. The official knew that he was risking his life by not following the king's direct orders. But he didn't need to worry. At the end of those ten days, it was clear that Daniel and his friends were much healthier than those who had eaten the king's food. And the strength God gave them far exceeded the strength of the others!

Some time later King Nebuchadnezzar had a dream that greatly disturbed him, and he called in his wise men to interpret its meaning. But they couldn't give him an answer, for they didn't even know what he had dreamed.

"Why don't you tell us what you dreamed about, and then we'll tell you what it means," the astrologers suggested.

But the king grew suspicious. As a test, he ordered them to tell both his dream and what it meant. When they couldn't, the king angrily decreed that all the wise men in Babylon were to be put to death. That included Daniel and his friends! But the king didn't know that God had given Daniel the ability to interpret dreams! So Daniel approached him and asked for time to interpret the dream. He then spent the night in prayer with his friends. In the morning, Daniel had his answer.

"Well?" Nebuchadnezzar demanded. "Can you tell me what I saw in my dream and explain what it means?"

Daniel replied, "There is no wise man on the face of the earth who could explain the mystery you have asked about—but God in heaven is the one who reveals such mysteries!" He then went on to explain the king's dream, which told of things to come.

Hearing the interpretation of his dream, the king bowed before Daniel and exclaimed, "There is no doubt that your God is over all the gods and is the Lord of kings, for He reveals mysteries when no one else can!" He then showered Daniel with gifts and burnt incense to him. He also made Daniel ruler over the entire province of Babylon and placed him in charge of all its wise men. The king gave Daniel's friends positions of honor as well, just as Daniel requested.

But some of the leaders in the kingdom became jealous and plotted to eliminate Daniel and his friends. Knowing that Shadrach, Meshach, and Abednego had refused to obey a royal decree requiring people to bow down and worship a golden image of the king, they brought this news to King Nebuchadnezzar. When the king questioned the three men and gave them another opportunity to bow down to his image, they refused. Furious, the king

> **Check it out! The city of Babylon was in the plain of Shinar. It's the same area where Noah's descendants tried to build the Tower of Babel. You can read about it in Genesis 11 or in the lesson in this book titled "My Way or the Highway!"**
>
> **The Hebrews often diluted their wine with up to ten parts of water in order to keep their law of abstaining from strong drink. The king's wine wasn't diluted.**

ordered them to be thrown into a blazing furnace.

"Who will defend you now?" he demanded.

"The God we serve is more than able to rescue us from your hand, O King," they bravely replied, "but should He choose not to deliver us, know that we refuse to serve your gods or worship the golden image you have made!"

To Daniel and his friends, the choice was crystal clear. They would choose God.

Footwork

God did choose to deliver Daniel's friends in a most remarkable way. Turn in your Bible to Daniel 3:19–30 and read the story. Now look closely at verses 28–30. What happened in King Nebuchadnezzar's heart? According to verse 28, what prompted this change of heart? Don't guess, but read it for yourself!

Fruit

Although Daniel and his friends had been "retrained" by their new culture, they didn't let that change their view of God or their desire to live for Him. In today's world, many people or things will try to "retrain" you and turn your heart away from God. Take a moment and think about what may be turning you away from Him right now. (Could it be friends or goals you have? Or perhaps habits, teachers, or being accepted by others?) Now, make a commitment to keep your focus on God and to live for Him in the culture He has placed you in. That's what Daniel and his friends did, and God helped them. Where is your life right now? Do you blend in so well that others can't see a clear picture of God in your life? Ask Him to help you change that today.

How 'Bout a Hand?
Taken from Daniel 4—6

Foundation

Stop and pray. Tell God about the fears and concerns you have as you hear about world news and threatening events, and ask Him to help you to trust Him during difficult times.

Focus

Do you ever wonder if God is really in control of the things that happen in the world today, including the actions and decisions of world leaders?

It had been thirty years since King Nebuchadnezzar's eyes were first opened to see God's power. Daniel and his friends were now nearly fifty years old! One evening the king had a terrifying dream and once again sought Daniel's help in interpreting it.

"Before me stood an enormously tall tree in the middle of the land," King Nebuchadnezzar said as he wiped the sweat from his brow. "And it could be seen over all the earth. It had beautiful leaves and abundant fruit—enough to feed all! Animals found shelter under it, and every animal ate from its branches."

The king stopped to eye Daniel and then continued. "Then I saw a holy messenger from heaven who said in a loud voice, 'Chop the tree down and remove its branches so that all the birds and animals will run away from it—only let the stump and its roots remain in the grassy field.' "

"seventy") is named after the 72

The king paused to recall the rest of his dream. "The messenger stated, 'He will be covered with dew and will forage for food like a wild beast—his mind will be like that of an animal until seven years pass by for him.' Please, Daniel, explain this to me, for none of the wise men in my kingdom can understand it."

Daniel hesitated, alarmed at the king's dream. Nebuchadnezzar was the tree in the dream. Although he had become powerful and had a vast kingdom, God was going to uproot Nebuchadnezzar unless he turned from his sins. "You will become like the wild animals, driven away from people and eating grass among the cattle," Daniel said. "Only when you acknowledge God's power and rule will your kingdom be restored to you. That is the meaning of the stump left in the field," he added.

God gave Nebuchadnezzar one year, but he didn't humble himself and turn from his sins. In fact, he even praised himself for the great kingdom he thought he had built. So God did as He had warned, and the king was sent away from the people, and lived like a wild animal. His body got soaked with dew and his hair covered him like feathers cover an eagle. His fingernails grew long and began to curl like the claws of a bird.

After seven years Nebuchadnezzar finally raised his eyes toward heaven and acknowledged God's authority. Only then did the king's sanity return. After this, his kingdom was restored, and he became more powerful and successful than before.

"I, Nebuchadnezzar, hereby acknowledge God and give Him glory because His ways are always right and just," the king proclaimed to all.

After several years passed, Nebuchadnezzar's son Belshazzar took the

---

After Belshazzar was killed, Darius came into power, and it was he who threw Daniel into the lions' den—with Daniel being a little over eighty years old at the time! You can read about what happened and God's miraculous rescue in Daniel, chapter 6.

Daniel's life encourages us to trust in God's powerful hand because ...

H—He

A—Alone

N—Never

D—Disappoints!

throne. Although Babylon was under attack by a neighboring country, the king felt little concern and threw a banquet for his nobles.

"These walls are strong, and we have twenty years' worth of food supplies stored up!" he boasted.

Then, in a moment of pride, he ordered that all the gold and silver goblets King Nebuchadnezzar had taken from the temple in Jerusalem be brought out for everyone to drink from. The guests celebrated with great enthusiasm, toasting and praising the Babylonian gods. Suddenly a hush fell over the room as a large, mysterious hand wrote words on the big plaster wall: *Mene, Mene, Tekel, Parsin.* Belshazzar nearly collapsed with fright and offered a large reward to anyone who could interpret the words. He ushered in his wise men, who were unable to understand them. Finally, the king summoned Daniel.

"I heard that you are one of those exiles from Jerusalem who found favor with my father, King Nebuchadnezzar," Belshazzar stated, secretly detesting the God Daniel represented. "If you can tell me what this writing means, I will make you the third-highest ruler in my kingdom."

Daniel replied that he desired no gifts or rewards. Then he proceeded to give the meaning of the mysterious words, first reminding the king of what had happened to King Nebuchadnezzar because of his pride. Then Daniel said, "Even though you knew this, Belshazzar, you chose to praise the gods, who are mere blind statues that are deaf and unable to respond, and didn't honor the one true God who has actual power over your life! Therefore, these words are His judgment to you. They proclaim that you have been weighed on God's scale and found to be lacking. God has brought your kingdom to an end and has given it to the Medes and Persians!"

Before morning had come, King Belshazzar had been killed, and Darius the Mede gained control of the kingdom. Believing that he held his destiny and the success of his kingdom in his own hands, Belshazzar lost it all.

Footwork

Turn in your Bible to Daniel 4:37 and read the statement King Nebuchadnezzar made. What did this powerful and influential king say? Who does God humble? Nebuchadnezzar spoke from personal experience!

Fruit

When you're tempted to fear the unknown or arrogant rulers who threaten you, remember that God isn't taken by surprise. He will eventually judge the arrogant and those who bully others. He can easily strip them of their power—and ultimately will—because He is the one who allowed them to rise to power. He knows when a gentle touch is needed (as in Nebuchadnezzar's case) or when a strong hand is called for (as in Belshazzar's case). Commit your life into God's hands. He will keep you safe! He holds your future (as well as that of all nations) in His hands, and He alone is capable of handling it all.

and inventor, Archimedes discovers th

Hosea

The book of Hosea is the first of twelve books in the Old Testament called the Minor Prophets. (Remember, the Minor Prophets aren't any less important than the Major Prophets; they just contain less material.) As you read through this book, you'll soon discover that Hosea isn't presented in chronological order in the Bible. That's okay. Not many of the prophetic books are. That's why it's important to understand what was going on during the time the prophet lived.

At the start of Hosea's ministry to the northern kingdom of Israel, King Jeroboam II was on the throne. In his long forty-one-year reign, he successfully extended Israel's borders, and the kingdom experienced a great time of prosperity. During this time, however, Israel had not only grown wealthy, but it had also become corrupt. While living in comfort, the Israelites had ignored the needs of the poor and had turned their backs on the Lord. (The prophet Amos, who also ministered during this time, addressed the issue of helping the poor.) Many blended the worship of God with the worship of pagan idols and saw nothing wrong with doing so! Because of the people's rebellion, God would judge them, but first He would try one last time to get their attention by sending them a very personal message to confront their waywardness and assure them of His love. This message would be vividly pictured in Hosea's own personal life. ————

Will You Be Mine?
Taken from Hosea 1—3

Foundation

Allow yourself time to be quiet before God and consider the ways He has faithfully shown His love to you, even when you least deserved it. Take a moment to thank Him for that.

Focus

Have you ever disappointed someone who loves and cares for you?

"Hosea, you are to marry, and the woman you marry will be unfaithful to you the way Israel is unfaithful to Me, who is her 'husband.' But through your marriage, I will deliver a message to My unfaithful 'wife', Israel."

Hosea remained quiet, pondering the words God had spoken to him. Unlike other prophets, Hosea hadn't been trained in the school of prophets; he was a layman—a common everyday person. But in spite of this, God raised him up to deliver a message to the people, and that message was of God's extraordinary love.

The wife I marry will be unfaithful to me, Hosea thought. The pain of that possibility was almost too much to bear. He imagined the pain God felt in choosing Israel as His "bride," only to see her become unfaithful to Him, changing her loyalties and worshipping other gods. "And You, Lord, knew what would happen even before You chose Israel to be Your people!" Hosea whispered in awe.

As God commanded, Hosea married a woman named Gomer, and just as God had said, she proved to be unfaithful to him. When Gomer gave birth to their firstborn son, God instructed Hosea to name the baby *Jezreel.* Although the name meant "God sows," it was more of a picture of God's coming judgment. In the Valley of Jezreel, God would take away Israel's military power, much like breaking the bow of an archer.

When Gomer gave birth to another child, a baby girl, God told Hosea to name her *Lo-Ruhamah,* which meant "not loved." Hosea knew that the word *ruhamah* signified a tender feeling of compassion. It was a word God had used on Mount Sinai to describe His own character—compassionate and willing to forgive. But now God needed to take more drastic measures to turn Israel back to Him, for although He was willing to forgive her, Israel cared little about seeking His forgiveness! So God would turn away from her. *Lo-Ruhamah.* Israel would be "not loved."

"Yet I will still express My loyal love on Judah, and I will rescue them," the Lord informed Hosea. "It will not be by military power or might but by My own hand."

After Gomer gave birth to another son and Hosea named him *Lo-Ammi* ("not my people") according to God's instructions, Gomer abandoned the family. She ran after the false lovers she had chased while living with Hosea—leaving three young children in his care.

I had given her everything, Lord, Hosea cried out. *I gave her security.*

> *Hosea used the term* **Ephraim** *thirty-seven times in his book. It's another name for Israel and is always associated with sin or backsliding.*

> *The word picture of God as Israel's husband was a message He gave through other prophets as well. Check out Jeremiah 3:14 NKJV ("I am married to you …"); Isaiah 62:5 (God rejoices over us "as a bridegroom rejoices over his bride"); and Hosea 2:19 ("I will betroth you to [Me] forever").*

I provided her with clothing and my protection. I gave her all I had—including my good name—and look what she has done!

God knew, for it was the very thing Israel was doing. Hosea was getting a firsthand taste of God's longing love for His people. And this taste was on Hosea's lips as he passionately proclaimed God's message, pleading with the Israelites to come back to the Lord and stop their unfaithfulness.

"If Israel does not turn from her lovers, I will punish her for the way she burned incense to the false gods while decking herself out in jewelry and forsaking Me," God stated. "I will make her life hard so she will say, 'I will return to my husband, for life was easier for me there.' Then I will bring her into the desert and there I will compassionately communicate with her. I will erase the names of the false gods from her mouth, and she will finally acknowledge Me and I will receive her back."

While Hosea was proclaiming that message, he walked by a slave market in the town square. There on the auctioning block was Gomer, his once beautiful bride. Shame was etched across her face, and her sunken eyes reflected a sense of sorrow. In an act of deep love, Hosea purchased her at a great price and brought her back home. In spite of everything she had done—rejecting his love, abandoning her children, and dragging his good name through the mud— he would take her back. This time their relationship would be defined by his terms of faithfulness, not hers. Now broken and spent, she would be restored because of Hosea's faithfulness—much like God in His faithful love would restore Israel once she had been broken.

Footwork

Open your Bible to Hosea 2:19 and read what God said to Israel. What does it say? *Betroth* means "to make a binding covenant in a marriage relationship." This verse shows us God's incredible love, even when His people (which includes you and me!) disappoint Him.

Fruit

Because we're human, we're prone to mess up and disappoint those who love and care for us the most. Sometimes we even disappoint ourselves. Thankfully, God doesn't abandon us in that helpless state. Hosea 14:4 says that He will "heal [our] waywardness and love [us] freely." But this means we must first humble ourselves and acknowledge our wrongdoing.

Have you walked away from God? Do you feel like you've backslidden lately? There's a simple cure:

1. Admit your guilt to God. Tell Him you're helpless and need His healing touch in your heart.

2. Return to God. Earnestly seek to include Him in every part of your day.

3. Press on to know God more fully. Read your Bible, His love letter to you.

God is asking, "Will you be Mine?" And He's waiting for your decision.

Joel

The book of Joel was written by a little-known prophet. We don't know much about Joel except that his father's name was Pethuel. Because Joel frequently mentioned the "house of the Lord," many believe that he didn't live far from Jerusalem. And his statements about the priesthood lead us to believe that he was possibly a priest as well as prophet. Joel's name meant "Yahweh is God," and that was precisely the message God gave him to deliver to the southern kingdom of Judah.

During Joel's time, young King Joash was on the throne. (For a great background on him, read the lesson titled "Excuse Me — Is This Yours?" taken from 2 Chronicles 23—24.) Assyria and Babylon weren't yet threatening powers, but Egypt, Edom, Phoenicia, and Philistia were. Joel, however, didn't address the threats from these surrounding nations. Instead, he addressed a much more immediate and devastating situation facing Judah. ————————————

Forward, *March!*
Taken from Joel 1—2

Foundation

Before you begin your exploration of Joel, ask the Lord to speak to your heart and give you eyes to see and ears to hear what He would have you learn.

Focus

Have you ever done something wrong and wished you could go back and fix it?

The sky turned black. The sickening noise could be heard for miles, and it meant only one thing—a locust plague!

"All you who live in the land, listen to what I have to say!" Joel proclaimed. "Then tell your children and instruct them to one day tell their own children—that it may be faithfully passed down from generation to generation."

The people listened to Joel's words with eager ears, for their land had been devastated. The winged invading army had stripped trees and shrubs bare. Able to jump two hundred times their three-inch length, the locusts scaled walls and even entered into homes, eating any wood they came across. They had already stripped the vineyards bare, so the priests had no grapes to use for their drink offerings. And since the grain in the fields and the olives on the trees had also been devoured, no grain

Joel, one of the earlier prophets of Judah, most likely ministered during the time of Elisha, who prophesied in Israel. See 2 Kings 2—7 for more about Elisha's life.

The Israelites often ate locusts and prepared them in various ways: roasted; boiled; stewed in butter; or ground up, mixed with flour and water, and baked into cakes. In the New Testament, John the Baptist ate locusts (Matt. 3:4; Mark 1:6).

Joel wrote, "Everyone who calls on the name of the Lord will be saved" (2:32). This same promise is found in Acts 2:21 and Romans 10:13 of the New Testament.

offerings could be made in the temple. The formal system of worship in Israel had come to a standstill.

Many looked skyward, but they could only see a thick blanket of insects that choked out the light of the sun and cast a deep, foreboding shadow over the barren land. Wave upon wave of locusts came. As they stripped the crops and pastures down to the dusty soil, cattle and sheep began to starve. Great despair filled the land, and it only grew worse as a drought dried up the riverbeds and shriveled the seeds that had been planted for future harvest. All hope seemed gone.

In the midst of this disaster, Joel exclaimed, "O priests, put on garments of sackcloth and mourn. Call a holy fast and gather everyone for a sacred assembly at the house of the Lord your God, and cry out to Him. For the day of the Lord is not far off and will come with destruction!" Joel knew that the locust plague was a warning from God, a way of turning His people back to seeking Him. God had used a plague of locusts in Egypt while the Israelites were still slaves. And Moses had given a final charge to the Israelites just before they entered into Canaan—the Promised Land: If they obeyed God, kept His commands, and didn't turn to false gods, they would experience the Lord's blessing. But if they disobeyed, He would send judgment to turn their hearts back to Him. One of the judgments Moses mentioned was a plague of locusts!

Since locusts only went where the wind carried them, the Israelites in Joel's time understood that the Lord had sent this plague as a warning that would not only apply to them now but would also be a picture of things to come.

Joel urged the people, "Seek the Lord your God with sincerity. Rather than tearing your garments, allow your heart to be torn in repentance before Him. You will find Him to be full of grace and compassion, for He is slow to anger and overflowing with love. He does not delight in sending calamity."

The people heard and understood where they had gone wrong. For Joel's words describing how God abounds in love (His loyal love) were the same words of comfort God had spoken to the Israelites generations ago right before He renewed His covenant with them—just after punishing them for worshipping the golden calf.

Joel continued, explaining how God would restore what was lost during the locust plague due to their sin and God's need to discipline His people. Even though the land would normally take years to recover from such a devastating plague, God would help His people. He would bring the rains and would cause the vats to be filled to overflowing with new wine and oil.

"I will restore to you the years the locusts have devoured," God assured the people. "There will be an abundance of food and everyone will see that the Lord your God has worked miracles for you."

Although God's people had turned away from Him to worship idols, once they repented and restored their relationship with Him, He was there to meet them in their need and lead them into the future. They would simply go forward from there.

Footwork

Turn in your Bible to Joel 2:24–28. What did God promise in verses 24–25? According to verses 26–27, what would be the results? Judah would no longer wallow in the consequences of her sin, but rather, God would intervene and restore her. Now look at verse 28. This is a prophecy of things to come—things that began in the New Testament. Through God's Spirit, who lives inside us by faith, we have all the power we need to live a life that pleases Him.

Fruit

We can't turn back time, but we can learn from our mistakes. In our lives we may have regrets about the things we've done or haven't done. God knows that, and as our hearts soften by experiencing the consequences of our bad choices, He is there with His faithful love to carry us forward. When we return to Him, He will restore and renew what we've lost.

Amos

The prophet Amos was a herdsman and a grower of figs. Not only did he herd sheep, but he also bred them and was known for the fine quality of wool he produced. Although Amos was from Tekoa, a rural area in Judah about twelve miles south of Jerusalem, God raised him up to deliver a message to the northern kingdom of Israel.

During the life of Amos, both kingdoms were doing well, and the Israelites prospered. As Jeroboam II (king over the northern kingdom of Israel) conquered territory to the north, he gained control over the trade routes and his kingdom's wealth began to increase. And with the increased wealth came an upper class of people who built expensive homes and lived lavishly. They had little concern for the poor and took advantage of those who worked for them as slaves to pay off their debts.

Amos ministered after the prophets Obadiah, Joel, and Jonah, but just before (and during part of) the ministries of the prophets Hosea, Micah, and Isaiah. While Hosea prophesied against Israel's idolatry, Amos concentrated on the social ills of the nation. His warning from God began with God's judgment on surrounding nations for their evil behavior. Then the noose began to tighten, and suddenly Israel was in the spotlight—and on the hot seat. Would Israel pay attention to Amos's message? Read on to find out!

That's Easier Said Than Done
Taken from Amos 1—7

Foundation

Take a moment to pray before you begin today's lesson. Ask God to give you a heart that sees things from His perspective.

Do you find it easy to overlook the needs of others?

"This is what the Lord says," Amos proclaimed. He eyed the people as he began his message. Would they even listen?

"Because Damascus has sinned relentlessly, I will not hold back on My wrath," Amos began, relaying God's message.

Damascus was the capital city of Aram, one of Israel's neighboring enemies. The Aramean armies were brutal in conquering lands. Like a threshing sledge, which was used to cut and separate the grain from its husks, so Arameans crushed everyone in their path, often torturing people who stood in their way.

"Because Gaza has sinned relentlessly, I will not back off or turn My wrath away," Amos continued, now listing the crimes of the neighboring country Philistia. The last straw in God's eyes was when the Philistines captured entire communities and sold them in a slave market to make money. People were auctioned off and then shipped to other parts of the world as if they were objects, not human beings. As Amos described God's judgment on these nations, Israel paid little heed, for Aram and Philistia were bitter enemies of Israel. They deserved God's judgment.

But then, Amos's message hit a bit closer to home with a judgment against Tyre.

Tyre, a leading city in Philistia, had at times been Israel's ally in battles. Then came God's judgment against the nation of Edom for its unnatural hatred toward Israel. (Edom was a descendant of Esau.) Next in line were the Ammonites, who had brutally killed women and their unborn babies when conquering lands, all for the sake of extending their borders. God would judge the Ammonites for their heartlessness. Last to be judged was not another Gentile nation but rather the nation of Israel, for the Israelites were no better than the people surrounding them—and in some respects they were worse!

"Listen to what the Lord holds against you, O people of Israel!" Amos proclaimed.

Amos then listed each and every one of Israel's wayward actions. The Israelites were guilty of everything from selling people into slavery to having creditors team up with court officials and unfairly rule against the poor. And if that wasn't bad enough, the Israelites took wine unjustly from the poor as fines and offered it up to false gods. They even combined their worship of God with the worship of idols. In all their actions, they not only ignored their covenant with the Lord, but they also had little concern for those the Lord created. They outwardly kept the ceremonial feasts and offerings to God, but what they offered wasn't pleasing to Him.

> *Plumb lines were used to measure how straight a wall was to judge whether it needed to be torn down. A plumb line consisted of a string with a weight at the end and when held in the air and left to hang down, would always give a true straight line.*

"I sent you hunger and famine," the Lord said, "yet you did not return to Me. I sent you a drought, but you did not return to Me. I even sent blight and mildew, but you still refused to return. After that, I sent locusts and other plagues," God added, "but again, you would not return!"

The next two judgments God would send to get their attention would be military defeat and, finally, devastation. These were the final measures Amos preached and warned Israel about. But the people weren't inclined to listen.

"The Lord showed me a vision," he proclaimed, explaining the vision of a plumb line that God had given him.

Israel was like a crooked wall that couldn't be fixed and needed to be torn down. Neither Israel's religious practices nor its political system measured up to God's standards, and Israel had run out of time. Like an old, condemned building, the northern kingdom would be demolished.

Footwork

Turn in your Bible to Amos 5:4. What does God say? Notice that He is giving the people a command, not a suggestion. Now skip down and read verse 14. What would the results be if the people decided to "seek good, not evil"? [*Hint:* In the NIV, the answer comes after the word *then.*] The Israelites had mistakenly thought God had been with them all along, even when they weren't living for Him. But their words (what they proclaimed to others) and their lives (how they actually lived) didn't match up. They were living by a double standard.

Fruit

Do you say (or think) "God is with me" when He really isn't? Many speak about living for God, but few actually back up their words with action. They find comfort in their religious activities and lifestyles but never lift a finger to care for the needy. All their religious talk and activity is empty, for their hearts are focused only on themselves.

If you truly love God, you'll be concerned about the things that concern Him. In the next few days, try giving up something that you feel you deserve or that you cherish, and give it to someone in need. It may be something as small as offering your seat to someone on a crowded bus. Whatever it is, big or small, people will see your actions and glorify God, knowing that what you did was much easier said (talked about doing) than done (actually doing it).

Obadiah

With only twenty-one verses, the book of Obadiah is the shortest book in the Old Testament. Obadiah was a fairly common name that meant "worshipper of Yahweh." It was such a common name, in fact, that there are thirteen Obadiahs mentioned in the Old Testament! We know nothing about the Obadiah who wrote this book, though some scholars believe that he may have lived in Judah.

The book of Obadiah is perhaps not as well known as other books in the Old Testament, nor was it ever quoted in the New Testament, but God has it included in our Bible for a reason. Its strong message of God's judgment against the nation of Edom (the descendants of Esau), who relentlessly and viciously attacked God's people, as well as its message of hope and encouragement to Israel, apply to all of us living today.

And That Takes Care of *That!*

Taken from Obadiah 1—21

Foundation

Take a few minutes to prepare your heart before beginning today's lesson. Ask God to show you areas in your life where you might be allowing pride to rule your heart.

Focus

Have you ever held a grudge against someone, or has someone ever held a grudge against you?

Obadiah knew the root cause of the hatred between the nation of Edom and the Israelites. It began hundreds of years earlier ...

"Jacob, I'm starving to death! Give me some of that lentil soup you made!" Esau demanded. He was a ruddy outdoorsman and had been out in the fields hunting all day. He was also the firstborn and Isaac's favorite son.

"No," came the measured reply from Jacob. As the younger twin, he enjoyed anything and everything that wasn't hunting and was clearly his mother's favorite. He also valued his godly inheritance and knew his brother didn't. So Jacob devised a plan.

"I'll give you some lentil soup in exchange for your birthright," he offered.

Hungry, and caring only for something that would immediately satisfy him, rather than things of lasting value, Esau agreed. "No problem! Of what value is a dumb birthright anyway?"

Later, Jacob would also trick their father in order to gain the blessing usually given to the firstborn son. When Esau discovered what his brother had done, he flew into a rage and sought to kill Jacob. Fearing for her son's life, Rebekah persuaded Isaac to send Jacob to live with distant relatives so that he could find himself a godly wife. That would take care of things—at least for the time being.

Esau (also called Edom) had married Canaanite women, disobeying God's command not to intermarry with foreigners. Eventually he moved far away to the southeast mountain country of Seir and settled there. Esau had little regard for the things of God, a characteristic that would be seen not only in his life but also in the lives of his descendants, the Edomites.

Although generations had passed since the incident between Jacob and Esau, a smoldering hatred between the Israelites (Jacob's descendants) and the Edomites had continued. In fact, it was the Edomites who refused to allow the Israelites to travel through their land as Israel headed toward the Promised Land. It was also the Edomites who later raided Israel and retreated to the safety of the cliffs they lived in. They had even

Edom *means "red" and refers not only to Esau's red hair and the red lentil soup he desired, but it also refers to the red cliffs in which he dwelt.*

The capital city of Edom was Petra, which means "rock." It was located in the red sandstone mountains southeast of the Dead Sea. Edom is part of the Arab nations today.

Herod the Great, King of Judea and a key figure in the New Testament, was a descendant of Esau. In an attempt to kill Jesus after He was born, Herod ordered the killing of all Israelite baby boys. See Faith Factor, NT for more details—or read about it in Matthew 2.

only one day's worth of oil.

encouraged and aided other nations in attacking their kin! For this God would judge them.

"Listen to what the Sovereign Lord has to say about you, Edom," Obadiah pronounced, reminding the Edomites of God's sovereign rule over the nations and His covenant with Israel.

Obadiah's message was one of judgment and doom for Edom. "You will be made small among all the nations and despised. You take pride in your secure dwelling places in the cliffs and think you are invincible, but God will bring you down! You cannot hide from His judgment," Obadiah challenged.

The only way into the capital city of Edom was through a one-mile-long, narrow ravine with cliff walls rising hundreds of feet on either side. The Edomites had built fortresses on those cliffs, making it nearly impossible for any enemy to attack. Because of this, the Edomites were arrogant and self-confident. They took pride not only in their fortress-city but also in their wealth (the treasures they had gained from raiding other nations and retreating back to the safety of their cliffs), their intelligence, and their military strength. They answered to no one—or at least that's what they thought.

"Your hidden treasures will be pillaged, your wise men will be destroyed, and your warriors will be terrified," Obadiah declared. "The very things you did to Israel, I will allow to happen to you! Because of your shameful acts and the violence you showed against your brother Jacob (the Israelites), you will be destroyed forever."

Footwork

Open your Bible to Obadiah. (This book is so small, it may be hard to find. But don't give up! Use the table of contents in the front of your Bible to help you find it. It's just before the book of Jonah.) When you find it, look at verse 12. What does it say? Now skip down to verse 15. What does this verse tell you about God?

Fruit

The Edomites held a grudge against the Israelites, and this motivated them to do wicked things. Driven by pride, bitterness, and anger, they sought to harm the people they hated. God warns us against holding grudges, for it's fueled by pride and pride is something God has little tolerance for. Why? Because God knows that pride destroys people.

This week, when you're tempted to be angry and hold a grudge against someone—don't. Instead, ask God to help you forgive that person. Although you may be able to get over the offense, others who are affected by your hatred may not be able to. Just look at the Edomites. Although Jacob and Esau made up (see Gen. 33), their descendants refused to give up the fight. Instead of holding a grudge, ask God to hold your heart. Tell Him all about your grievances. Ask Him to help you forgive, and trust Him to change the other person (and you). God will take care of the rest!

jonah

Faith facts

Some people will try to tell you that the book of Jonah is just a made-up "fish story." Don't believe them! Jonah is a historical book about a real person. In 2 Kings 14:25, we learn that Jonah lived during the reign of King Jeroboam II. Real cities, such as Nineveh, Tarshish (modern-day Spain), and Joppa are also mentioned in his book. Even Jesus called Jonah a prophet and referred to his ministry.

Perhaps the biggest struggle people have is the idea of someone being swallowed by a gigantic fish and surviving. Actually, sperm whales have been known to swallow large objects, including a fifteen-foot shark. For Jonah to have experienced this isn't as far-fetched as some think.

Jonah, who lived in the northern kingdom of Israel near the lake of Galilee, was probably one of the "company of prophets" trained by Elisha near the end of his ministry (see 2 Kings 6:1–2). Jonah was a well-liked prophet in Israel. His messages were positive, and people enjoyed hearing prophecies about the nation's expansion and prosperity. God, however, planned to send him on another mission to deliver a message of judgment to Israel's most feared enemy …

Who Cares
Taken from Jonah 1—4

Foundation

Before you read about Jonah today, ask God to speak to your heart.
Thank Him for His loyal love, and ask Him to give you a greater
compassion for others and to see people from His perspective.

Focus

*Have you had an "I don't care!" attitude toward someone or
something?*

"You're sending me to the *Assyrians?*" Jonah challenged. Surely God
was mistaken. The Assyrians were brutal people. They prided
themselves in torturing their enemies, and often they either burned
them to a crisp, cut off their heads, or both. It wasn't uncommon for an
Assyrian king to heap a pile of heads outside the city gate as a trophy
of his conquests.

*And You want me to bring them a message of judgment so they will
repent of their evil deeds?* Jonah half prayed, half argued with God.

The Assyrians were bitter enemies of Israel, and Jonah knew the
prophecies of Hosea and Amos concerning Israel's destruction at the
hands of the Assyrians.

*I'll have no part in helping an enemy that will later destroy my
nation!* he determined.

So instead of obeying God and going northeast to Assyria, Jonah

and Confucius's philosophical

boarded a ship traveling west to Tarshish (Spain). The journey to Assyria would have been a long and inconvenient five-hundred-mile trek over land. The journey to Tarshish by ship was easy and fast, and conveniently went in the opposite direction. Jonah settled back for what he thought was going to be a relaxing ride. He was wrong.

"You! Wake up!" the captain of the ship shouted, trying to be heard over the thunderous crash of the waves and the roar of the wind. He jostled Jonah until he finally stirred. "Everyone is praying to their gods except you. Pray to your god, whoever it may be, for my ship is about to break apart and sink in this storm!"

While Jonah had slept, unconcerned, the experienced Phoenician seamen had pitched much of the ship's cargo overboard. Believing the tragic storm was a result of divine judgment against someone onboard who had done wrong, the sailors drew lots to see who it might be. All signs pointed to Jonah.

Jonah confessed his wrongdoing. "I tried to run away from the one true God, who has power over all nature, and He sent this storm." Then he told the sailors, "Throw me overboard!"

At first the sailors refused to do as Jonah suggested and rowed harder to get back to shore. But when the waves got even worse, they pitched Jonah overboard, and the storm instantly stopped. Just as quickly, a large fish came up out of the water, swallowed Jonah, and carried him away.

While in the stomach of the giant fish, Jonah had time to think—and repent. God had a job for Jonah to do, and He was serious about it. He wanted His message preached to even the vilest of people—

> *Nineveh was five hundred miles northeast of Israel. Tarshish (on the southern tip of Spain) was nearly two thousand miles west of Israel—nearly four times farther away!*
>
> *Before Jonah arrived in the city, Nineveh had experienced two famines (765 and 759 BC) and a total solar eclipse (June 15, 763 BC). Events like these were often considered signs of divine anger, possibly making the Assyrians more than ready to receive Jonah's message.*

people He apparently cared for. When Jonah finally understood that, the Lord commanded the fish to vomit Jonah onto dry ground.

Again, the Lord told Jonah, "You are to go to Nineveh and tell the people what I say to you." This time Jonah obeyed!

"In forty days, God will destroy this city!" Jonah announced on his first day in Nineveh. To his surprise, the wicked people responded to his warning. They turned from their sins and sought God's forgiveness through prayer and fasting—and God granted it.

When Jonah preached in Nineveh, his skin would most likely have been bleached from the stomach acids of the fish he had been in. This would only add to the power of his message of doom!

"See, Lord, this is exactly why I didn't want to warn these people, for I knew that You are a compassionate God and would forgive them!" Jonah complained. He would much rather have seen God rain down His judgment on the Ninevites, but instead, He poured out His love.

With that, Jonah climbed to the top of a nearby hill and waited for God to destroy the city. But He never did—at least not until the prophet Nahum's time!

Footwork

Turn in your Bible to Jonah 3:10 and take a close look at what this verse says. What did God feel toward the Assyrians? Why? Now read 4:1–2. What five things did Jonah say about what God is like?

Fruit

Jonah didn't want to go to Nineveh, for he knew that if they repented, God wouldn't carry out what Jonah said would happen. Selfishly speaking, that could look very bad for him as a prophet! Also, Jonah simply didn't care about the Ninevites—but God did. From the very beginning, God had a unique purpose for the Jewish nation. They were to share God's message with other nations and be a blessing to the world. Unfortunately, they forgot that calling and disobeyed God, even worshipping the false gods of the nations they were to reach for God.

Often, we think of the Old Testament as a book that only talks about God's harsh judgment, and we wrongly conclude that His concern for the non-Jewish (Gentile) nations doesn't show up until the New Testament. But that isn't true, and the book of Jonah is a perfect example. God cares for all those He has created.

This week, pray for one person you know who needs God's message of love and compassion. Perhaps this person is running from God, hasn't heard about Him yet, or isn't interested. Ask God how you can be a part of reaching that person.

Who cares? God does—and so should you!

Micah

Faith facts

Micah came from a small village about twenty-five miles southwest of Jerusalem and prophesied during the reigns of three kings of Judah—Jotham, Ahaz, and Hezekiah. King Jotham was a fairly good king, although he failed to remove all the high places of idol worship in the land of Judah. King Ahaz was a wicked king who ignored the prophet Isaiah's advice to trust God and made copies of foreign gods for all the people in Jerusalem to worship. King Hezekiah was a very good king who tried to turn the people's hearts back toward God by calling for national repentance.

The prophets Micah and Isaiah prophesied during the same period in Israel's history, and God sometimes gave them the same message: Judgment for Israel and Judah is coming, but in the future, God will send a Deliverer, one who will rescue and redeem sinful man. ————

Now It's *My* Turn
Taken from Micah 3—7

Foundation

Stop and pray. Ask God to speak to your heart as you venture into today's lesson. Ask Him to change what needs to be changed in your life.

Focus

Does it ever frustrate you to be under someone who isn't a good leader?

Helpless. That's what they were—utterly helpless. Micah knew the conditions of the people's hearts in both Israel and Judah. He had watched the people stray from their love of God and follow false ideas that only led to dead ends. He had watched the leaders—who were unconcerned about the injustice, poverty, and abuse around them—take advantage of the people. The leaders weren't just part of the problem; they were the cause of much of it!

"Woe to you who decide to do wrong and carry out your plans!" Micah began. "You try to take another person's land and house for yourself. You take what isn't yours, desiring to increase your own power and position. In doing so, you break the covenant God made with your ancestors before bringing them into this land."

Micah had no doubts the people would understand what he was referring to. Their ancestors had come from being slaves in Egypt before the Lord freed them. Because of this, they were never to enslave one another. Nor were they to take land that belonged to another tribe or family. When God brought them into Canaan (the Promised Land), He gave them land to divide among their families. That was to be their "portion," or inheritance. But the rich were now seeking to take other people's land from them. They even enslaved the poor who couldn't pay off their debts. This broke part of God's covenant with them on how they were to live.

"Because of your actions and disregard for how God wants you to live, the very thing you have done to others by enslaving them and taking their land will be done to you!" Micah warned.

Not all the problems in Judah were caused by the rich abusing the poor. All the people—rich and poor—were guilty of disobeying God and living wicked lives. The condition of their hearts was wrong, resulting in a hopeless, wicked bent away from God. Much like a waterfall, this wicked bent started with the leaders, where it flourished, and trickled down to everyone else. Everyone was guilty. But for now, Micah would turn his attention to the leadership.

In Deuteronomy 16:19, God commanded against using bribery to influence others. The leaders in Jerusalem ignored this command.

In Micah 5:2, Micah predicted the birth of Jesus, which was fulfilled more than seven hundred years later! Many other prophets also foretold Jesus' birth and life, and all of these prophecies were fulfilled as well.

"Listen to me you who lead these people," he declared, "You know that you should love good and hate evil, but you are doing just the opposite! You love evil and hate good! And you prophets—you false prophets!—you tell the people what they want to hear if they give you enough money or food. You have no regard for the truth. When God's judgment comes and the people ask why, you will get no answer from God. You will be ashamed when people find out that you aren't true prophets after all," Micah warned.

"O leaders of Jerusalem, you do not love justice; you love only what brings benefit to you. As a result, you judges of the court take bribes and unjustly rule in favor of whoever pays you the most money! You priests teach about God for a fee, and you prophets raise money by telling fortunes. This should not be! God requires you to be just and equitable, but instead you are only out for money. You then take the money you get and toss some in God's direction for an offering as if nothing is wrong. Something is wrong! It's the condition of your hearts!" Micah challenged. "Your bad example has spread to others who are following you, and because of hardened hearts and wickedness, Judah will be disciplined by God."

Micah paused a moment and reflected on the situation. Then he prophesied about a time in the future when God would provide a remedy for the people's wickedness.

"Lord, ho can compare to You? No one else can forgive sins and fix the hearts of people," Micah noted with hope. "You will once again shower us with Your compassion, and will remove our sins far from Your presence."

Micah trusted that even though the kingdom of Judah would be judged, God wouldn't crush it. One day from its seed (from the royal line of Judah) would come a Savior who would change the course of history and mankind's hearts.

"Out of Bethlehem will come one who will be Ruler over the nation of Israel, one who has been around since before the creation of time. He will be like a shepherd over His flock, giving security to all who are His. His greatness will be known all across the world, and true peace with God will be found through Him alone."

Footwork

Open your Bible to Micah 6:8 and read it. According to this verse, what three things does God require of us? Each of these was in the covenant God made with Moses and Israel before bringing the people into the Promised Land. And it's summarized in Deuteronomy 30:15–16.

Fruit

God took the lead and paved the way for us—showing not only how to live in relationship with Him but also providing the means of making that happen! That means is through Jesus, and you can find out more about God's wonderful provision in a special message in the back of this book. When Jesus comes back to earth, everything will be restored to His original plan, but that hasn't happened yet. So what are we to do in the meantime? How are we to live now? Micah 6:8 answers those questions. Walking humbly with God is being in a relationship with Him on His terms. Loving justice and having mercy are all results of living a life that's in line with God. Judah failed at this because both the leaders and the people lost sight of Him.

Write Micah 6:8 on an index card and memorize it this week. On the back of the index card list the three actions across the top: "Act justly" (do what's right in my dealings with others), "Love mercy" (look out for the needs of others), and "Walk humbly with God" (walk in humble fellowship with God). Then underneath each point, list three practical things you can do this week to begin living that way.

By sending Jesus, God paved the way for you to have a relationship with Him. Now it's your turn to take action and seek to live for Him. (Don't worry, if you know Jesus, you have the Holy Spirit to help you live a life that pleases God. Your job is to follow.

Nahum

Faith facts

Although we aren't exactly sure where this prophet was born, it's interesting to know that the city named Capernaum literally means "village of Nahum." One hundred years after the prophet Jonah addressed the great city of Nineveh, Nahum did too—but with a different message.

In His mercy, God had given the Ninevites four opportunities to turn from their evil ways and acknowledge Him. The first opportunity came under Jonah, and the Ninevites repented—at least temporarily (see Jonah 3:6–10). The second opportunity came when Assyrian king Tiglath-Pileser took some of the Israelites into captivity (see 2 Kings 15:29). The descendants of the Ninevites who repented under Jonah would have heard about the Lord through the captives. Unfortunately, they chose to either forget or ignore God's warning. Then, King Shalmaneser deported all the Israelites from the northern kingdom to Assyria. The Ninevites would surely have heard about God from some of these exiles (see 2 Kings 17:23–28)! Finally, the last opportunity for the Ninevites to repent came when the Assyrian king Sennacherib fought against Judah. After blaspheming the Lord God, his army suffered judgment, and his own sons killed him in a heathen temple on his return to Assyria (see 2 Kings 19:37).

Now, Assyrian king Ashurbanipal was on the throne (669–633 BC), and the prophet Nahum was sent with a message: Having been given many opportunities to turn and acknowledge God, judgment was now coming for Nineveh.

As you explore this book, don't fool yourself into thinking it's only a doom-and-gloom judgment message. It's so much more than that! In the book of Nahum we see a wonderful aspect of God's nature. Read on to discover what that might be!

352

Believe It ... or Not
Taken from Nahum 1—3

Foundation

Take a moment to prepare your heart before reading any further.
Ask God to help you see Him for who He is, and thank Him that
He is faithful and true to His Word.

FOCUS

Have you ever been warned about something but didn't
believe it would actually happen?

Nahum reflected on the city of Nineveh. It seemed almost impenetrable. Its
100-foot-high walls were so thick and wide, three chariots could ride on
them side by side. If that wasn't enough, a moat 150 feet wide and 60 feet
deep surrounded the enormous walls. Hundreds of guard towers were
positioned all along the walls, making it nearly impossible for Nineveh to
fall to an enemy attack. Clearly, Assyria was one of the most powerful
nations in the world, and Nineveh was one of its greatest cities.

Naham now directed his thoughts towards God's character, proclaiming,
"Though the Lord is powerful and slow to get angry, there is no way He
won't punish the guilty."

He was clearly aware that God's anger against Nineveh wasn't new.
Nearly one hundred years earlier, God had warned Nineveh about its
wicked and violent practices. He had even sent his prophet Jonah with a
warning of coming judgment if the Ninevites refused to repent. But the

people in the city did repent and humbled themselves before God. Unfortunately, their repentance was short-lived. As Assyria gained power as a nation, it also increased in arrogance. Soon the people had forgotten about God altogether and had gone back to living in brutal violence, terrorizing nations around them and torturing those they captured. (See the lesson in Jonah for a description of their practices.)

God's "escape clause" of judgment for the nations was given in Jeremiah 18:7-8. Nineveh had escaped once, but now its wickedness had come full circle, and it would face destruction.

Six hundred years before Jesus was born, the Medes and the Babylonians captured Nineveh exactly as Nahum had foretold! A rise in the Tigris River caused a flood that carried away part of the city wall, making Nineveh vulnerable to enemy attack.

"We're a mighty city!" the people declared smugly.

"No one has been able to stand up to the king of Assyria!" the king bragged.

It was true—at least from a human perspective. The Ninevites could easily endure a twenty-year siege and feel no inconvenience. Nahum would tell them otherwise.

"The Lord is good and protects those who place their trust in Him," Nahum stated, reminding the people of the true nature of God. In His mercy, God had given them a second chance to repent, just as Jeremiah stated God would do for any nation that repented of their evil deeds after being warned. He would relent from uprooting, tearing down, and destroying them. In Nineveh's case, however, that time had come and gone. Nineveh would now be destroyed. "God will destroy the city with a massive flood," Nahum prophesied. "For God has turned against you, Nineveh!"

Nahum then described what God had shown him in a vision. Fortresses surrounding the city would be easily captured by the Babylonians, and the great city of Nineveh would be destroyed not only by a flood but also by fire. All the gold and silver the Assyrian kings accumulated from taxing other nations would be carted off to Babylon. The Ninevite officers and guards would become so afraid, they'd flee overnight much

as the last independent Egyptian rule

like locusts that settle on the walls in the cool of the evening but fly away when the heat of the sun comes. Many people would be killed, and Nineveh's destruction would be final.

Just as Nahum prophesied, so it had all happened—much to the Assyrians' disbelief!

Footwork

Turn in your Bible to Nahum 1:3 and read it. This verse describes two things we can be sure of concerning God's character, and one thing we can count on that He will do. What were those three things? To Judah this was a comfort; to the Assyrians, it spelled disaster!

Fruit

God said that the destruction of Nineveh would be complete. Interestingly, the rubble of Nineveh eventually became so overgrown with grass that Alexander the Great marched over it and Napoléon camped near it without even realizing it! Some might find that unbelievable, but we shouldn't. God does as He says He will do, whether we choose to believe Him or not.

God has provided a way for us to be in a right relationship with Him (through faith in Jesus), and He tells us what will happen if we choose to reject Him. God leaves the choice to believe Him or not up to us. What choice will you make?

HABAKKUK

Little is known about the author of this prophetic book, although some believe that the musical references in the last chapter suggest that Habakkuk may have been a priest who was involved in the worship ceremonies at the temple in Jerusalem.

Unlike the other prophetic books, Habakkuk doesn't contain a message of warning or judgment directed toward people. Instead, it's a book full of complaints and questions directed toward God—questions that have been in people's hearts down through the ages. As you'll see, God heard and responded to the questions and complaints that burned deep within Habakkuk's heart. Because of this, Habakkuk wrote a prayer of praise to God for His awesome power and love, as well as His faithfulness.

Habakkuk contains many encouraging words for those who are going through difficult times or feel all hope is lost. Enjoy your time in this thought-provoking book!

I've Got a Question for You

Taken from Habakkuk 1—3

Foundation

Take a moment to prepare yourself before venturing into today's lesson. Stop what you are doing and don't read on. Talk to God and ask Him to speak to your heart, showing you what He wants you to learn about Him.

Focus

Have you ever had an unanswered question that burned deep within your heart?

"Lord, how long are You going to allow this evil to continue? Why don't You act?" Habakkuk complained.

He could have poured out his complaints to his friends, but he didn't. Although he was frustrated, annoyed, and perplexed, he took his feelings directly to God—and God was able to handle them.

Habakkuk lived in a volatile time. The northern kingdom of Israel was long gone, and the southern kingdom of Judah reeked with the smell of its own wickedness. The Babylonians, having conquered both Assyria and Egypt, were now the leading world power and were every bit as evil as the Assyrians had been. They took pride in their military strength, delighted in looting and taking captives, and had no regard for God. The Babylonians

ncluding Caesar, Virgil, Horace,

were an arrogant and dangerous enemy, greatly despised and feared by their enemies. But Habakkuk wasn't complaining about them—at least not at this point.

"Lord, why do You make me look at all the injustices being done by those living in Judah? Why don't You do something about all this wrong? I see violence all around me, but You do nothing about it. Your Law has been ignored, and the wicked rule over the righteous so that no one has an understanding of true justice. How long will You allow this evil to continue?"

"Habakkuk," God responded, "What I'm going to do is beyond your ability to believe, for I plan to raise up the Babylonians as a tool of judgment against Judah."

Habakkuk was dumbfounded. "The Babylonians?" he repeated. All Habakkuk could think of was the violent nature and arrogance of the Babylonians. They scoffed at rulers, made their own laws, and laughed at fortified cities while invading them.

Yes, God was right. Habakkuk couldn't believe it. Why would He use such a wicked nation to devour those who were more righteous?

"Even though Babylon has the ability to easily destroy us, we will not perish, for You are everlasting and keep Your covenants," Habakkuk acknowledged. Although he was confident of God's character, he reeled under the news of God's method. It seemed so unjust! "Why do you use the wicked to administer discipline on Judah?" Habakkuk complained.

Babylon seemed like a fisherman dragging a net through the water and snagging helpless fish, and then emptying the net just so he could fill it again—and again and again. So it was with Babylon. Babylon would destroy nations and keep on destroying them with no end in sight. Habakkuk was perplexed. God's use of

> *These words in Habakkuk: "The righteous shall live by … faith," freed a monk named Martin Luther from his failing attempts at striving to win God's favor. Those words sparked a change in Luther, who then ignited the Protestant Reformation in 1517 by nailing his Ninety-five Theses on the door of the Castle Church in Wittenberg, Germany.*
>
> ---
>
> *Habakkuk 2:4 is quoted three times in the New Testament. Check out Romans 1:17; Galatians 3:11; and Hebrews 10:38.*

Babylon would only reward Babylon's treacherous actions! Where was judgment for Babylon? What was God thinking?

But then Habakkuk's attitude changed from outrage and disbelief to trust and confidence in God's character. "I will stand and watch for You, Lord, like a guard who watches for the first sign of an approaching enemy," he earnestly stated. "I will look for the earliest and clearest information You have to give me regarding my questions and complaints."

At that point, God instructed him to write down on clay tablets what He was going to reveal. "This is so a herald can carry it to other cities and spread its message. Even though the events I am about to reveal will happen in the future, they will happen," God stated.

With that, the Lord gave several "woes," describing the actions of the Babylonians and the judgment that would eventually befall them.

In the end, Habakkuk's complaints and questions were replaced with a confident trust in the God who was in charge.

"Those who do right will live, have peace, and feel secure because they trust in God and God alone," the prophet repeated under his breath, full of awe. Habakkuk couldn't help but think of God's words to him—words that stated with certainty that God was indeed in control. One day, there would be no more questions, but until that time, Habakkuk would keep bringing His to God.

Footwork

Turn to Habakkuk 3:17–19 and read what these verses say. Fig trees not budding, no grapes on the vines, no olives or produce, no sheep or cattle—all of these represent circumstances that seem hopeless and disappointing. Now look at verses 18–19. What did Habakkuk say he would do in verse 18? What did he believe that God would do for him in verse 19?

Fruit

Often life can get confusing, and when it does, we tend to carry around big question marks in our minds: "Where is God?" "Doesn't He care?" "Doesn't He see what's going on?" "Why is He taking so long to do something?" "Does He really know what He's doing?" Even though we may never admit we have those questions, the Lord knows we do. He invites us to bring them to Him. Sometimes He may answer them; sometimes He may not. But regardless of whether or not He answers our questions, we need to trust Him. As God reminded Habakkuk, "The righteous will live by … faith [will rely on God and be faithful to Him]" (2:4).

Although we may have many questions for God, He has only one question for us: "Will you trust Me?" As Habakkuk learned, sometimes the real question at hand is different than we might think!

Zephaniah

Zephaniah, a contemporary of Jeremiah and Habakkuk, prophesied before the fall of Judah and just before God's judgment on Nineveh. We learn about Zephaniah from the first verse of his book in which he traces his lineage back to the godly King Hezekiah (who would have been his great-great-grandfather). Since most prophets listed only their father's name, the fact that Zedekiah traced his lineage back four generations indicates that he possibly had high social standing. It also means he would have been a distant relative to King Josiah, under whose reign he prophesied.

Zephaniah was one of the very last voices just before Judah's destruction. The fact that God sent all those warnings through previous prophets shows that He is not only just (meaning He must punish wrong), but He is also merciful (meaning He gives us every opportunity to avert punishment). The heart of Zephaniah's message takes this wonderful news even one step further.

Ahhh. Now We're Talking!
Taken from Zephaniah 1—3

Foundation

Take this time to prepare your heart. Talk to God—really talk with Him, and tell Him what is on your heart. Ask Him to share with you what is on His.

Focus

Do you ever wish that life could be perfect—right here and right now?

Zephaniah sighed. Things were far from perfect in the kingdom.

Although Judah had improved its borders outwardly, inwardly it was in a state of terrible decline due to the bad influences of recent kings. Manasseh was one such king. Instead of worshipping God, he built altars to Baal and began worshipping the sun, moon, and stars. He even put such altars in the temple courts. To top it all off, Manasseh placed an Asherah pole (for worshipping the false god Asherah) in the temple itself! When King Manasseh died, his son Amon, named after one of the Egyptian gods, continued his father's wicked practices. Even after Amon's death, the evil influences of Amon and his father continued to live on. On the scene, however, came a new leader—Josiah, who took the throne at the age of eight and who would grow up to become a good king.

When Josiah turned sixteen, he began to follow after God and within four years initiated a sweeping reform in the land. He sought to purge Jerusalem and the kingdom of Judah of the false gods and idols Manasseh and his son had erected. After King Josiah ordered the priests to cleanse and restore the temple, the high priest, Hilkiah, told the king that a copy of God's Law had been found. King Josiah read it to the people and led the nation in repentance and renewal of their covenant with God—but it was too little, too late. Even though King Josiah had reestablished the worship of God in Judah, he didn't fully abolish idol worship, so when the king died, the people returned to their former practices.

Zephaniah sighed again. *No, things are far from perfect.*

Zephaniah's words would be the last warning Judah would receive before God brought His judgment upon them.

"God's hand of judgment is against all who live in Jerusalem," Zephaniah announced. "You who worship the sun, moon, and stars, you who combine the worship of the one true God with the worship of your false god Molech, and you who neither worship idols nor worship God—all of you will fall silent before the Sovereign Lord, for now it is His turn to speak."

Zephaniah told Judah that God was preparing them like an animal to be consecrated and sacrificed to an invited guest—and that invited guest would be Babylon! Since the neighboring nations were no better, Zephaniah then proclaimed a message of judgment for them as well. His first announcement was against the Philistines to the west. They would be destroyed, and their land would be given to the remnant of the house of Judah. This was bad news for Philistia but encouraging news for the Israelites. God hadn't forgotten the covenant He made generations

In the pagan cultures of Old Testament times, star worship was believed to help harness the powers of nature. In Deuteronomy 4:19, God clearly warned the Israelites against worshipping the sun, moon, or stars. He alone controls all of creation!

The Cushites were Ethiopians—descendants of Ham (Gen. 10:6)—who lived in the upper Nile region, today's southern Egypt, Sudan, and northern Ethiopia. They were the southernmost people known to Judah at that time.

before with their ancestor Abraham. God's people would one day occupy the land, which meant that they wouldn't be utterly destroyed in the coming judgment. God would preserve a remnant from Judah.

Next, Zephaniah addressed Moab and Ammon, nations that lay to the east. These people were descendants of Lot's daughters and, thus, blood relatives of the Israelites. However, they were enemies who insulted, threatened, and mocked God's chosen people. God would destroy their land and it would lie barren forever. The Cushites to the south (the Ethiopians) would be killed in battle, and the Assyrians to the north would be destroyed so that Nineveh would be as dry as the desert. The once proud city full of irrigation canals would be no more.

God's harsh judgment against the nations and Judah was to purify them so that in the future all nations would call upon the name of the Lord and serve Him together, shoulder to shoulder. God would make things perfect, but it would be in His time and under His conditions. That plan would involve events in the immediate future as well as the distant future.

"The LORD your God in your midst, The Mighty One, will save; He will rejoice over you with gladness, He will quiet you with His love, He will rejoice over you with singing" (Zeph. 3:17 NKJV). Zephaniah encouraged the people with those words, for God had shown him a better time was coming.

Footwork

God gave His people a comforting promise through the prophet Jeremiah, who lived during Zephaniah's time. This promise is for us as well! "'I know the plans I have for you,' declares the Lord, 'plans to prosper you and not to harm you, plans to give you hope and a future'" (Jer. 29:11). You just read Zephaniah 3:17 at the end of the previous section. Now go back and read it again. According to this verse, what will God do for those who are His?

Fruit

Life is full of disappointments, and as much as we try, it can never be perfect or able to fully satisfy us. But there is One who can satisfy—One who extends His love and mercy to us. In Zephaniah we learned that the Lord delights in, cares for, and loves those who are His. Are you one of His? I'm not asking if you're Jewish, but rather, are you someone who has responded to God's offer of a relationship with Him? If you aren't sure or are uncertain how you can become one of His, turn to the back of this book. You'll find a special message there just for you.

Haggai

The book of Haggai is only two chapters long. And Haggai's ministry was short too. It consisted of four messages given over a span of four months. Unlike the prophetic books we've already explored, Haggai didn't warn the people of God's impending judgment, for judgment had already come. The Babylonians had destroyed Jerusalem and taken the Israelites (those living in the southern kingdom of Judah) as captives to Babylon. Now, however, a new time was coming and a new set of challenges awaited God's people as they returned from exile back to Jerusalem. It was under these circumstances that Haggai delivered his messages of challenge and encouragement. What did the people need to be challenged about? Why did they need encouragement? You'll just have to read the lesson to find out!

Be sure to check out www.cookministries.com/FaithFactor for three bonus lessons titled "Ah-Hah!" "Join the Team," and "You Win the Prize!" These lessons will provide an intriguing backdrop to the last three books in the Minor Prophets: Haggai, Zechariah, and Malachi. (While you're at it, encourage a friend to check out this Web site too!)

is thirty-four-year rule, Herod

I Didn't Think . . .
Taken from Haggai 1—2

Foundation

Preparing your heart before you dig into God's Word is important
and necessary. So don't skip this part! Take a few minutes to talk
with God. Thank Him for His loyal love and faithful attention, even
when you don't always offer the same in return.

Focus

Are you easily distracted?

What wonderful news! After seventy years of living in captivity, the
Israelites learned that King Cyrus had issued a decree giving them
permission to return to Jerusalem to rebuild their temple. Hearing this
news, Zerubbabel (the grandson of King Jehoiachin and of the royal
line of David) organized and led the first group—totaling almost fifty
thousand people—back to Judah. Before long, the priests were able to
once again offer sacrifices on a rebuilt altar in the midst of the rubble.
In the second year, they laid the foundation of the temple, but when
they faced opposition from their enemies they abandoned the task.

"It's just not time to rebuild God's house," they said as an excuse,
and took the paneling that was intended for the temple and used it in
their own homes. And so the temple sat untouched for sixteen years.
The hearts of the people grew distracted as they disobeyed God,

dismantles the temple to build a

Many years after the Babylonians took the Israelites of Judah into captivity, King Cyrus of Persia conquered Babylon and became the new ruler. Interestingly, Cyrus's decree to free the Israelites was foretold long before Judah was even taken captive!

A simple way to remember the message of Haggai is to remember to THINK:
T—Take time to pray.
H—Hang on to God's standards.
I—Imagine the blessings and consequences of your actions.
N—Never think you can just drift through life.
K—Know that God will bless you for your obedience to Him.

neglecting the task He had given them and focused instead on establishing their own daily life and routines.

Haggai would challenge their apathy and self-focus. "You say it's not time to build the Lord's house, but is it time for you to build your own? The Lord's house lies in ruin and He is not pleased. Have you not noticed?" Haggai pressed. He continued explaining how they had planted seed, but reaped little harvest in the fields. And they drank, but could never get their fill because of the drought in the land—the drought God sent to get their attention. "Stop and think about your actions!" he urged.

Zerubbabel, the high priest, and all the people heard what Haggai had to say, and they knew he was speaking by God's divine authority. They understood that the reason for their failure was because they had neglected the Lord. Haggai's words gave them a renewed sense of respect for God as they were reminded of God's promise to be with them. With this new perspective came new motivation, and within twenty-three days of Haggai's message, work on the Lord's temple began once again. Never before had the people responded so quickly to a prophet's message!

The next month, as the people were sifting through the rubble and the temple began taking shape, their hearts became discouraged. Many had heard stories from their ancestors describing Solomon's grand and glorious temple. What they were building seemed like a small and shabby garage in comparison.

But the Lord gave Haggai a message of encouragement for the people. "This is what the Lord Almighty says," Haggai stated. "'Work hard and do your work for Me, for I am in your midst. The glory of the temple you are building will far exceed the former glory of Solomon's temple.'"

Far exceed the glory of Solomon's temple? they wondered. *But how can that be?*

"I will grant peace in this temple," the Lord reassured them. It would be to this temple that the Messiah would come in the future, filling it with His glorious presence.

After this, Haggai gave two more messages to encourage the people to keep their focus on the Lord and not become distracted. He knew that their faithful obedience would result in experiencing God's blessing in their lives.

Footwork

Open your Bible and read Haggai 1:4–5. What does it say? Is this something God might need to say to you right now?

Fruit

God challenged the Israelites to give careful thought to their ways. Giving careful thought to the way we live isn't something we tend to do very often. It's so much easier to get caught up in the daily activities of life that we neglect the things of God. Watch that you don't become distracted by what seems enjoyable or by what comes easily. These things will only cause you to lose your focus and become complacent in your relationship toward God. So how can you give careful thought to your ways? Set priorities!

This week make it a priority to meet with God. This can be done several ways, and how you do it is strictly up to you. Perhaps you might set aside a time for Bible study or prayer—or better yet, both! Whatever you do, try setting an egg timer and focus your thoughts for that specific amount of time. You may also want to begin journaling in a notebook. Simply begin by telling God your fears and discouragements. As He gives you a verse or promise from His Word, write it in the margin on that page. You'll be amazed at what you discover! Consider beginning each day with a simple prayer: *Lord, walk with me throughout my day today. Help me stay focused on You, sensitive and obedient to Your leading. Amen.*

Zechariah

The book of Zechariah is the second of three postexilic books (Haggai, Zechariah, and Malachi) and was written by the prophet Zechariah. Born in Babylon and of the Levitical (priestly) line, Zechariah was most likely a young man when he joined Haggai and the nearly fifty thousand Israelites returning to Jerusalem under Zerubbabel's leadership.

Like Haggai's message, Zechariah's message was to his fellow exiles, but unlike the older prophet, Zechariah didn't focus on the rebuilding of the temple. Instead, he concentrated on rebuilding the people's relationship with God.

Zechariah began prophesying at the halfway point of Haggai's short four-month ministry, and his messages came from God in the form of eight visions (chapters 1—6), four messages (chapters 7—8), and two burdens (chapters 9—14).

Some consider this book difficult to understand because parts of it refer to end-time events. But don't let that be a discouragement to you! Although there are many prophecies in the later chapters that point to the future coming of Jesus the Messiah as well as His millennial rule, we'll limit our exploration to the beginning chapters of this book. (You can explore the others on your own!)

You Go First!
Taken from Zechariah 1—5

Foundation

Prepare your heart before reading today's lesson. Ask God to give you the courage to take the appropriate steps needed in your life at this time.

Do you ever find it difficult to take the first step?

Zechariah paused as he began recording the message God had given him. It was common practice to date things according to the reign of a Jewish king. However, Israel had no king on the throne at this time. The Babylonians had taken the Israelites from their land and placed them under King Nebuchadnezzar's rule. When King Cyrus of Persia conquered Babylon, the Israelites then fell under Persian rule. King Darius of Persia was now in command, and Zechariah would date his message accordingly. Although he knew this was the time of the Gentiles (non-Jews), Zechariah looked forward to the day when Israel would once again have a king on the throne.

"In the eighth month of the second year of King Darius's reign, the word of the Lord came to me, and God called me to deliver these messages to you," Zechariah began. He then began to tell them how their forefathers angered the Lord because they didn't listen or pay attention to His commands. "Even when He coaxed them to return to Him, they continued to follow their own rebellious ways. Do not be like them!" Zechariah warned "But return to God, and He will show you His favor and make His presence known to you!"

Zechariah was thoughtful for a moment. How well he personally knew the trouble Israel had gotten into, for he had been born during their years of captivity in Babylon. Although Zechariah hadn't seen the Promised Land until now, he had heard reports from others while growing up.

"Do the prophets live forever? No!" God stated. The prophets were there only for a short time, so the Israelites needed to respond to God's messages while they had a window of opportunity. They needed to step out and act upon what God was telling them to do.

Zechariah knew it was because of the Israelites disobedience that the temple had been destroyed and it was because of disobedience that the rebuilding of it had been delayed. Although during the Babylonian captivity, many realized they had disobeyed the Lord and knew the judgment they received from God was both just and merciful, it wasn't necessarily enough to transform their hearts.

Had they really learned what God intended for them to learn? Zechariah sighed. Not only did the people need encouragement to obey God and rebuild the (outer) structure of the temple,

"Israel" and "Israelites" refer to the descendants of Judah who God preserved through the Babylonian captivity. The northern tribes (formerly called Israel) were wiped out forever.

Shebat was the Babylonian word for the eleventh month of the year, a word the Jewish exiles had adopted. The eleventh month was February.

they needed to understand their own place in God's eyes and rebuild their (inner) relationship with Him. God had a job for Israel to do, and that job was to be the vessel through which His message would spread throughout the entire world. Did they fully understand that? God would make certain they did.

"On the twenty-fourth day of Shebat, the word of the Lord came to me in eight visions," Zechariah penned, describing how all these visions came during the same night.

The first five visions dealt with comfort, while the last three dealt with judgment. These were the visions God gave Zechariah: The vision of the horsemen among the myrtle trees meant that God would rebuild Zion and His people. The vision of the four horns and the craftsmen meant that God would judge the nations who oppressed Israel. Not only would God protect and glorify Jerusalem (according to the vision of a man with a measuring line), but He would also cleanse and restore Israel through a coming Messiah (told through the vision of Joshua, the high priest, being cleansed).

Zion *was the name of the mound where the Jebusite fortress stood when King David captured it (see 2 Sam. 5:7). David named the fortress "the City of David," and later, "Jerusalem." Zion is another name for Jerusalem and sometimes refers to the Israelites themselves.*

The vision of the golden lampstand meant that God's Spirit would empower Zerubbabel and Joshua as leaders, and the vision of the flying scroll indicated that individual sin would be judged. Furthermore, the nation's sin would finally be removed (as told in the vision of a woman in a basket), and in the end days, God's judgment would come on the nations (indicated by the vision of four chariots).

Zechariah trusted that these powerful visions would tell the Israelites not only what they needed to do but also what was to come in their future. For the Israelites to complete their work on the temple, they needed to understand the importance of what they were doing—and have a knowledge of the one true God whom they served. God was challenging them to take the next step, and He would lead the way. Would they follow?

Footwork

Turn in your Bible to Zechariah 1:3 and read what it says. What was the first thing God told the people to do? Now flip ahead to Zechariah 4:6. This is an all-important reminder about whose power the Israelites were to rely on as they stepped out to do what God had commanded them to do.

Rome. Roman government changes from a

Fruit

The Israelites had experienced power of their own (and failed), as well as the power of other nations (and suffered). God challenged them to rely on a power they weren't accustomed to: the power of His Spirit. He alone was the One who could change hearts. He alone was the One who held their future. God would rebuild His relationship with His people, but it wouldn't be by their own willpower, or by their grand schemes and empty promises. It would be by His Spirit.

Where are you in your relationship with God? Does your life need some rebuilding? Perhaps you need to return to God—or turn to Him for the first time. Are you experiencing His power in your life? If not, it's never too late to take the first step. "Return to [Me]," God says, "and I will return to you" (Zech. 1:3). His help is only a prayer away.

Lord, I've tried to change myself, and I can't. Forgive me for thinking that I can live life in my own power. I need You, and I want You to be in control of my life.

Malachi

You've now reached the end of the Minor Prophets and the last book of the Old Testament. If you've landed here because you're skipping around, now would be a good time to go back to the beginning (Genesis) and work your way forward. If you've worked your way from the front of *Faith Factor, OT* to the end, good for you! You've not only gained a wonderful grasp of the entire Old Testament, but you've also laid an excellent foundation for understanding the New Testament. (And if you're ready for more, check out *Faith Factor, NT,* which will take you through the second half of your Bible—the New Testament.) The name Malachi means "my messenger," or "my angel." Although the prophet doesn't give historical markers (such as kings ruling, or natural disasters) in his writing, we can make an educated guess on an approximate date for his book by the fact that Malachi uses the Persian word for "governor." It is safe to say Malachi wrote his book during the postexilic time (536 BC), possibly after the temple had been rebuilt.

Concerning this last book of the Old Testament, Malachi would be the last prophet God would send to His people for a long time—four hundred years in fact! When God sent a prophet again, it would be John the Baptist, who would announce the coming of the Lord Jesus. (See the book of Matthew in the New Testament for more about this.)

So what was the message God left with the Israelites? What were His final words before a long period of silence? Read on to find out!

The sport of sumo wrestling begins

Is This *All?*
Taken from Malachi 1—4

Foundation

Stop and pray before you begin this last lesson. Ask the Lord to show you what might need to change in your thoughts, words, or deeds.

Focus

Have you ever felt empty inside, wondering if there's more to life than what you've been experiencing?

It had been one hundred years since King Cyrus's decree—one hundred years since the first group of Israelites had journeyed from Babylon back to Jerusalem to begin rebuilding the temple. Although the temple was now up and the walls surrounding Jerusalem were almost fully restored, the morale of the Israelites was down, and their relationship with God was slowly crumbling …

"God doesn't love us," some of the people muttered under their breath, "for He has yet to fill our rebuilt temple with His glory!"

"And we're still under the rule of the Persians!" others added with discouragement. "Where is the Promised One who will set us free, delivering us from our enemies—the One whom the prophets spoke about?"

The Israelites had taken their focus off God and placed it onto their circumstances. Living by their own understanding and expectations, they

n Japan. ● 20—19 BC — Herod the

had forgotten God's loyal covenant love for them. This soon led them to forget other things as well.

Tithes *were the "firstfruits" God required and involved giving off the top first to God, and then keeping the remainder for oneself.* Offerings *were given above and beyond the tithes out of a heart of joyful gratitude and trust.*

God's last words in the Old Testament (Mal. 4:5–6) were words of hope. They pointed to a future Messiah whose coming would be announced by someone who would be like the prophet Elijah. Matthew 17:9–13 and Luke 1:17 in the New Testament tell us that prophet Elijah was John the Baptist.

"This is what the Lord says to you," Malachi began, "'A son gives honor to his father, and that is fitting—just as a slave gives honor to his master. I am both a father and master over you, but where is the honor and respect I deserve?'"

The prophet waited a moment for his words to sink in and then directed his focus toward the priests, pressing the matter further.

"You have despised God's name," he charged them.

Although their job as priests was to lead the people in worshipping God correctly, they had encouraged only halfhearted worship. Instead of requiring the Israelites to obey God's command and offer Him only the very best of their flock (see Deut. 17:1), the priests looked the other way and allowed people to offer unwanted, sickly, and lame animals. But God didn't look the other way. What was meant to be an outward expression of loving devotion, celebration, and trust toward God had become an empty ritual, an act of disobedience, and an insult to Him. It wasn't long until the people's habit of going through the motions clouded their thinking and dulled their hearts.

Instead of keeping their covenant vows to their wives, men divorced them.

"I have a hatred of divorce," God stated plainly and clearly. There were only a few things God ever expressed hating, and divorce was one of them. He knew that it harmed both people and destroyed the beautiful word picture He designed marriage to be—a picture of His unconditional love for His people.

Instead of bringing a joyful offering celebrating God's blessings, the people held out on God. *If we give God a portion of what we have, we'll no longer have what we need—and we can't afford that,* many mistakenly believed. As a result, they missed out on God's provision for them and settled for less than what they could have had.

"Don't just give Me part, but bring all of your tithe," God encouraged. "And see if I will not open the windows of heaven and pour out a blessing beyond your imagination!"

But the people refused to obey, so God refused to bless them.

Because the Israelites doubted God's covenant love for them, they soon fell into a pattern of dishonoring Him. Once this happened, it was only a matter of time before their hearts became disillusioned.

"Of what use is all of this, anyway?" they grumbled as they went through empty, outward motions of worshipping God. Their disillusion quickly turned to disgust, and then their hearts became distanced from God. But even though they had lost the sense of God's presence in their lives, He didn't abandon them.

Footwork

Although we may lose sight of God, He never gives up on us. Turn in your Bible to Malachi 3:3, and read what it says. Although this verse talks about the priests (Levites), it applies to us as well. A refiner of silver and gold didn't just stick the precious metal into the fire and walk away; he stayed right there, carefully watching over the metal and applying just the right amount of heat to burn off the impurities. The job was finished when the refiner could see a perfect reflection of himself in the metal.

placing it on a mammoth square

Fruit

Sometimes we go through life with mistaken ideas about who God is and what He expects of us. Often these wrong ideas come from playing church and just going through the motions. Sometimes they come from never hearing God's truth in the first place. Do you doubt God's love for you, or His just and righteous nature? Do you dishonor His name by the halfhearted way you live your life? Have you been going through the motions of religious activities that seem empty and meaningless? Is there a distance between you and God?

If you answered yes to any of these questions or wonder, "Is what I'm experiencing all there is?" there's something you need to know. What you've been experiencing isn't what God intends for you and isn't "all there is." He longs for you to know Him in an intimate way. He will take you as you are. He will remove your impurity. He will slowly change you so you can begin to reflect His glory. God isn't interested in outward, empty activity; He's interested in your inward life, your heart attitude. Are you ready and willing to experience that? Tell Him about it right now.

Appendix

A SPECIAL MESSAGE JUST FOR YOU!

The fact that you're reading this page either means you desire to know more about how you can have a personal relationship with God, or you turned here by accident (or even curiosity). Either way, I'm glad you did. Whatever your reason, this message is especially for you!

Before you can enter into a right relationship with God, there are a few things you first need to know about yourself and about Him. These are straight from God's Word—in *both* the Old and New Testament:

1. You cannot possibly live a good enough life to earn your way into heaven. In fact, in Ecclesiastes 7:20 and Romans 3:23 we learn we are all sinners and fall miserably short of meeting God's requirements of perfect holiness.

2. Because God is holy and just, He cannot accept us in our sinful condition. Isaiah 59:2 and Romans 6:23 tell us the result of sin is death and separation from God. Just like death separates us from our loved ones, spiritual death separates us from the presence of God. It keeps us from being able to have a right relationship with Him. As you can see, this creates a huge problem.

3. The good news is that God did something about this problem. Because of His great love and mercy (see John 3:16 in the New Testament), He provided a way for us to have a relationship with Him and offers this eternal life to us as a gift (Romans 6:23). Because sin had to be punished, God sacrificed His own Son to pay the penalty of our sins in our place (Isaiah 53:3; 1 John 5:11–13). It is a gift we cannot earn and did not deserve (Ephesians 2:8–9).

4. Just knowing about this gift is not enough. We must receive this gift (Ps. 130; John 1:12). Just as a gift is not ours until we accept it, we must choose to accept God's gift of eternal life in Jesus.

In John 14:6 we learn that there is only *one* way to have our sins forgiven so we can enter into a relationship with God and live with Him in heaven. Jesus is the Way, the Truth, and the Life. No one comes to God except through Him. What God pointed to in the Old Testament through the sacrificial system, He brought to fulfillment in the New Testament through Jesus. We receive God's gift of eternal life by placing our faith and trust in what He has provided. When we do this, we become children of God and enter into a relationship with God forever.

ARE YOU READY TO DO THIS?

Simply pray to God and tell Him what you desire. This requires no special formula or words. God offers you the gift of salvation and is waiting for you to accept it.

Tell God you are sorry for your sins and for not living up to His standard of perfect holiness. Ask Him to forgive you for your wrong actions, attitudes, and thoughts (selfishness, anger, pride, jealousy, etc.). Claim Jesus' sacrifice for you as your means of forgiveness. Ask God to forgive you, and tell Him you want to enter into a relationship with Him and become His forever. (Psalm 51:1–4, 7, 10 offers a great model prayer.)

Thank Him for what He has done and promises to do. In 1 John 1:9 we are told that if we confess our sins, God is faithful and just to forgive our sins and cleanse us from unrighteousness. Psalm 32:1–2 states: "Blessed is the person whose sins are forgiven and whose unrighteousness is no longer counted against him!"

If you have done this, you've now begun your new life with God. He accepts you as blameless and holy—your guilt is gone! Just like a newborn baby needs to grow, you need to grow too. You do this by reading your Bible, praying, and seeking to live the kind of life that pleases God. God is there for you. He will help you grow in your relationship with Him.

Congratulations! You've just begun an exciting journey!

Bibliography

Anthony, Michael J., and Warren S. Benson. *Exploring the History & Philosophy of Christian Education*. Grand Rapids: Kregel, 2003.

Walvoord, John F., and Roy B. Zuck. *The Bible Knowledge Commentary, New Testament*. Colorado Springs: Scripture Press, 1983.

Walvoord, John F., and Roy B. Zuck. *The Bible Knowledge Commentary, Old Testament*. Colorado Springs: Scripture Press, 1985.

Bruce, F.F. *Paul: Apostle of the Heart Set Free*. Grand Rapids: Eerdmans, 1977.

Keener, Craig S. *The IVP Bible Background Commentary, New Testament*. Downer's Grove, IL: InterVarsity Press, 1993.

Walton, John H., Victor H. Matthews, and Mark W. Chavalas. *The IVP Bible Background Commentary, Old Testament*. Downer's Grove, IL: InterVarsity Press, 2000.

Johnson, Joni A. *World History & Literature*. Dayton, OH: Blue Earth Publishing, 1997.

Life Application Study Bible. Wheaton, IL: Tyndale, 1996.

Master Study Bible, NASB. Nashville: Broadman & Holman Bible Publishers, 1981.

NASB Open Bible, Expanded Edition. Nashville: Thomas Nelson, 1985.

NIV Study Bible. Grand Rapids: Zondervan, 1995.

Hyndman, Rob J. *The Times: A Chronology of the Bible,* Rob J. Hyndman (online PDF material) www-personal.buseco.monash.edu.au/~hyndman/bible/times/contents.htm.

Gundry, Robert. *A Survey of the New Testament,* 3rd ed. Grand Rapids: Zondervan, 1994.

Stanton, Mary, and Albert Hyma. *Streams of Civilization, Vol. 1*. Arlington Heights, IL: Christian Liberty Press, 1992.

Chisholm, Jane. *Usborne Book of the Ancient World*. Tulsa, OK: EDC Publishing, 1991.

Word Sight, "Bible Time-line," Word Sight, http://www.wordsight.org/btl/000_btl-fp.htm.